Travels With My Harp

The Complete Autobiography

MARY O'HARA

SHEPHEARD-WALWYN (PUBLISHERS) LTD

First published in 2012 by
Shepheard-Walwyn (Publishers) Ltd
107 Parkway House, Sheen Lane,
London SW14 8LS
www.shepheard-walwyn.co.uk

British Library Cataloguing in Publication Data
A catalogue record of this book
is available from the British Library

ISBN: 978-0-85683-285-7

Typeset by Alacrity, Chesterfield, Sandford, Somerset
Printed and bound through
s|s|media limited, Wallington, Surrey

Contents

Acknowledgements

I wish to express my gratitude to Brigid Marlin for permission to reproduce her painting on the front of the jacket and to Catherine Reeve for the use of her photo on the back flap. I am grateful to family and friends for the use of photos to illustrate the book.

I would also like to thank Coryne Hall for her help in editing the manuscript and Jean Desebrock for the attractive design.

Second Thoughts

INTRODUCTION TO THE COMPLETE AUTOBIOGRAPHY

'MEL,' EXCLAIMED my sister Joan, 'why on earth are you writing your autobiography at your age? That's something you do when you are in your eighties.' She was right of course. But gauging that she was not in a receptive mood, I didn't even attempt to explain the pressure I was under. That was in 1977 – over thirty years ago. By the age of forty-two, I had experienced what some might call a 'successful' musical career, an early and very happy marriage, early widowhood, spent twelve-and-a-half years as a nun in a Benedictine monastery, and now was having another unexpected and successful career in music. I was beginning to lead a very busy life flitting between recording studios, radio and television stations and concert halls. I was getting tired of all the interviews and answering the same questions over and over, especially about my monastic sojourn. Up till then my life had been full of surprises, chock-a-block with the unexpected. How does one know that this is not the end?

But that's not why I agreed to write my autobiography when publishers came knocking on the door on the heels of that first TV interview I did with Russell Harty on the BBC. At first I kept refusing, saying I was far too busy; I was in the middle of a UK concert tour. Jo Lustig, my very capable and persuasive manager of just a year, assured me that once I put it all down in book form, people could refer to the book and stop asking me the same questions repeatedly. I was naïve enough to believe him because I wanted to believe him. And I did not have to lift a finger (or in this case, a pen), he said, for he had the perfect ghost writer for me, a journalist friend of his. I would talk to her now and again between concerts and eventually an autobiography would appear, supposedly written by me. That's how ghosts worked, he said. So, finally worn down, I signed on the dotted line. In those early trusting days I signed anything presented to me.

The publishers paid my manager the money. The manager shared it between the four of us – the ghost, her agent, himself and myself. I talked to the ghost and the ghost wrote what she wrote. I kept asking to see what she had written but I kept being fobbed off. That was how ghosts worked, I was told.

I was uneasy with this ghosting procedure. And then one day I spotted a magazine article about me written by my ghost and it impelled me to take action. She'd over-dramatised what, in anybody's view, was already quite simply a very dramatic story. I made a decision. The test of authenticity would be the way she treated my stay at Stanbrook Abbey. If she misconstrued the spiritual element, then no matter what, I could not continue with this ghosting arrangement. I demanded to see the typed manuscript and, as I suspected, she had indeed missed the bus. There was no way I could append my name to what she had written as my book. I quite understood that it was difficult for an outsider to get inside my mind, either during my stay at Stanbrook or during the whole period after my husband's death. I made a further decision: I'd write the book myself. As I drove home between concerts, I called into Stanbrook Abbey and explained the problem. They put me on to a lawyer friend of theirs, Michael Rubenstein, a quiet but firm man experienced in legal matters such as I was bound to face. It took some patient and protracted negotiations with my manager and some monetary exchanges to just get my own files back. My late husband's letters, photographs of my family, my diaries – the return of everything had to be painfully negotiated, leaving my bank account fairly well depleted. For a brief period I considered approaching a professional writer friend, whom I knew really understood the inner me, to ask him to take over the ghosting but when I discovered it would involve yet another agent I dropped that idea.

I realised I'd have to write the book myself. When I contacted my publishers, Michael Joseph, they were relieved and said that all along they were hoping that I would do so. On my way up to London to see them, I wrote the first chapter on the train. 'That's your voice,' Alan Brooke, the managing director, exclaimed. 'This is what we want.'

I had learnt a valuable, costly lesson: never trust others with your life story. You do the interpretations yourself. This 'problem with the book', of course, sowed lasting distrust between myself and Jo Lustig, which was a pity, for he was a competent manager. Eventually we parted company. But now I was obliged to write my own story from scratch – and fast too, because the publishers' advance was dissipated. And that's how I came to write my autobiography at the age of forty-two. And I have never regretted doing so. I called it *The Scent of the Roses*, the last line of the song 'Farewell, But Whenever You Welcome the Hour' by the early 19th-century Irish poet Thomas Moore and a very popular song, like all the Moore's Melodies, in the Ireland of my youth. The song is about enduring friendship and love through the thick and thin of life.

> Let Fate do her worst, there are relics of joy,
> Bright dreams of the past which she cannot destroy.
> Which come in the night-time of sorrow and care
> And bring back the features that joy used to wear.
> Long, long be my heart with such memories filled
> As that vase in which roses have once been distilled.
> You may break, you may shatter the vase, if you will,
> But the scent of the roses will hang round it still.

It was a sentiment with which I empathised but though the title made a lot of sense to me personally, it could mean little to anyone who did not know the song and the provenance of that phrase. But I've always liked 'The Scent of the Roses/Farewell But Whenever.' It was the song that Joan Baez told me she treasured most on one of my early recordings, *Songs of Ireland* – the album that my husband Richard and I were working on together only weeks before he died.

Thirty years on I now see that there are advantages to writing one's autobiography in later life. For one thing, the passage of time gives one, for want of a better expression, a sociological perspective, the story becoming as much about one's own times as it is about oneself. It enables one to filter, revise and temper one's interpretations of people and events. I find this particularly true about the memories I have of my mother. It was only much later in life that I came to the conclusion that the *start* of my mother's problems was post-natal depression – a medical condition almost unheard of in the Ireland of the 1950s, let alone the 1930s. I've discovered too that the drink problem for both my parents started early on. Again, much later in my life, someone mentioned to me my father's propensity for gambling

on horses as a young man, which must have been held well in check
by my mother, for I neither heard nor saw a sign of it when I was
growing up and which could account for her holding the purse strings.
All these things may have contributed to the marriage difficulties, and
in the light of this new knowledge many other past events have taken
on new meanings. Which is why I was tempted to call any updated
version of my autobiography *Second Thoughts*. Instead I decided to call
it *Travels With My Harp* – for reasons that will become obvious as I
progress through my life.

Did I feel a great urge to update my memoirs? Not at all. In the
late 1970s I had given it my best shot. I am now very happily remarried and contentedly retired. Having returned from a six-year stay in
Africa in 2002, I'm fully occupied in catching up on my reading and
learning Spanish instead of Swahili, which I did in Africa. Having just
completed five volumes of my harp accompaniments and given talks
about *Travels With My Harp* in Australia, Europe and North America,
perhaps I can rest on my oars, a la '*Óro Mo Bháidín*', which, to my
great delight, has morphed itself into 'Sleepyhead', a hit number
by the American electropop band Passion Pit. A case of my former
manager Jo Lustig, now dead, having the last laugh, perhaps?

In 2001, the Australian playwright John Misto wrote a play about
me called *Harp on the Willow*. It deals with my marriage to the
American poet Richard Selig and the monastic sojourn brought about
by his premature death. The play had a very successful run in Sydney
in 2004 and in Melbourne in 2007, starring Marina Prior in the lead
role on both occasions. There was another very successful production
of the play by the highly regarded Wyong Drama Group in 2010.

To coincide with the Melbourne occasion, I had been asked if I'd
consider bringing people up to date on what has happened in my life
since 1980. Not surprisingly, I missed their deadline by several years
but in 2009/10, the Burns Library at Boston College held a six-month
Mary O'Hara exhibition which gave the project sufficient impetus for
me to complete the task. Since 1980 many interesting things have
happened to me but also many more things have come to light about
the events described in *The Scent of the Roses*. The task of sorting (and
reading) my letters and papers for this exhibition furnished me with
a new understanding of many past events; research for my talks in
2005 also unearthed long-forgotten experiences. I discovered files and

documents containing correspondence and articles that I hadn't remembered reading before. Perhaps, I thought, the authors of some of the interviews came to know me better than I did myself. Browsing through this material helped inform my knowledge considerably and gave my memory a welcome nudge. In this present updating of my memoirs I have used this extra information, these newfound insights, and woven them into my previous writings. In fact at one stage I wondered if a compilation of past press interviews might not prove a lot more interesting than any memoirs I might put together. However, I resisted this temptation.

Much of the content of my earlier book, though augmented by new or reinterpreted information, does of course remain the same. The latter half of the book is new and covers the last thirty years of my life. I want to thank all those innumerable friends and, above all, my husband Pat, who patiently encouraged me to finish this project – 'if only for the archives' they kept insisting.

Inis Mór, Aran Islands. January 2012
www.maryohara.co.uk

The Scent of the Roses

PROLOGUE 1980

MID-MORNING, Easter Thursday. In the sunlit Methodist Hall the tension was almost tangible. A singing competition of the Sligo *Feis Ceóil*, the annual Festival of Music and Drama, which attracted competitors from all over Ireland, was drawing to its close. Anxious mothers sat beside their small fidgety bairns who had been thoroughly scoured and relentlessly groomed down to the last white sock (and gone through their songs until they could sing them in their sleep). Some pestered their parents with whispered questions such as 'Mummy, who do you think will get First?' But the fond mamas had their eyes and attention riveted on the god-like adjudicator, an august musical pundit down from Dublin, seated in potent isolation in the centre of the Hall, scribbling (endlessly it seemed to the watchers) page after page of criticism. The most miserable person in Ireland at that moment was competitor number 28, sitting near the back of the hall – a slender, pale and freckle-faced little girl of eight, with a huge bow on the side of her straight light-brown hair. Heavens above, she was thinking, she hadn't wanted to enter the wretched competition at all, but realising that to have said so would have made no difference, she'd gone ahead with it. Even at that tender age she'd sensed it was good for her character to do things, innocuous in themselves, but which she personally disliked doing. Oh but the terrible shame of it: she hadn't even been *recalled*. Out of those dozens of competitors only about ten had had their numbers called out. This meant that the adjudicator, dismissing the remainder as not good enough, would listen once more to the performances of the selected few and then decide who would get First, Second and Third prizes and 'Highly Recommended'.

The little girl, number 28, wished the ground would open and swallow her up. Floors had never obliged before so why should they be expected to do so now? If only she could slip away unnoticed, run home and play tennis by herself against the side of the house, as was her wont, and forget the whole affair. But since her mother was sitting beside her, escape was ruled out. She'd just have to sit through the rest of the humiliating business of hearing the adjudicator call out the names of the prize-winners and analyse their performances.

The hush of expectancy now deepened as the adjudicator, with a bundle of papers in his hand, finally made his way to the platform. He paused for a moment, glancing abstractedly over the top of his spectacles at the sea of ultra-attentive faces before him. Then he spoke. 'I've recalled twelve competitors to decide which of them should receive second, third and fourth prizes. I didn't recall competitor number 28 because, after she'd sung, there was no doubt whatsoever in my mind that she'd be the winner of first prize. I've given her 98 marks out of 100.'

CHAPTER 1

That Child Won't Live

I DON'T KNOW if my mother ever harboured notions of my becoming a singer: I very much doubt it, but if she did she never mentioned it to me. But I do know from others that she was worried I might not survive babyhood, though I personally have no recollection of being a sickly child, or frail, or mal-nourished.

I was an Easter child, born in Sligo, a small town on the west coast of Ireland. It had been a busy port before World War II, with an extensive trade in timber from the Baltic, weekly services to Liverpool and Glasgow, trade in grain from South America and Australia and various goods from Europe. From remote times, the O'Haras were settled in the Barony of Leyney in County Sligo. Thurlough Carolan (1670-1738), the noted Irish composer and harpist, composed *'Cupán Uí Eaghra'* for Cian (Kean) O'Hara (1657-1719) who was High Sheriff of Sligo in 1703 and 1713. Cian's son, also named Cian (1713-1782), was a Drury Lane playwright of some note and is best known for his drama *Midas*. Our branch of the family, however, is descended from Oliver O'Hara, who took part in the Irish rebellion of 1641. Later, when Cromwell, the victor of the English Civil War, gave Irish Catholics the ultimatum of 'going to hell or to Connaught', the O'Haras were not immediately affected as they were already in Connaught, but Oliver O'Hara's family did forfeit their lands for participating in the rebellion. A section of the family conformed to the new religion and so retained their property. Soldiers figure along the line, including my great grand-uncle who, in 1863, fought as a cavalry officer in the Union Army in the American Civil War.

My mother (who by the time I was born had three children under the age of four) relied on our neighbour Lily Hession, a mother of

1

seven children, as the resident expert on all child ailments. My mother did not breastfeed and relied completely on cow's milk. When I, the latest O'Hara newborn, could not keep the milk down, an SOS went out for Mrs Hession. Lily's daughter Eileen remembers her mother arriving back from her visit somewhat distraught and making the solemn pronouncement: 'That child won't live.' This stark phrase stuck in Eileen's mind. Eileen came to a concert of mine in Poole on the south coast of England in 1980 and, not having met since childhood, there was a lot of history to rake over. I casually mentioned that I'd recently seen a herbalist who had taken me off dairy products because, she said, I was allergic to them. Taken aback, Eileen butted in: 'But, didn't you know that, as a new-born baby, you almost died because you were allergic to dairy products?' And it had taken me forty-four years to discover this!

By any account, my parents' marriage was not the happiest of alliances. It is still very difficult to understand why they married. My father was a mild-mannered man; my mother was wilful with sometimes a tyrannical streak. I often think that if Father had married somebody who was more of a home-maker it would have provided him with the foundation he needed to make him truly happy. And if perhaps Mother had shared her life with someone firmer, she too might have thrived; she needed to be controlled. Although there were admirable qualities on both sides, they tended to negate each other. Some years ago my father told me that at one time they had both considered doing medicine at university. But as far as I can judge neither would have been the right type. Their temperaments were unsuitable. The medicine dream was an aspect of their partial inability to come to terms with everyday life.

John O'Hara, as his family referred to him, had a restless nature and had always wanted to travel. He attended Summerhill College, Sligo, but left at sixteen and qualified as a 'wireless operator' at the radio college in Cahirciveen, County Kerry. Though the course usually took a year, he applied himself diligently and qualified in a record three months. The college principal was impressed enough to ask him to stay on as an instructor, but, as his only reason for doing the course was to get away to sea, he declined. For three years he sailed the world with the merchant navy. On the high seas he had plenty of time to think and study. He matriculated and entered University College,

Galway, where he met Mai Kirwan, a commerce student, who was to become my mother.

Mai Kirwan is reputed to have been very attractive and vivacious. Photographs confirm this. I've heard her referred to as a college beauty and very charming. She was musical, having played the piano in her school orchestra at Taylor's Hill Dominican School in Galway. Educated and consequently in one sense a liberated woman in her day, she was at the same time not *really* liberated due to her temperament.

John O'Hara graduated with degrees in civil engineering and geology while Mai Kirwan graduated with a degree in commerce. During their marriage, I seem to remember money being a source of dissension. Mother always appeared in my childhood eyes to be the aggressor with my long-suffering father never asserting himself, hoping in vain for a quiet life. She had a temper and he didn't. Only recently did I get to hear about my father's heavy gambling on horses during the very early years of their marriage. Not the most auspicious of starts.

After he qualified, John O'Hara, still hankering for adventure, planned to become a professional soldier with the British Army in India, but at his interview he was persuaded to change his mind. He ended up with the British Colonial Service and was posted to Nigeria. Mai Kirwan took a teaching job in the west of Ireland. They must have kept in touch and in two years John O'Hara came back to Ireland, married Mai Kirwan and together they returned to West Africa. He was twenty-seven and she was twenty-nine. Even then, Mother was beginning to show signs of neurotic behaviour.

Father told this story. They were on board the West African mail steamer, which had just started to sail down the Mersey with the pilot on board. Mother decided she'd investigate the as yet unseen cabin. Seeing the low bulkhead, she turned on Father and snapped: 'The ceiling is too low; get me off this ship at once.' He replied, 'If you really mean it, then you'd better hurry up so that you can leave with the pilot and get down by the Jacob's ladder.' Mother stayed.

This irrational strain in her character lingered on. Years later we were living close to the harbour in Sligo. For some reason or other Mother was in bed during the day and the heavy dray horses pulling their noisy carts over the cobbled stones alongside the house got on her nerves. She ordered Father to go to the Town Hall and get the traffic stopped. He never did.

It seemed an extraordinary partnership. I do think that Father really loved Mother in his own way. All his life he was very loyal and faithful to her, and he never mentioned the constant friction to anyone outside the family. If ever he overheard us children grumbling among ourselves about what we deemed to be our mother's irrational behaviour, he'd pull us up gently.

I have a theory that Mother did not have a strong maternal instinct and wanted only one child. This was my eldest sister, Joan. Thinking about it years later as an adult, it seemed to me that Mother saw Joan as an extension of herself. There was a companionship between them that was not shared by the rest of us. Joan had the dubious privilege of having her cot in Mother's bedroom. Later on, when my brother and I came along and we were taken out for walks by the 'girl' (our 'live-in' maid, though we were never allowed to refer to her as 'maid'), Mother would say, 'Now the babies are all out we can sing and dance together,' and she and Joan would dance around the room.

Mother found child-bearing and rearing difficult. When the second child was born, fifteen months after Joan, it was too much. She couldn't cope, so Angela was reared by our paternal grandmother. There was always antipathy between Mother and her mother-in-law, but it was one-sided and it didn't stop us visiting Granny, who lived nearby. I was extremely fond of Granny. Poor Angela had a difficult life and died young but that is another story. Sometime during the war Angela came to live with the rest of us for a short while, but she and Mother did not get on and soon she was away again. Perhaps their fiery temperaments were too alike. So, from the start and until her death in 1972, Angela was to me, most of the time, a remote figure and I never had the opportunity to really get to know and understand her. When my brother Dermot appeared on the scene, Mother spoiled him in a different way from Joan – I think she felt sentimental towards him because he was the only boy. I was one year and twelve days younger than he, (though for many years I was telling people there were just twelve days between us), and we were very close, right up to the time we went to boarding school.

Eileen Hession, some years older than me, remembers me in my pram as a thin, snotty-nosed little baby – which throws light on something puzzling my mother said to me in my early youth: 'I was ashamed of you when you were a baby. I used to keep you hidden in the pram,' she remarked. I didn't dare ask why. I must have recovered rather quickly because snaps of me show a healthy, chubby, cheerful baby. As a child I remember being kept in bed sometimes with tonsillitis and I recall my paleness being remarked upon. Angela, given to rhyming, used to chant: *Pale Bale* (my mother's pet name for me) *is frail*.

I think I must have sensed very early on that I would have to stand on my own two feet and fend for myself. Which is precisely what I proceeded to do at the age of seven months. My first steps were not only taken alone but were running ones. It was a mild December day and the family had driven out to Strandhill, a seaside resort five miles outside Sligo. Leaving me lying safely on a rug on the strand, the grown-ups started to take a walk along the edge of the sea. Suddenly, there was a noise and turning round they saw me running towards them. To this day I love speed.

Very early on I also learned to pull myself up in my pram and would sit there unusually straight-backed, grinning at the world. Worried that I must have something wrong with my back, Mother took me to the doctor but all was well. Later, I cultivated an upright stance and my boarding school reports, which got progressively worse, had one redeeming gleam of light. Beside the word deportment, the word 'excellent' invariably appeared.

I do think children ought to be told not only that they are loved but also that they are attractive, or at least made to feel they are. I grew up assuming that I was physically inferior to everyone else – the Plain Jane of the family. Some of this was due to the fact that Joan was blessed with an abundance of self-confidence about her appearance – about everything, in fact – which was wonderful and always endorsed by Mother's compliments. As a teenager she had her poetry published and one of her plays publicly performed in Sligo – by a group called 'The Sligo Unknown Players'. As a small child it always puzzled me how they could continue to be called 'Unknown' after we saw them perform. Now and then I'd overhear Mother quoting admiring remarks made by others about my sister's looks. Matters were not improved by my mother's tendency to dress me in Joan's cast-off clothes, which, since her colouring is completely different from mine

(Joan looked marvellous in browns and dark colours) only emphasized my paleness. When I was older Mother once told me that when, as a small child, I fell and hurt myself I would run straight to Joan. I am delighted to know this now but when I was first told about it, it seemed very strange indeed because I recall finding Joan a distant person who rarely smiled – almost a stranger. Decades later when I mentioned this to my sister she said: 'Yes, and I used to *push* you away.'

It was only in adult life I discovered that at this period of her life Joan was preoccupied with her own problems.

Mother was conventional and curls were the 'in' thing in those days. My hair was very fine and straight and would probably have looked well with a proper cut, but curls were a must. She went to town where bows were concerned. Very large multi-coloured objects became permanently attached to the side of my head. I didn't object to these, perhaps because I couldn't see them. Then one day when I was about eight, Mother decided I must have a perm. This was an awesome business, and secretly I felt I was getting preferential treatment. Stoically I endured the hot irons clamped tightly to my head and after several hours I emerged from my first visit to the hairdresser with a halo of fuzz. Everyone was delighted, nobody more than I. In fact, in the long term, it did my hair good; and from then on, bit by bit, it became naturally wavy, and today there are times when it is decidedly curly, especially in damp weather.

Another time when I was very small, Mother suddenly got the whim to cut my hair very short and put me into a pair of shorts. I suffered this humiliation in silence, but after the job was completed I disappeared. Eventually, I was found hiding behind the pantry door, crying quietly. My explanation was, I'm told, 'You're trying to make a 'shame-boy' out of me.'

Although there were no really halcyon days that I can recall, nevertheless Dermot and I shared many happy childhood times. Father was a great pal to us, and we played a lot together. Dermot and I used to tumble about on Father's bed and he was unendingly patient with us. We were extremely lively, but he never once admonished us for all the shouting and squealing and pulling at him that we delighted in. If he failed to wake up when we yelled into his ears, we would pull up his eyelids and shout into his eyes!

As a small child my father would take me out for a walk while my mother took Joan elsewhere. One day Father said to me: 'Would you like to come with me to Liverpool?'

I was delighted and off we set. Very soon we were at the huge, now empty, timber warehouses by the docks. Written in large letters over one was 'LIVERPOOL'. I didn't hold it against him though!

Dermot and I frequently got into trouble together; like the time, when we were three or four, our next-door neighbour found us lying on our backs systematically eating her carefully grown peas, row after cherished row, which ran alongside our fence. She chased us away into a field of shin-deep nettles, and when we came home in tears smarting from the stings we rightly got little sympathy, so we comforted each other over our bowls of soup.

People sometimes ask me if I ever smoked. My answer is that I gave up cigarettes when I was three years old. Dermot and I used to puff away *under the bedclothes*. My parents, who were both heavy smokers, noticed that their supply in the spare bedroom was dwindling. They suspected the maid until one day the little clandestine mound of cigarette butts, secreted in some private corner by my brother, was found. He got punished, I didn't.

Joan would come home from school full of her new learning and eager to impart it to us two little receptive ignoramuses. She made us sit before a blackboard where she would chalk up her day's knowledge and, reversing her role of a short while before, make us be the pupils. She told me that she had a little cane and whacked us if we gave the wrong answers!

Later on when we were a bit older, she started writing plays which we all performed for the family. The one I remember best had a farmer in it, played by the maid, who was swathed in a curtain and shod in Mother's white leather mosquito boots. I was a rather superior fairy and, adopting a dramatic stance, was carefully coached by Joan to stare at a certain Victorian print on the wall and proclaim with raised magic wand, 'I am the fairy Zakufranzpenromanisk.' Dermot stole that show, dressed up as an exceedingly pretty fairy in a confection of yellow tulle, wearing bright red lipstick. Halfway through his bit he got an uncontrollable fit of the giggles and the 'curtain' had to be drawn.

I started going to school aged four. Dermot started at the same time. I remember it vividly. Father drove us there and, having said good-bye, left us at the little gate which was too small for a car to drive through. It was the national school, St Vincent's, run by the Ursuline convent and staffed by some members of the community, but mostly by lay women. We must have arrived late for there was no one to be seen anywhere. For some reason I was carrying Dermot's coat over my arm. We knocked on the door of the Low Babies' section of the building (next year we'd be in High Babies). At the sound of Father's car starting, Dermot let out a wail, dashed into the yard and belted towards the gate crying his heart out, leaving me alone with the coat to face the music. My new teacher, conducting me inside, put me at a desk near the front. Smiling to hide my painful shyness I produced a hankie and held it pressed to my face. The teacher, Miss Ruhane, gentleness itself, finally managed to get the hankie away but I spent the rest of the morning with my face buried in my hands, my head down on the desk, too bashful to face all these new children.

I was full of admiration for these self-confident ones. Even Dermot, when he was finally lured back, settled down with no apparent self-consciousness and with his customary charm. I can see him now, walking into the Low Babies' classroom, having attended to the necessities of nature, his trousers still undone, and in an enviable matter-of-fact way heading straight to the teacher's desk, loudly requesting, 'Please, Miss Ruhane, will you do me braces?'

It was about this time that we moved to Harbour House, formerly the Harbour Master's house. It was a large, eighteenth-century stone building, supposedly haunted by a sea captain. Some areas inside were in permanent twilight and there was a particular passage between the breakfast room and the kitchen which was decidedly stygian and figured in my nightmares. I couldn't go down this passage at night without a tightening of the abdominal muscles and *very* loud singing, moving at top speed. At night, when I was sent upstairs to fetch something, I would sing with such volume and intensity that I'd forget what it was I'd been told to bring down and would have to call out 'What did you send me up for?' Joan told me that she was so scared in Harbour House after dark that if she happened to find herself alone, nothing – not even inclement weather – could persuade her to stay inside. She would simply wait outside, swinging on the railings, or sauntering up and down, till someone arrived home. Father said he believed the house was haunted: for instance, doors would close unaccountably. The four large attics were so spooky that I couldn't so much as look at the winding stairs leading up to them once darkness had fallen. In the morning we would ask Father, 'Did you see any ghosts last night?' and he would reply something like, 'No, but I saw some pixies.' (These were the Little People or fairies which we used to read about in our story books.)

'What did you say to them?'

'Well, they asked me if I would like to be a pixie too, but I said no thanks because I think Mary and Joan have enough pixies already.'

He was referring to our little woollen pointed hoods which were also called pixies. This would have us laughing delightedly and our fear of the dark night and the ghosts would be temporarily allayed.

The Sligo National Primary School was just down the road from Harbour House. Looking back, the schooling system seems a curious set up. There was St Vincent's, the national school, where the teaching was excellent, and it was free and attended by a mixture of pupils from both professional and working-class backgrounds. Not far away, separated only by a camogie pitch, was a small private fee-paying primary school, and then there was the big secondary school, which catered for day-students and boarders. Each member of our family started off at St Vincent's, until he or she was ready for the secondary school. But I only stayed there until I was eight. One day during recreation I was accidentally charged into and broke my collarbone. Mother decided the school was 'too rough for Mary', and I was sent instead to St Anne's, the private school further down in the grounds, where I spent the next two years before joining my two older sisters at secondary school.

My early years coincided with the war. Father, always seeking adventure, joined the British Army as a commissioned officer and for some time was stationed in Northern Ireland. We used to drive up and spend long weekends with him in Ballycastle, County Antrim. I recall loaves of white bread being smuggled into the Free State in the boot of the car. There are other memories too. There was 'Snowball', a charming woman who stayed in our hotel. Years later we heard that she had been a spy for the Germans.

After training in Ballycastle, Father was posted to India. From there, he wrote to each of us. I looked forward to his letters (which towards the end I could read for myself), which were chatty and affectionate and always ended up with 'take care of Mumsy' or 'do what Mumsy tells you'.

Mother was left on her own to cope with three young children. As I've said, Granny was rearing Angela. Mother very often had me sleeping with her in her bed so we developed a camaraderie of sorts. I recall with pleasure the umpteen times she took me with her into town shopping and the cosy sit-down ice-creams we had together in the *Café Cairo*. Invariably after her shopping in Sligo town she would come home bearing cakes and bars of chocolate for us. Then there was what I called 'the bouncy thing', which I adored. On the way into town she would hold out her arms and stiffen them. Holding on to her hands, I would leap into the air. I loved that part of the trip. And Tuesday was 'comic day', a really big day for us. Who would get to read the *Dandy* or the *Beano* first? Dermot usually won.

I was not a great reader (Joan was a voracious one), but there was one particular book that I read over and over again. It was called *Long, Long Ago* and was the Greek and Roman myths retold for children. I'd probably be very disappointed in the illustrations now, but to me at that time, they were exquisite. It takes no effort to conjure them up seventy years later: 'While Proserpine danced the great king watched her', and poor old Pluto looking so innocent and well-intentioned. 'Prometheus chained to a rock' – with that vulture at his liver. 'Europa and the bull' – all those daisy chains; yet another chain: the one binding the diaphanously clad blonde-haired maiden to the sea cliff where she waited for the unseen monster to come and gobble her up. But of course, Perseus always got there first.

I think it must have been during this period that Mother's drink problem set in but I was far too young to realise with what demons she may have been wrestling. Because I had been at boarding school and Mother died when I was seventeen, there was no opportunity for an adult's relationship with her and I'll never know for sure what lay behind the problems of my parents' enigmatic marriage. Alcohol abuse predominates in my memories. I developed ways of disengaging my inner self from the misery, as a means of survival. I think I was affected but not damaged by it all. And there was a very positive side to it. From an unusually early age I could see something was radically wrong, and I learned a lot about what a marriage should be from observing one that was, to my mind, a disaster.

Mother would sometimes make me miserable by getting me to sing for her friends. Out of shyness I hated doing it but I'd never refuse. As a four-year-old she taught me *lots* of songs like 'Little Sir Echo' which we sang together – I being the Echo, of course. Then there were the innumerable times when Joan and I stood around the piano in the sitting-room and we sang the latest popular songs with Mother accompanying us. Songs like 'The Umbrella Man', 'At the Balalika' and numerous others, some of which I was later to record and sing on television and in concert.

I was given the day off from school when Father came home from India. There was great excitement. He had trunks full of exotic presents for us: carpets and rugs, silks, rings, silverware, swords, sandals, to name just a few. And there was all the news to tell him. Very soon, however, the disagreements resumed. Even as a very small child I used to pray that my parents would separate. I knew I would stay with Father – everyone knew I sided with him in the interminable conflict. Joan, I assumed, would stay with Mother. Both parents by now were drinking heavily. I took to playing tennis 'out the back' on my owney-o, bashing the tennis ball against the side of the house. I was happy there, all by myself, absorbed, and away from the tensions inside. It was my big release. By the standard of the times we were comfortably off. There were many times when Father would have preferred to go abroad again and sometimes they reached a stage where a house was purchased, whether it was Sheffield or Malta or wherever, and at the eleventh hour Mother would have a 'health crisis' and say she was not going and would 'take to the bed'. They were always senior well-paid positions and Mother thwarted many of his best plans. He was a very gifted man – if only Mother could have been flexible and met him half-way. Of course, as I now know there were failings on Father's side too. But I can only write as I recall. Mother's failings were more glaring in my youthful, inexperienced eyes. Perhaps she tried harder than any of us ever knew.

Years later, when I was in the monastery, I started having a recurring dream. In it Mother had become a totally reformed character: an attentive caring wife and mother. She never spoke a harsh word and was frequently engaged in gardening, something I don't ever remember her doing. Perhaps this was a sign that she had attained complete happiness at last. This dream had an unfailingly soothing effect on me.

Every Easter week found Sligo in the febrile grip of the annual *Feis*, which is the gaelic word for festival. There were two organisations: the *Feis Ceóil* and the *Feis Sligigh*. Both involved competitions for singing, reciting, the playing of musical instruments and dancing. There were solo, duet and ensemble contests. The Sligo *Feis Ceóil* was the older institution and the standard was reputedly as high as, if not higher than, that of the Dublin *Feis Ceói*l. Competitions were in the Gaelic language in the *Feis Sligigh*.

As a child I dreaded Easter because the very word evoked thoughts of a week of unmitigated discomfort, occasioned by my having to perform at innumerable competitions. Competitiveness is alien to my nature, so I would never have voluntarily entered the *Feis* arena. It was my school teachers who did me the bad/good turn. I considered it a penance: all that relentless assault on the nervous system. But it was also a blessing in disguise, for it trained me successfully to cope with and effectively control that agony of nervousness which is the common lot of most performers and artists, whose ranks I was destined to join nearly ten years later. The exhilaration of winning was tempered by the knowledge that one would be 'entered' again the following year. The Christian significance of Easter was lost on me then and I would have looked at you with incredulity if you had told me that twenty years hence the Easter mysteries and particularly the Resurrection, would assume such importance for me.

Preparations for the *Feis* started months ahead: some parents I suspect may even have built their year around it, becoming obsessed with the performances of their offspring. With single-minded dedication they would have their child licked into shape well in advance of the Big Event. Then, at the appointed hour, they would lead them forth to the venue, thoroughly scrubbed and dolled up in their best outfits.

While their children went through their paces, some parents could be observed in the audience following every syllable and mouthing it with them. The rivalry could be quite acute. One year it was bruited that certain parents had invited the adjudicator to tea! Rank bribery was intimated. The high-tension point of each event was that awesome interval between the final competitor leaving the stage and the adjudicator mounting the platform to announce the results. Breathing was more or less suspended. Then the winner was announced and the charged atmosphere cleared. The audience discussed and compared notes among themselves and slowly the hall would empty while people waited patiently for the next competition.

The ability to bi-locate would have been invaluable for those of us who found we had been entered for two or more competitions at more or less the same time on the same day. Believe me, it did happen. I've already described my winning of a singing competition at the Sligo *Feis Ceóil* at the age of eight. In the same year I had been entered for a *Feis Sligigh* competition at the Town Hall. No memory of sunlight there but a sense of dust and dryness everywhere. My first song was '*An Caitín Bán*', a lament for a little white kitten. The other was about a little girl called Mary, '*a bhíos i gcónai 'gáire*' (who was always smiling). That adjudicator also caused me unnecessary agony, this time by reading out the prize-winners in reverse order. I wasn't even among those highly recommended, or third or second prize-winner. Then, I heard my name and number read out as First prize-winner. To compound my painful confusion at this unexpected turn of events, shot through with pleasure of course, I heard the adjudicator say, 'Would this competitor please come up on stage so that I may congratulate her.' Veiling the acute shyness with my customary giant-sized smile and with thumping heart, I gracefully climbed on to the stage and received my prize. But I made a less graceful exit, slipping on the wooden steps, bumping my head and landing on my back at the foot of the stairs, completely winded. I was carried outside by the adjudicator, with worried mother close at his heels. As a concerned crowd gathered, I regained my breath and the adjudicator gently remarked, 'You have a lovely voice and I hope you'll never get a swelled head.' I almost did...

In 2009, the steering committee of the Sligo *Feis Ceóil* wrote to me. As one of those who had won the Children's Cup, they asked me to jot down my childhood memories of the *Feis Ceóil*.

> My memories are mostly of nerves, I have to admit, and the inner dread that descended on me as Easter Week approached. I was sent in for various competitions each year coached for the singing ones by the gentle Mother Brendan at St Anne's, never daring to say: 'Oh please Mother don't send me in again.' And how very glad I am that I covered up my reluctance because the exercise stood me in great stead when later I became a professional performer.
>
> About the Children's Cup: I'll have to take your word for it that I won it. I honestly don't remember having done so. What I do recall is almost winning it the year it was won by a boy whose voice was already on the verge of breaking. Rumour was rife in Sligo that he'd won it because his mother had invited the adjudicator to tea that Sunday before the competition.
>
> Among the other things I remember was the time my brother Dermot who had gone in for a recitation competition was recalled but couldn't be found. He'd fled as soon as he finished his piece and went home to play ... sensible boy.

'Out the back' was our favourite place for sulking, being alone or nursing a hurt. During the war Mother tried to economise on children's new clothing. She gave one of her suits to a tailor to have it reduced and made into a 'new' suit for Dermot. Now, 'reduced' is the operative word for the man did more or less just that with the jacket. He turned up the hem leaving the pockets where they originally were and, worse still, also left the waist as it was. The first day Dermot was put into the outrageous garment he vanished almost immediately – and was missing all morning. He was finally located 'out the back' in tears. When he was asked what the broken heart was all about he said: 'It's this suit. I wish that a lion would come and eat me up – me and this awful suit.' He'd been listening to those verses about the little boy who let go of his nurse's hand and was eaten by the lion at the zoo. Thereafter this monstrous garment was referred to by all and sundry as 'the lion suit'.

It's probably true of many mothers that they don't realise how sensitive little children are about the clothes they are made to wear, and how hurt they can be. My Confirmation Day was a mortifying experience. Mother had decided that, for the ceremony, I should be clad in Joan's once-best dress. It was an expensive silk dress, but salmon pink – beautiful on Joan but a disaster on me with my different pale, nondescript colouring and skin tone. In a newspaper article, years later, Joan described me as having been a 'fawn-coloured child'. It was also short. I loathed the garment but knew better than to say so and provoke an argument I couldn't win. Being wartime, ever since the supply of petrol for civilians had ceased, the car had been laid up on blocks in the coach house. There was only one taxi service in town and the man had been booked to bring my brother and myself to the cathedral. For some reason the taxi failed to turn up. It was getting perilously close to the hour of the service, so Mother decided to get out her bicycle and ferry us on the carrier through the rain, one at a time. The cathedral was a good ten minutes' cycle away. By the time we were both deposited inside the door, Dermot was lachrymose. The ceremony had begun. The boys in an assortment of garments were seated on one side of the church. On the opposite side sat the girls in serried ranks, all wearing – to my utter consternation – *long white dresses*, complete with *white shoes* and socks. Dressed glaringly in my short salmon-pink dress, white socks and *brown* sandals, feeling like a cross between a fish out of water and a Christian martyr, I had to march up the aisle in full view of everyone and join this radiantly white troop of potential soldiers of Christ. I deserved an award for bravery.

Out for a walk one day and skipping ahead of my mother and her friend, I overheard the latter remark: 'Mary's got dancer's legs.' Since compliments (I took it to be one) were thin on the ground where I was concerned, I was thrilled but too diffident to enquire what was meant. Mother decided I should learn ballet. This prospect gave me unspeakable pleasure. There was one woman in Sligo who taught ballet, and Mother made arrangements for me to begin lessons. Then, unexpectedly, my would-be teacher left town. That was that. I took it all philosophically. I would have loved to have tried dancing. It seems to me to be the most satisfying form of self-expression, engaging, as it does, the entire body from head to pointed toe; also the silence of the art appeals to me. It wasn't until I was nineteen and living in Dublin that the opportunity of having lessons presented itself again. I attended ballet classes there and enjoyed every second of them, but by then my singing career had begun to take off and occupied most of my time. Besides, I'd always been told that dancers must start as young children and not be too tall and I am five feet seven and a quarter inches in my stockinged feet. I think perhaps one reason why I enjoy tennis so enormously is because of the grace of the game. Some movements on court approximate to the dance.

I've always had a natural aptitude for sports. When I moved on into the senior secondary school in Sligo, I started to play *camógaí* (Gaelic spelling), also called hurling, a ball and stick game, played by women. The only time I took part in the Annual School Sports, I won the running competition. I loved movement, and when I was chosen to act as goal-keeper in my first and second year at day school I was too inhibited and diffident to say I hated the inactivity and could I please be allowed to play out in the field. So for two whole years I endured this penance, until I was sent off to boarding school.

As we grew older I played less and less with Dermot. I was at St Anne's school and he was at the Christian Brothers' school on the far side of town and immersed in a world of gangs to which, of course, little girls were never admitted. Dermot had an endearing habit of getting some words slightly wrong. He announced one evening that he was 'clergic' to eggs. And my favourite one: he was trying to do his homework and the rest of us were being noisy when he flung down his pen and cried, 'Can't you have a bit of *constipation* for someone who is trying to study?' He was a very affectionate little boy and very protective of me. When I broke my collarbone and he heard the news from a school companion who said, 'I hear Mary was taken home in a coffin', he was so frightened and angry that he fought the other boy. And later, when I had to have my appendix out, he burst into tears, ran upstairs, locked himself in the lavatory and cried for hours.

On the two occasions that I spent in hospital, Mother did not visit me. For some reason she could not face it, but I was prepared for this, remembering her reaction to my first accident. I'd been wheeling a dolls' pram when a very plump girl I was playing with sat on the pram causing the whole thing to tip over. My hand caught in the handle and, unable to free it, I was dragged down the slope of the concrete road for several yards. Spurting blood, I dashed into the house and

Mother was so upset that she promptly disappeared, leaving Father to deal with me. He held my finger under the running cold water tap. The finger was broken and the chemist fixed it up. Mother didn't accompany us, and I fully understand now that she just did not feel able to cope. She knew I was fond of her and I knew she was fond of me, but I took it for granted that she would stay away from the hospital and that Father would take over as usual. She was inordinately fearful of illness. She suffered from bronchitis, but would never have her chest examined in case she had tuberculosis. She grew up at a time when the disease was rampant in Ireland and entire families died of it. I do think she could have benefited from psychiatric help, but in those days and in that part of the world, ailments of that nature were synonymous with mental sickness and treatment was not available as far as I know. She was subject to black depressions.

I had a reputation at school for being gentle and biddable, but I must often have been very difficult and fractious at home; I remember Mother once turning on me saying, 'You're a street angel and a house devil.' Boarding school was soon to put an end to that.

Father wanted to send Dermot to Stonyhurst, the Jesuit School in England. There was some family hitch at the last moment and Dermot was sent instead to Blackrock College, Dublin. The following year when I was thirteen it was decided that I too should go to boarding school. I was sent to Sion Hill, run by the Dominican Sisters and next door to Blackrock College. That was handy for everyone, especially for my parents visiting us. As things turned out, with Joan now also in Dublin at the Abbey School of Acting and Dermot and myself at boarding schools there, my parents decided to move to Dublin. Going to boarding school was something I'd never dreamt of. Joan told me that she used to wish she'd been sent to one, so in a way I felt privileged.

It was the end of an era for the family, an end of living in Sligo.

CHAPTER 2

Ploughing a New Furrow

FOR ME GOING to boarding-school was doubly exciting. I was intrigued by the Cash's name tapes that had to be sewn on all garments and the lengthy list of clothing required. I was excited by the shopping it all entailed. There was the novelty of living away from home and it afforded me an escape from the tension in the household.

Obviously, at that age, I did not know my mother, nor perhaps even my father – not the full story anyway. As a teenager I nurtured many negative memories of my mother and it was only recently, when a gynaecologist friend explained to me that she exhibited all the symptoms of post-natal depression, that I began to enumerate the positive memories that, in my youth, I had pushed to °the back of my mind. I resented the constant attacks on my father, verbal and sometimes even physical, the sarcastic remarks with never a show of affection either by word or gesture. In 1980 when writing the first draft of my autobiography, why did I not recall the ample evidence of the affection she showed me? Perhaps I subconsciously resented the special place my sister Joan had in her life. I don't know.

Here I am, aged seventy-four, asking myself all sorts of questions about my memories of my mother. Yes, I did feel self-conscious arriving as a boarder at Sion Hill dressed in a hand-me-down, though expensive, coat of Joan's, dyed navy. But very soon, Mother bought me an expensive and beautiful princess-line winter coat that was so admired by some of my more glamorous schoolmates that they used to borrow it for special occasions. It was well worth waiting for. And, instead of the dull mass-produced long white dresses that came from a leading Dublin store to be worn on Prizegiving day, Mother had a very pretty one made especially for me by a private dressmaker. Boarders had regulation week-day and Sunday uniforms. Mother, who was fashion conscious and dressed smartly, did not care for the dull run-of-the-mill Sunday uniform and had mine specially made. Wary of my mother's reaction, I never reported to her the disapproval of the Mistress of Schools, who expected everyone to be dressed the same. And what about the special party she gave for me and for my little friends when I was about ten? Or the lovely cakes she made specially for me and brought with her when they drove out to visit me at Sion Hill on Sundays. That sort of thing.

I was put on a train in Sligo and met in Dublin by friends of the family who drove me to Sion Hill. Everyone was kind, welcoming and pleasant and in no time I settled in. Going to secondary school was a turning point in my life. It may be an exaggeration to say that there I kicked over the traces, but something akin to that did happen. I sprouted wings.

I had always done very well at school in Sligo. Academically, the standard there was very high. Sion Hill was not in the same league. After the first few days of classes I could see that in Third Year in my new school they were covering the same ground I'd already successfully traversed in the Second Year in Sligo. So I simply sat back and lazed. My days of being a diligent student were over. At the end of that year I sailed through the school examinations without doing any work. The following year I got honours in the National Intermediate Examination Certificate – without doing much work. The rot had set in and thereafter it became increasingly difficult to apply myself to my studies.

If my brain was not being exercised enough, my body certainly was. Father had brought back some fine hockey sticks from India, but the game was not played in the Sligo school and the sticks had lain there unused. One of them arrived with my luggage at Sion Hill. The first day on the field I discovered that, although I am not left-handed, I have more power and control on my left side and since hockey is right-hand swing I recognised the game was not for me. I swapped my hockey stick for a *camógaí* stick (a lovely springy one which lasted me

all those four game-packed years), and a new world opened up for
me. I found that I simply adored the game. I was nimble-footed and
revelled in the swiftness and speed, and from then on played either
centre field, or much more often, left wing. *Camógaí* was more in tune
with my temperament than hockey. Like the latter, it too has its discipline, yet it is less restricting. For instance, unlike hockey, the player
may swing her stick as high as she likes on either side; the ball may
be bounced on the stick whether standing or running. In my opinion
camógaí is the more spirited game; rather like having wings instead of
being on wheels. It certainly had a liberating effect on me. Later, the
summer term brought tennis and an attendant new dimension of
pleasure. A lot has been written about the virtue of games for growing children; I can vouch for their salutary effect on me. Out on the
camógaí pitch and tennis court I became unshackled, and knew a glorious sense of freedom. I loved games for their own sake, which is also
the way I feel about singing. Two things mar that pleasure: competition and organization. For example, I would prefer to rally for a
couple of hours rather than play sets of tennis. And organization:
it was an honour to have been voted Games Captain by my school
fellows during my last year at Sion Hill but it most certainly took a
lot of the zest out of playing. I am not an organizer and I disliked the
responsibility that 'being in charge' entailed. But, nevertheless, I spent
any free time I had out on the playing fields. It was fortunate for me
that games at Sion Hill were so encouraged. During my years there,
our First Eleven *camógaí* team was never beaten by any other Dublin
school.

Not long after I arrived at Sion Hill it was discovered that I could
sing, so I continued to be put through the *Feis* mill, this time the
Dublin *Feis Ceóil*. My singing teacher, who also had a degree in French,
was a very amiable, firm yet gentle person called Sister Angela Walsh.
She continued to teach until she was almost ninety. She was quite frail
and had very bright eyes. One of her great maxims was 'Live the song',
which is what I always aimed to do. Until she died in 1983, I counted
her amongst my most cherished friends.

I have often thought how important it is for parents, teachers, or
indeed anyone in authority, to feed the self-confidence of young
people. Once as a young widow of twenty-two, I returned to Sion Hill
to participate in a charity concert given by Sister Angela's ex-pupils.

An older singer, whom I didn't actually know, waited off-stage while I sang 'She Moved Through the Fair', a very difficult song to sing well. I had been, as usual, shivering with nerves in the wings awaiting my turn, and felt relieved when everything went off well. As I came off, this older singer remarked: 'I liked your little song.'

Though cut to the quick by this put-down, I maintained my composure. But when the concert was over, I cried my eyes out and wanted to give up singing there and then. Sister Angela reassured me, dried my tears and urged me to ignore the remark. I mention this paltry incident only to show how really fragile my self-confidence was, even though I had by then a highly acclaimed series on BBC TV under my belt, TV and recordings in America, as well as three best-selling records.

Every year Sion Hill, together with the attached Domestic Science Training College, put on a pageant. Scripts were written by one of the nuns. Each year I secretly hoped there would be a part in the pageant for me and when eventually I was chosen to play St Francis, I was thrilled. To this day I can recall the chloroform-like smell of the glue with which the beard was stuck to my chin. It was a very small role with some lovely lines I had to speak about love and Brother Sun. I was fourteen and one of the seniors waiting with me in the wings remarked: 'You look great as a fella. I could easily fall for you.'

It was 1951, my penultimate year at Sion Hill. The annual pageant was going to be based on the life and work of Thomas Moore, who, in his poems depicted the harp as a symbol of Ireland. For that reason, harps and harpers had to be found. Unfortunately, both had by then gone out of fashion in Ireland. The forward-looking prioress of Sion Hill, Mother Jordan, had earlier decided to introduce the harp to the school, probably with the pageant in mind. Researching for my Talks in 2005, I chanced upon some interesting correspondence between Mother Jordan and Mr Malachy McFall of Belfast, the only harp-maker left in Ireland at the time. He didn't have any new harps and could offer her only one second-hand Tara standing harp for £65, a pretty stiff figure in those days. So, the school scoured the country high and low and collected old harps from barns, outhouses and attics

– most of them riddled with woodworm – and managed to 'fit' three small Brian Boru knee-harps to three young singers in the pageant, Deirdre Flynn, Kathleen Watkins and me. Then it was suggested that, rather than using the harps as stage props, we should learn to play them and thus be able to accompany ourselves as we sang 'Moore's Melodies' – not that far removed from what the harpers of old did. The school had found someone to teach the harp for the event, in the person of Máirín Ní Shéa, known to us students as Mrs Ferriter, herself one of the last of a dying breed of Irish harp enthusiasts. I do not know of any tradition of women singers in Irish culture, much less a tradition of women accompanying themselves on the harp. We were ploughing a new furrow.

The success of the school pageant was such that, Máirín was kept on as a full-time teacher and gradually over the ensuing years, she found she had classes full of budding harpists. Thus was born a trend that eventually helped revive the harp in Ireland as an accompanying instrument. The idea appealed to many who saw the revival of old Irish cultural traditions as important to the country's sense of nationhood. Máirín Ní Shéa did more for the revival of the Irish Harp than anyone else I know of in the early 1950s. The sheer novelty of singing and accompanying oneself on the Irish harp aroused curiosity and drew many listeners – and spectators.

Déirdre, Kathleen and I were not particularly pally starting off, but finding ourselves frequently thrown together during the ensuing couple of years, friendships were formed and, to this day, we have kept in touch and meet occasionally. They opted not to take up music professionally but have followed my work closely and have been my lifelong supporters. In 2008 they came to a talk I gave at the Carolan Harp Festival in Nobber, Co. Meath.

It is doubtful if we'd have got on Radio Éireann's programme 'Children at the Mike', which we did each of us in turn, if it weren't for accompanying ourselves on the harp. When Máirín arranged the broadcasts in the late spring of 1952 my two songs were: 'Habit Shirt' (Gaelic, despite the title) and '*Árd Tighe Cuain*', a beautiful exile's song from County Antrim. After I left school, my sister Joan presented me with her own English translation of the latter. She called it 'The Quiet Land of Érin' and as time went by I became identified with this song. In 1956 I used it as the opening and closing theme melody for my

BBC Television 'Starlight Series' – and indeed for innumerable subsequent radio and television programmes.

Aged sixteen and in my last year at Sion Hill, I did the minimal amount of work, even using the harp lessons as an excuse to give up the piano. For whatever reason, I found it difficult to apply myself to study. My teachers attributed it to the situation at home. When I sat for my history examination paper and read the questions I decided I could not answer a single one. So, while everybody else scribbled away industriously, I produced my knitting needles and got on with finishing my white tennis socks. When the papers were collected, mine was in its pristine state of blankness. The supervisor, with a glare of disapproval, took the tennis sock from me and pinned it to the examination paper. In due course I was summoned into the un-amused presence of the Mistress of Studies, who promptly despatched me back to the now deserted examination room to re-do the test. To my astonishment, I passed.

Bit by bit in my final year, I began to drop subjects. I had already jettisoned Harmony, partly because of disharmony between me and the teacher. She saw I wasn't applying myself. I'd have dropped every subject if I could have got away with it. As far as I know everyone else took seven subjects in their Leaving Certificate examination but I opted for the minimum allowed – which was five. Although I got honours in Irish and French, my marks for the other subjects were nothing to boast about.

I could never be classified as wild: I never went out of my way to infringe any school rules or regulations. It just happened. From the time of my arrival I became more and more irrepressible. My transgressions were largely of the schoolgirl giddiness variety: talking in class, in rank, in the dormitory after lights out (I had only one midnight feast and found it utterly boring), reading comics under the desk lid while class was in progress (I always made sure of a seat at the back so as to engage undisturbed in such undercover pursuits); running when I was supposed to be walking and so on.

Then there was the now baffling episode of the pony tail. Without the slightest intention of setting a trend, one afternoon I innocently gathered my hair into an elastic band at the crown of my head and presented myself at my desk in the study hall. Its effect on the presiding Sister was startling. It was, I suppose, a hitherto unknown hairstyle. Anyway, I was called up to the Sister's desk and roundly reprimanded. After I'd left, during a visit to my old school I was told that the said sister had found it difficult to keep a straight face while the ponytail bobbed up and down as I argued earnestly with her over the offending coiffure. The next day the school was peppered with juniors sporting pony tails. The damage, whatever it was, had been done.

Another time, in town for some reason, two companions and myself, as pre-arranged met up with some Belvedere schoolboys. We went off with them to the cinema. Afterwards as we were saying our innocent good-byes in the shrubbery, the lights of an oncoming car revealed the delinquents and, of course, we were reported to the authorities. Next day my companions and I were dramatically called forth from the study hall and each one interviewed separately by the Prioress. She was such a remote figure that this was the only occasion I can recall having dealings with her – which indicated the enormity of the misdemeanour. My parents were sent for and told about the incident. I don't remember any further repercussions.

I had a hefty appetite (though you would never have thought it to look at me) and was the best eater at my table in any given year. Everything I ate was quickly burnt up – games and nervous energy I suppose, what we nowadays refer to as a 'fast metabolism'. When autumn came we threw our *camógie* sticks up at the walnut trees and the fruit tumbled down. We used our desk lids to crack open the shells. There was a well-stocked apple orchard that also suffered from our periodic raids. Being one of the more gracile ones, my job was to slither through a gap in the hedge and collect the windfalls. Having stuffed the tops of our gym-slips to capacity, the other method of transport for the plundered fruit from orchard to school dormitory was the capacious elastic-ended legs of our uniform school knickers. If any of the Sisters noticed my curious and uncharacteristically slow gait on an autumnal afternoon around 4.15pm (the apple-gathering hour) they made no comment.

A few months before I was due to finish school, soon after the incident with the Belvedere boys, we were all leaving the refectory in rank, and supposedly in silence, and yours truly was of course talking.

Suddenly, Sister Petra, the Mistress of Studies, made a noise like a clap of thunder with her wooden clappers. We all stood rooted to the spot. 'Mary O'Hara,' she said, 'the community has decided that if you continue to break as much as one more minor rule we cannot shoulder the responsibility of you any longer.' That shut me up for a bit, but not for long. We were all terrified of her. She became a good friend of mine after I was widowed. I had come to appreciate her, as one often does with teachers, in a very different light. Her friendship meant much to me.

Despite my supposedly incessant contravention of school rules and the annoyance it must have caused, I know that the Sion Hill community nevertheless loved me – and none perhaps more than Sister Angela. After my husband's death I was showered with letters from them. One wrote: 'Nuns seldom cry, but you would have been touched by the number of people here who wept when your telegram reached Sister Angela.' They had never even seen Richard. I was deeply moved. The connection between myself and Sion Hill from the time I left school until my marriage – and Richard's death – had been a very tenuous one, through my sporadic singing lessons and a letter about once a year to Sister Angela. But after Richard's death I kept in closer contact. Over the intervening years I have been the recipient of considerable love and friendship from several people there – and I know that my life has been the richer and warmer for it. I never think of myself as their past pupil but as a friend.

CHAPTER 3

The Harp

B Y THE TIME I finished boarding school in the summer of 1952
my sister Joan was established at the Abbey, Ireland's National
Theatre, as a gifted young actress. She'd known since she was
five years old what she wanted to be. My lack of motivation bothered
Joan and she suggested I do a course at Jill Fisher's School of Beauty
Culture. Consequently, that winter I attended classes. I passed my
diploma but neither collected the certificate nor ever made use of it.
However, it proved an invaluable asset, helping in later life with my
stage make-up.

Next Joan got enthusiastic about my doing art. I liked art but my
talents in that area were as yet unexplored. I'd always thought it a
shame that at Sion Hill the choice lay between music and art.
Naturally, I'd chosen music but I regretted having had to forego art
classes which I'd enjoyed as a junior. So, off I trotted to be enrolled in
the College of Art in Dublin.

Encouraged by Sister Angela, I continued my singing lessons, but
it never crossed my mind to continue with the harp until one day, out
of the blue, a casual remark from my mother gave me pause. She said
something like this: 'Oh, by the way, I hear that the others [meaning
Déirdre and Kathleen] have continued having harp lessons. What
about doing the same yourself – if you feel like it?'

My mother was in no way pushy and, had I decided not to bother
going back for more lessons, she'd have left it at that and never mentioned it again. But it was as if that stirred something in me and I
thought, 'Sure, why not?' So, back I went and I am very glad that
I did.

The big event that winter took place in January 1953. Máirín (Mrs Ferriter), Déirdre, Kathleen and I were flown to London to take part in the entertainment side of the publicity for the first '*An Tóstal*' ('Welcome' in Gaelic), launched by the Irish Tourist Board to boost the tourist industry. It included tea at the Irish Embassy and an appearance on the BBC TV programme 'In Town Tonight', produced by Richard Afton. The harp proved to be a 'great draw.' It got us into all the media, even Pathe News, something I only discovered by accident when, back in Dublin, I went to the pictures at our local cinema. And there we were, strumming away. Three years later Richard was to play an important role in my career by bringing me over from Dublin to make my first solo appearance on British television in his Variety Programme 'More Contrary', which resulted in my being signed up for the rest of that series and led later to my own television 'Starlight Series'. On this first occasion he took us all to lunch at the Café Royal and saw to it that we were comfortably set up at the Piccadilly Hotel. There we tasted the sensuous delight of our first heated bathroom floor. Déirdre and I, who shared a room, cavorted ecstatically about the suite, scantily clad, delighting in the warmth of the rooms – for central heating in those days was virtually unheard of in Ireland and it was warm only near a fire, beyond the radius of which chill and draught prevailed.

Even after the London appearances with '*An Tóstal*', which got very good press, I never entertained the notion of earning my living as a singer. However, shortly after our return from London something very unexpected started the ball rolling. My sister Joan, between her acting appearances at the Abbey Theatre, had been presenting a weekly commercial programme on Radio Éireann. It was called 'The Gateaux Programme' and one day the producer said to her: 'Joan, we really could do with a singer on the programme, do you know of anyone?'

'Well,' said the loyal Joan, 'I have a little sister who sings and plays the harp.'

'Oh ... right, bring her in and we'll have a listen.'

So in she brought me. I sang a couple of songs and the producer's verdict was decidedly positive. Over a period of several weeks I recorded some two dozen songs for this weekly commercial programme.

Around the same time, Mairéad Piggott, producer of Radio Éire-ann's 'Children at the Mike', asked if I would do a fifteen-minute programme of Irish songs (in Gaelic) on my own. They were satisfied enough with the result to want more and, from then on, a blue con-tract form would arrive in the post periodically. That's how RÉ did things in those days. During this time I also started singing as soloist with the Radio Éireann Light Orchestra (more blue contract forms on the doormat). 'Take the Floor' ditto. This was a light variety pro-gramme in which I took part many times. Besides myself on the harp, it included the Presenter (Dinjo), the actor Éamonn Keane, a story-teller, Rory O'Connor and his Dancers (believe it or not on radio), another singer (*a capella*), Teresa Clifford, and a comedian. Gael-Linn was another popular sponsored programme for which I recorded indi-vidual items from time to time.

Researching for a talk I gave at the World Harp Congress in Dublin in 2005, I came across a little red notebook that lists most of the songs I recorded for radio during this period and what I was paid. For instance there were two dozen songs listed for which Gateaux paid £2.00 each – a princely sum then for a teenager. Brendán Mac Lua, who in those days manned the reception desk at Gael-Linn and who later became a very successful editor/owner of the newspaper, *The Irish Post* in London, told me years later that he had resented my breezing in, on and off, to record a song or two and getting paid more than he did for a whole week's work. I was also approached with offers of work from other commercial programmes following the success of the Gateaux programme. By now I was taking part in Variety Concerts around the country. Not having an agent, concert organisers around the country contacted me through Radio Éireann. What with these broadcasts, my regular Radio Éireann fifteen-minute programmes and intermittent guest appearances with the Radio Éireann Light Orchestra, I recognised the need to build up my repertoire. Every week I went to the studio and recorded several new songs for the commercial programmes but, of course, RÉ's own broadcasts always went out live. Quite unplanned, I found myself earning my living as a singer and harpist, so one can see how my Irish Harp played an important role in first bringing me to public broadcasting and the attention of an ever-widening audience at home in Ireland and, very soon, abroad too.

Early in 1953 I decided I needed a harp of my own. As there were none to be had in Ireland at the time, I had to turn to a harp-maker called Henry Briggs, an Englishman living in Scotland and making Irish harps. What could be more politically ecumenical! He eventually made a second one for me and this time I travelled to Glasgow to collect it, meeting Mr Briggs for the first time. Both harps started life as a sycamore tree in a Scottish woodland. His first harp remained my favourite and is now on display at the Burns Library, Boston College. It is the one featured most often on the cover of my recordings and books, including this autobiography. My other Briggs is now in retirement in Wicklow, Ireland, with my nephew, the writer Sebastian Barry.

In that same red notebook I came across this draft of a very businesslike letter (clearly dictated by my father – you can tell from the style, it's not that of a seventeen-year old girl) but addressed by me to the Irish Minister of Industry and Commerce, which is worth quoting:

Dear Sir,

I was one of the Tóstal harpists who visited Britain in the Spring of this year. I endeavoured without success to purchase a harp in this country and had no alternative but to order a new instrument from Mr Briggs, Musical Instrument Manufacturer of Glasgow. I expect delivery of same within the next week.

Under the circumstances I would be very much obliged if you would issue to me a permit enabling me to import the harp (which is a Tara standing Harp) duty free.

Yours faithfully,
Mary O'Hara

That letter emphasised the fact that in 1953 there were still no harps being made in Ireland. This soon changed, however, with more and more young girls clamouring for harps on which to accompany themselves. It was years later that I discovered that I was being held responsible for this phenomenon.

I did precious little work at the College of Art, but I had a great old time. I consorted with painters like Owen Walsh, and classmates like

Brian Bourke, and others, some of whom later made names for them-selves. One morning, having tuned in to a radio broadcast of mine the previous night, Brian said to me: 'My God, Mary, you're schizophrenic. I listened to you last night and you were singing one thing and play-ing another.'

I became pally with Michael O'Nolan, who for some reason I knew as 'Tilly', younger brother of Brian (aka Myles na gCapaillín and Flann O'Brian) author of *At Swim-Two-Birds*, *The Third Policeman* and *An Béal Bocht*. Tilly's sketch of me appeared in the *Irish Times* and I was surprised on my recent visit (2009) to Boston to see it hanging at the Burns Music Library, Boston College. I also sat for Tilly. Later, when I became better known, I was told he was kicking himself for painting over it.

My friendship with Tilly was purely platonic but one day while I was sitting for him in the large dining room at his home, his mother wandered in with her carer. She glared at both of us in turn and mut-tered darkly to him: 'I'm going to tell your father about this.' His father had been dead for years.

My only other connection with the Ó Nolan family was that a sister of theirs, Mother Rosario OP (whom we called Rosie) taught me at boarding school how to darn a sock. At the College of Art I met up again with Brigid Marlin, a classmate from Sion Hill and today a renowned painter. This time we became fast and lasting friends. We used to go off for coffee together and one morning, walking up Grafton Street in high spirits, she started to sing 'If I were a black-bird, I'd whistle and sing...' She claims I rudely interrupted her, muttering: 'Thank God you're not a blackbird.'

Around this time I was introduced to Seán Óg Ó Tuama, who was to become a key figure in my musical career. He was related by marriage to Máirín Ní Shea, our Sion Hill harp teacher, through whom I first met him. We became and remained, to the time of his death in April 1980, very good friends. Seán Óg was a gifted and generous-hearted man. Science was his profession, music his passionate interest. In my opinion, nobody in the mid-twentieth century Ireland did more to foster a knowledge and love of traditional Irish song than Seán Óg Ó Tuama.

For years he held a Saturday afternoon class in the Royal Irish Academy of Music (RIAM), an imposing building in Westland Row, Dublin 2. The class was free and open to all and sundry. Seán Óg stood before us and taught the songs by singing a phrase at a time, which we then repeated. His fund of songs seemed endless and he had them published later in a series of song-books called '*Claisceadal Cois Life*' and for the first few years, needing to build up my repertoire for my radio broadcasts, I bought the booklets and attended his *RIAM* classes whenever I was back in town. To my way of thinking learning a traditional song from someone as informed and as steeped in Irish culture as Seán Óg, is incomparably better than learning from the printed page. Besides, many of these songs had never before been written down.

In a very real sense Seán Óg and exponents like him, by transmitting them the way they did, have kept these songs alive. His singing voice may have left much to be desired, but behind the voice was a keen mind and a heart charged with an intense love of his country and its music, so that he was more than a mere teacher of notes. The Gaelic '*Amhrán Mór*' (big/great songs) – which I always sang unaccompanied – are the ones that elicited the highest praise from music critics wherever in the world I sang them in concert. These I learnt from Seán Óg Ó Tuama. From the start, one of my favourite Gaelic songs had been '*Róisín Dubh*'. It bears one of those symbolic titles that belong to a time when it was the habit of poets and ballad writers to refer to Ireland under concealed names. I like the idea that when the order went forth from Dublin Castle that ballads (being powerful political instruments) were not to be sold at markets, balladeers adopted the simple ruse of selling bundles of straw wrapped in a broadsheet with the ballad on it. During Jacobite times the allegorical ballad was at the height of its vogue, culminating during the early years of the last century in Yeats's play *Cathleen Ní Houlihan*.

In view of all the work I was getting, I felt I owed it to my audience to be as competent as possible, which is why I decided to take lessons on the orchestral harp from Mercedes Bolger, who had just returned from a season with the Hallé Orchestra and was at the time harpist with the Radio Éireann Light Orchestra. A shy and amiable person, Mercedes and I became good friends and remain so to this day. I continued with her lessons until my work and,

eventually my engagement to Richard Selig, took me away from
Ireland altogether.

For a very brief period after leaving Sion Hill I participated in Variety
Concerts organized by various Irish Societies in England and Scotland
around St Patrick's day, together with Máirín Ní Shéa and her sister
Róisín, another ardent Irish Harp enthusiast. We were clad in the same
long, green, stylised Irish costumes, hired from Ging's theatrical out-
fitters in Dublin, which I irreverently referred to as 'our flowing togas'.
During that early stage we all sang and played the harp in unison but
very soon I had become a solo performer, largely because of my radio
work, and I started to get separate engagements on my own. A newspaper cutting of this period shows the three of us sitting at our harps
under the caption 'Trio Takes a Tour' – 'Róisín and Máirín Ní
Shéaghdha and Máire Ní Eadhra of the O'Shea School of Harpists,
Sion Hill, Dublin, take their harps to England and Scotland for a tour
which begins on St. Patrick's Day. And, in Glasgow, they have an
appointment with a B.B.C. recording unit.' It states that we also had
concerts in Liverpool, Sheffield and London.

Recently, I was reminded of other such engagements, not with the
Ní Shéaghdhas, when someone sent me a cutting from what was then
the *Manchester Guardian* (1954). I include this rather schmaltzy-worded
notice, headed 'Irish National Concert' simply because it marks the
first attention my work received from the foreign press.

> Sure, you could hear the angels sing at the Free Trade Hall last night.
> And Irish eyes were first smiling, then tearful, as Michael O'Duffy,
> Martin Dempsey and the Gaelic League Choir poured out their songs
> from over the water.
>
> But singing sweetest of all was Mary O'Hara, the girl with the
> eloquent harp, a voice like a nightingale, and enough native charm to
> melt the Blarney Stone.
>
> With that harp, that voice and that grace, sooner or later she has
> to be christened the Irish Angel.

Whenever I was back in Dublin needing more songs, I'd ring up
Seán Óg and, over a cup of coffee somewhere, we'd carefully go over
together the latest Gaelic song I had chosen to learn. He was a native

Gaelic speaker. In my own phonetics, I'd meticulously write down (on a serviette, usually) the correct pronunciation of each syllable. Through him and, for the first time, I became aware of the subtlety of the Irish language, especially its phonetics and how important vowels are and how the slender and broad consonants sound so different, something we do not have in English. Just as with learning the orchestral harp with Mercedes Bolger, so with learning the Gaelic, I felt I should do this as thoroughly as possible. I was beginning to learn more about the Gaelic language and Irish song generally and regretting that I was not a more attentive student during my Harmony classes at Sion Hill. Maybe my boarding school would have been proud of me now. I was belatedly becoming the model student.

In January 1953, Mother was admitted to hospital for surgery. As time went on she had become dependent on barbiturates and alcohol which led to her death at the age of only fifty-one. A week before she died she was operated on for cancer but there was nothing the surgeon could do, the cancer had progressed too far. She died in February. Her death certificate stated cause of death: sclerosis of the liver. Never expecting her to die, Joan and I visited her regularly, Dermot less so, but my distraught father was constantly by her bedside holding her hand. She died very peacefully. We were all in the room when she died, all very silent, while the young nurse who attended her was on her knees by the door quietly weeping.

Early the following year, as soon as he could after straightening out his affairs, my father returned to West Africa to his old job with the British Colonial Service, but this time to the Gold Coast now named Ghana. Dermot and I shared the house in Dublin. Sadly, we had grown apart and were most of the time at loggerheads.

In April 1953 Joan married Frank Barry, a Dublin architect. Her years of sharing a bedroom with me were at an end. No more for her the discomfort of having to put up with the foibles of a younger sister. We had only one set of curlers and they belonged to me. Joan wanted to borrow them the night before her wedding but I was too mean to lend them! I put them in my own hair. But I did lend her my special green sweater for her honeymoon. Since falling in love with

Frank, Joan had blossomed and the relationship between us improved immeasurably. It was as if I was getting to know her for the first time in my life. The cold, distant eldest sister of my childhood had become warm and responsive. We became great friends, and there were few things I enjoyed as much as visiting Joan and Frank in their flat in St Stephen's Green and going places with them.

Saturday night was dance night, either at a tennis club or at the College of Art. I had the occasional date, though no lasting interest in any particular person. I had my short-lived crushes (always carefully hidden), but I was easily turned off. The type of shoes they wore or the colour of their shirts, a mismatched tie or other such trivia would invariably put me off. Obviously the right person hadn't yet come along. I knew I would recognise him when he did.

On 1st June 1954 I went to visit Father in Africa. He had invited me out for the summer and I was jubilant at the prospect. Some of my friends were apprehensive and kept warning me of possible dangers but my father made light of all this.

Father met me at Accra, where we stayed a few days at the home of an RAF friend. Then we set out for Secondi, about two hundred miles away, where Father had a house. On the way I had my first introduction to the colourful West African mammy wagons. These are open-sided lorries which transport everything from humans, to domestic animals and general merchandise, in one happy pot-pourri. An endless variety of imaginative slogans decorate the sides of these wagons – 'Sea Never Dry', 'Jesus Saves Us', 'Freedom Forever', 'Caution Best', 'Kwame Nkrumah the Saviour', 'Sweet pas Takoradi Harbour', 'Love Thy Neighbour' and so on. Before I was born, my parents had brought back a drum from Africa. It looked forlorn and out of context in our west of Ireland home. Now for the first time, I was to see and hear drums in their proper setting. 'In the beginning,' says African folklore 'the creator created the drummer, the hunter and the smith.' In the Gold Coast I witnessed drums indeed talking. They are used to warn of danger, call the people to council, bring news from afar, provide rhythm for the tribal dances and give prestige to ceremonial gatherings. The drums I saw were made from hollowed logs with animal skin or an elephant's ear stretched across the top and held taut by pegs. I was told of a West African legend that the man-in-the-moon is a drummer.

When we finally reached Secondi, Kofi the cook greeted me with a shy smile and a splendid meal. My favourite dish to this day is West African curry, and Kofi was a past master at producing it. The basis of this dish is chicken, guinea fowl, native goat, or rabbit. The meat is stewed in palm oil, which is derived from crushed palm kernels and is a heavy, deep reddish-brown coloured liquid. Madras curry powder is mixed into this and swimming around in it are whole, hard-boiled eggs. An accompanying mountain of fluffy rice is served in a separate dish. But it is the variety of side dishes which is the crowning gastronomical glory. Fruit of every available description – mangoes, avocado pears, pawpaw, oranges, limes, grapefruit, bananas, pineapples – and vegetables: tomatoes, garden eggs, okras and ground nuts. For those for whom the dish is still not fiery enough, little saucers of hot red peppers and spices are on the table. This meal is ambrosial.

I was there in the rainy season, and when it rained it did so with a vengeance – the tropical, torrential rain that hitherto one had only seen in films. But the days of glorious sunshine far outnumbered the wet ones, and I took advantage of all the swimming, sunbathing and exercise in the fresh air. I had never been in better health. My catarrh vanished, the attendant swellings under my eyes, which are, I believe, connected with sinus trouble, completely disappeared. I slept well, ate supremely well and came back to Europe after those three months with a smashing tan, fortified against the awful colds and chest coughs to which I was victim winter after winter.

Arrangements were made for me to give a recital at the British Consulate. I practised with a Danish woman, a very good musician, who accompanied me expertly on the piano. My programme included traditional Irish and Scottish songs, a Mozart, some Elizabethan songs, a Max Reger lullaby in German, and others. It was very well received. A black member of the audience wrote me an enthusiastic letter afterwards saying, 'Your voice is beautiful and you sing like a devil.' Could he have meant angel? Later I broadcast some songs over the Gold Coast radio. The studio was not air-conditioned and the piano accompanying me suffered from the effects of humidity and many rainy seasons. The broadcaster preceding me gave a learned dissertation on tropical fish.

During my stay, Father moved to a new bungalow in Takoradi which, being close to the ocean, was much more spacious and open. There I learned to swim (self-taught). There too I made my first abortive attempt at learning to drive. With Father as driving instructor, I took my first lessons on Takoradi airstrip, but the lessons ended abruptly when I almost overturned the car on the way home. I misjudged a corner and ended up in the ditch. I don't know how I managed it. As I was due to leave West Africa the next day, I didn't sit in a driver's seat again until I'd resumed my singing career after I emerged from the monastery, twenty years later. Driving is now one of my great delights.

Back in Dublin I resumed singing and was kept comfortably busy throughout that winter and spring of 1955 with ever more radio broadcasts and Variety Concerts. In those days, the Radio Éireann studio was above the GPO in Dublin city centre, so many a time the harp and I travelled together on the Clontarf bus into town. Harps are delicate little things and should be protected from the hard knocks of life. I'm ashamed to confess, not so with my harp. It survived many a hard knock on those Dublin buses because I had to leave it at the back of the bus under the-not-always-watchful eye of the conductor – he had other work to do. Often if the bus came to a sudden stop, there would be the inevitable loud thump: the sound of the harp crashing to the floor – invariably followed by a mad rush on my part to rescue it. Bent blades often resulted. I must have been a familiar sight, easily identifiable by my appendage and I was frequently approached in the street and on the bus. Gradually, because of my radio work and the Variety Concerts, people came to associate me with the Irish harp. The harp is a picturesque instrument and it guaranteed media attention. Sometimes being labelled 'Irish harpist' rather than 'singer accompanying herself on the Irish harp' irritated me, but I had to accept that. Decades later, some years after I started singing again, I was surprised and very flattered, I must admit, when the Irish conductor Proinsias O'Duinn invited me to contribute to a series of programmes he was doing on Radio Éireann on Contemporary Irish Composers. He further startled me with a most unexpected compliment: 'You're the only one who makes the harp sing.'

I like to think now, not that I made the harp sing, but that the harp sang for me. We got on so well together. It's been said that the harp is the nearest instrument to the human voice. Mine has always been so responsive, biddable, so in tune with the mood of the song I was singing: playful and cheeky as in 'Maidrín Rua', joyous and triumphant as in 'Lord of the Dance', heartbreaking as in 'Ae Fond Kiss'. I had no agent or manager – things just happened. At this period, as well as getting a lot of air-time, I was also receiving plenty of media exposure, making the covers as well as inside of some of the popular magazines of the day.

I sometimes broadcast as soloist with the Radio Éireann Singers and on one of these occasions Seán Ó Riada asked me if I would accompany them during a performance of one of his pieces. In John's (in those days we knew him as John Reidy) contemporary composition I was required to count seventeen and a half bars of silence before coming in with a vigorous discord; then another dozen and three quarter bars of silence, followed by a dissonant twang from me. After that some more silence before my next contribution. The strain of counting those bars of silence was severe. During rehearsals I managed to come in at the right time, but when the live performance was in progress I slipped up somewhere in my figures and from that first inaccurate entry to the bitter end I didn't know whether I was coming or going. Exacerbation and resignation vied for supremacy on John's poor distraught face as he conducted his esoteric work to the end.

It was during this period that I took ballet lessons at a new school run by Cecil Salkeld, the only Ballet School in Dublin at the time. I loved it but the broadcasts were getting in the way. I was still not sure what I wanted to do in life, so I was keen to experiment. At the suggestion of Jill Fisher, I took up modelling and was accepted for a course at one of the top Dublin modelling agencies. At the time I was self-conscious about my bottom. I felt it stuck out slightly when I was in a straight skirt and, during the training, I sought to remedy this by placing a small, flat woollen cap inside my skirt at the small of my back. I got away with it for about a week, until one day in class the instructor detected it and, to the great amusement of the others, she extracted the woollen cap.

Having successfully completed the course, I got several bookings and did three fashion shows in a row – quite successfully, as far as

I could judge. My fourth booking clashed with something far more significant – a date with Richard Selig. I chose the date instead. That was the end of my brief modelling career, and I never went back.

CHAPTER 4

Dublin

I HAD STARTED broadcasting with Gaelic song and moved on to Irish songs in English, but was fast running out of suitable material. I was getting a lot of radio work through Ciarán Mac Mathúna, the popular Radio Éireann producer, who from time to time included songs in English and Scots Gaelic in his programmes. Early in 1955 he wanted me to sing a Hebridean song, 'The Uist Cattle Croon' on one of his programmes. Calum Maclean, a Scottish friend of his, was in Dublin just then, doing some work at the Irish Folklore Commission – the Irish counterpart of the School of Scottish Studies in Edinburgh – and Ciarán arranged for me to take some lessons from Calum in order to get the authentic Scots-Gallic pronunciation. Calum was a Hebridean Islander, a renowned folklorist and a native Gaelic speaker. Irish Gaelic is very close to Scottish Gaelic (sometimes called Scots-Gallic) – Irish being the mother language – but the pronunciation and accent differ considerably. It was a gloriously fresh spring morning as I crossed St Stephen's Green, making for one of the Georgian houses where the Folklore Commission has its headquarters. When I entered the room, a small, slightly built man, with large brown eyes and a long, pale, Highland face, was seated at a desk with his back to the window.

I sat beside Calum and proceeded to go painstakingly through the song, syllable by syllable. After the programme went out over the air I had an enthusiastic letter from him saying how pleased he was and would I consider going to the Hebrides to learn more of their songs: 'I want you to do for our Gallic what you've been doing for your own Gaelic.' His brother, he said, was the local doctor on South Uist and would see to it that I was put up in one of the crofts. Calum didn't even wait for an answer, and another letter from him followed on the heels of the first, saying that his brother Alistair would be delighted if I would stay with him and his family. I accepted the invitation and was expected in South Uist towards the end of July. This wholly serendipitous event opened up for me a new facet in my singing career.

I planned to stay just one week, as I had a broadcast coming up and needed to be back in Dublin. I flew to Glasgow and spent the night with friends. From there I took a train to Oban in time to get the boat to Raasey where I broke the journey to pick up Alistair's eight year old son Robbie. The Macleans are natives of this small inner island and Calum's brother Sorley, the noted Gaelic poet, and his family were there that weekend.

Like many of the islands, Raasey is Calvanist (South Uist is a Catholic island). Calvin and his followers have what to many appears to be a kill-joy attitude to life. They forbid singing, playing musical instruments and even such innocent recreation as swimming, on Sundays. So when I took Robbie along with me to go swimming that Sunday morning, I unwittingly risked courting their tacit disapproval. Later on in the evening, Calum's uncle Hector, a farmer who lived further up the hill, discretely arranged for me to come and sing for him. While the preacher's voice could be heard resounding through the valley, Uncle Hector, who was milking the cows at the time, carefully closed the cowshed door and with someone on the look-out, I sang the only Scots Gallic song in my repertoire at the time, 'Bó Luarach Thú' which, appropriately enough, is a milking song. Next morning, as arranged, I sang for the rest of the family. Robbie and I then continued the boat journey to South Uist.

It was a good week. The Maclean children and I went swimming whenever it was warm enough. There is nothing to compare with the miles of deserted silver strands in the Outer Hebrides. Heavenly.

As it turned out, I didn't have to go far to collect material. Alistair's wife, Rena, a native of Skye, taught me several lovely songs at her kitchen table. In fact things were going so nicely that I decided to accept the invitation of my host and hostess to extend my stay and cancel my radio broadcast with RÉ in Dublin. Then an odd thing happened. Never before (or since) had I been offered two live broadcasts on the same evening, but towards the end of the week, I received a contract for a second broadcast for the same day. Having discussed the

matter with the Macleans, we decided it would be best for me to fly
to Dublin for the two broadcasts and return afterwards to South Uist
for a further two weeks.

I flew from Benbecula and was met at Dublin airport by my brother-
in-law, Frank Barry. He had been approached by Trinity College
undergraduates, the amateur actors with whom I had worked in
Dublin some time earlier, to see if I'd go with them to Edinburgh.
I have no recollection how I initially got involved with the Trinity
students and their Amateur Dramatic Society. I was wondering aloud
about this recently, while staying with Christopher Fitz-Simon and
Anne Makower, old friends in Dublin. Christopher, now a writer and
retired professor, was in 1955 a student at Trinity College in Dublin.
He explained that as a member of The Trinity Players, he helped to
stage three W.B. Yeats one-act plays during the lunch hour at the university theatre: 'To fill the gap between plays, while changing scenery,
we roped in Mary O'Hara to sing and accompany herself on her Irish
Harp. For two weeks there wasn't a single empty seat in the hall.'
He very kindly attributes the full houses to my participation. It is a
mystery to me why this period is so completely blank in my mind
though I have good recollection of the Edinburgh appearances.
However, I can't deny it happened because I've recently come across
the press-cuttings.

Now they were putting on the three Yeats one-act plays as a fringe
production at the Edinburgh Festival and, again, they wanted me to
perform between the plays. They would pay expenses but could not
afford a fee. I remember feeling decidedly insulted by the 'offer', for
I could see it only as a stop-gap: to keep the audience entertained
while the students shifted scenery, so I summarily said 'no thanks'.
But Frank wisely pointed out that, as there would be two performances, one at 5 pm and another at 11 pm, I would have the splendid opportunity of being free every evening to go and see performances
by internationally top-ranking actors and musicians if I so wished. It
was an inviting prospect, so I told him I would think it over. As it
happened my subsequent decision to accept was to have significant
repercussions on my singing career and private life. A couple of days
later, I fulfilled my two broadcasting engagements.

Anyway, as Christopher pointed out, my bit with the Trinity Players in Edinburgh, as in Dublin, was to sit and perform at the very front of the stage, between the plays, while close behind me, separated by a thin curtain, objects were shifted about for the next play. With apologies to William Shakespeare, if he and you will permit a pun, I could say I 'suffered a *scene* change' when, on a high note in '*Eibhlín a Rún*', I received a hefty jab in the back. Of course I warbled on. But when at one point, the harp seemed on the verge of tipping over into the pit, one chivalrous knight in the front row sprang to the rescue and steadied it. It was my introduction to the novelist Sir Compton MacKenzie, who later invited me to be one of his house-guests for the rest of the Festival. It was from his home that I got my first broadcast for BBC Radio Scotland and my first appearance on BBC TV (1955), sharing the set at one point with a handsome Highland sheep. While preparing a Mary O'Hara web page, we recently chanced on a pile of old press-cuttings from those far off days – among which was this from *The Scotsman* (1/9/55):

> The outstanding performance, this year, was that of Miss O'Hara, a young Irish lady who played the harp and sang with the T.C.D. Players, and who has now left Edinburgh for Dublin. Everyone who saw and heard her assures us that she undoubtedly stole the whole, giddy Festival show...

I must say, at the time, I was very much unaffected by all the fuss. Not having an agent or manager to seize the opportunity, I was happily living from day to day, not concerned with the future and certainly not fully realising I was quickly becoming a professional singer by default. In those days, as far as I am aware, the concept of 'star' had not been born. For one thing, the mass media was not as pervasive then as it is today.

The summer of 1955 was incredibly hot and sunny by Irish standards. The farmers groaned but the rest of the population rejoiced, and often we would go swimming at midnight. To this day I meet people who can remember the 'great summer of 1955'. But I was to remember it for another more personal reason, which was to determine the course of the rest of my life.

The morning after the two radio broadcasts, I was strolling through Stephen's Green enjoying the radiant morning and mulling over the Edinburgh Festival proposition. If I accepted, then of course I'd forfeit the rest of that holiday on South Uist. Should I? Should I not? A voice broke in on my thoughts: 'Hello Mel, I'm glad I met you because I've been trying to contact you.' It was the poet Tom Kinsella. He wasted no time on preliminaries: 'There's a young American Rhodes Scholar called Richard Selig, a minor poet at Oxford who wants to meet you.'

Now, at that time the idea of having to meet another American was anything but welcome. Only a couple of weeks earlier I'd managed to fob off an American, and oddly enough he too was called Richard. He had been one of a group of international students attending a summer school at University College Dublin. I had taken part in a one-act play *An Imaginary Conversation*, put on by the undergraduates – in fact I was the only person in the play who was not an undergraduate – and had met this man along with many others at a reception in Newman House. He kept asking me out and finally I agreed to go to the cinema. I thought *Bad Day at Black Rock* would never end... After the pictures we repaired to a trendy coffee shop and while I was sitting there, trying not to look too bored, a friend studying at Oxford passed our table and said hello. As he went to pay his bill at the cash desk the young man with him turned and gave me a long, penetrating, singularly unselfconscious look. Although I couldn't have known it then, this was Richard Selig.

So when Tom Kinsella posed his question, I had an immediate and ready answer. 'Tom,' I said, 'I'm not interested in meeting your American. I've just got rid of one!'

Undaunted Tom pressed on: 'Mel, he's *very* good-looking and has a jaw like Rock Hudson.'

'Well,' said I, 'I happen not to like Rock Hudson, neither his looks nor his jaw.'

Tom went on to explain that Giovanni Costigan, an American professor from Seattle who had taught Richard Selig at one time, was giving a party in his rented flat in Fitzwilliam Square. The excuse for the party was, he said, so that Richard and I could meet. Tom and I went our respective ways and I'd still not committed myself to the arrangement. When I got home there was a message that some stranger had phoned. Next morning as I was coming downstairs the phone rang. When I picked it up a voice said: 'This is Richard Selig.'

Oh God, I thought, it's that American! His accent was very, very slight. I think his years in England had resulted in a neutral sort of accent entirely his own, and very pleasing to the ear.

Richard went on: 'There's a party tonight at Tom Kinsella's.' (So they'd changed the venue.) 'Would you have dinner with me at The Bailey beforehand?' Richard, I was to find out later, always came to the point.

Now, I did *not* want to go but I couldn't see how I could gracefully get out of it. I envisaged another weary evening similar to the one with the other American. Moreover, this wouldn't end with dinner but would drag on into a party. And I didn't enjoy parties anyway.

'Oh Lord,' I thought to myself, 'what am I going to do?' I was trapped. Warily, I agreed to meet him.

How would we recognize each other was the next question down the phone. Aha, I thought, this'll fix him! Then, out loud: 'You'll have no trouble identifying me. I am disfigured with freckles and I am inclined to drool!'

He laughed, 'I too have freckles and I'll be wearing a pea-soup green suit.'

What I didn't know then was that he had not only seen me (at that café) but had also heard me sing. He was renting a room in Waterloo Road, and from this Dublin base, Richard had travelled to the west of Ireland, hired a bicycle in Sligo and headed for Drumcliffe Churchyard to visit the grave of W.B. Yeats, whose poetry he'd admired for years. He also visited Galway and Connemara. Back in Dublin, he circulated amongst the Dublin intelligentsia, the young poets and artists of that colourful city. As it happened, a thin wall separated Richard's room from that of John Reidy, the composer mentioned earlier. John, who later adopted the Gaelic version of his name, Seán Ó'Riada, was to do so much for Irish/Gaelic music before his early and untimely death. One evening, Richard had been chatting with some acquaintances in the flat below his, with the wireless on in the background, when my voice came across the air. Silencing the others, he listened. He didn't know whose voice it was until, at the end, the announcer read out the names of those participating. It was the earlier of the two live broadcasts of that previous Monday evening

– the ones I'd come back from the Hebrides to do. So, he'd heard my name mentioned on and off by mutual friends, then seen me and later heard me singing; and had decided now that he wanted to meet me.

Richard was very direct. After we'd got to know each other I once asked him why he'd stopped in his tracks to listen to my singing. 'Because', he said, 'I had to listen. There was a sadness in your voice.' The song was a Gaelic lament, *'Caoine Cill Cais'*.

Our date was for eight o'clock. Typically, I arrived late. I was wearing a sleeveless cotton dress. My hair was long and flying all over the place because I'd just washed it. Since those three months under the African sun people had often remarked on how much more golden red it had become (my father had auburn hair). The thin red Alice band I wore on it was for decorative rather than functional purposes. As usual I was without stockings and minimally shod in very open, flat sandals.

Sensing that I'd be late, Richard sat in Davy Burns, the fashionable pub across the road frequented by the Dublin literati, and watched my arrival. Much later he told me that I reminded him of nothing so much as a young wild pony.

I swept upstairs and went to the appointed room. There was no young man in a pea-soup green suit. I went off to the ladies to do a small repair job with the comb. When I came back to the room, minutes later, sitting at a table was a serious-faced young man, smoking a pipe and clearly waiting for me. I was very impressed by his unusual good looks, but all evening I was careful to conceal this. Had I not been told I would never have taken him for an American. On the contrary, he looked very 'county' to me. Later, when I discovered how cosmopolitan he was, this made sense.

I don't remember what we said to each other, but I recall the meal. It was vast and excellent. The Bailey was at that time one of the two top restaurants in Dublin. But in spite of my customary shyness I felt a certain 'at-homeness' in his company. My habit of sitting up very straight caused Richard to ask at one stage 'Do you by any chance have a poker down your back?' During coffee, Richard Murphy, the Irish poet, came in with his wife and joined us. He and Richard were both Magdalen men and shared the same tutor.

Having finished the meal, it was time now to head up to The Green for Tom's party. 'Aren't you going to bring the harp?' Richard asked.

A rhetorical question as it turned out. Stifling annoyance, I said, 'Do I have to?' I had to. The instrument was still in the studio where it had lain since Monday night. Radio Éireann was a good ten minutes' walk away. We collected the harp and made our way back through the city to Tom's place. Every time we had to cross the road, Richard took my hand. It was a friendly, matter-of-fact, protective gesture.

It was close to midnight and the party was in full swing. My brother-in-law Frank was sitting on the floor in one corner and I gravitated towards him. Joan had given birth to her second child Sebastian that very week and was still in the nursing home. Both of them, my sister especially, were forever plotting and hoping that I would develop a sustained interest in someone worthwhile. So Frank asked as usual, 'Mel, is he an egg and rasher?' (Dublinese for 'smasher'.) This time it was an unqualified 'Yes.'

Richard had deposited himself in a far corner and was soon surrounded by people. So far as I knew for the rest of the night I might as well not have existed, but I didn't let it bother me too much. That's it, I thought. And anyway, I was good at hiding my feelings. Later in the evening individuals were called on to sing. I sat on the edge of Tom's bed and sang 'The Quiet Land of Érin'. Richard obliged with two American folk songs I'd never heard before, and which I thought were very lovely: 'Black is the Colour of My True Love's Hair' and 'The Riddle Song', also called 'I Gave My Love a Cherry'. He had a sort of Gene Kelly voice – a husky baritone. In 1976, when I gave a recital at the American Embassy in Dublin and needed American songs, I remembered 'The Riddle Song', made an arrangement for the harp, sang it there and have kept it in my repertoire ever since.

At about three in the morning people started drifting outside for soup. As I came to the centre of the room I found Richard there too and in a rather cool voice he asked if I'd like some soup. I said I would. Thinking we would be away for about thirty minutes or less, I didn't even bother to bring my little straw handbag. We wandered into the warm night. We couldn't locate the others so we had soup on our own in a little coffee shop on Stephen's Green at the top of Grafton Street. When we'd finished, Richard suggested we go for a walk. We headed down the now deserted Grafton Street and on through the city till we reached the docks. We sat down on a bench and talked a bit. We continued our stroll on into Sandymount and beyond. With the dawn, we turned back and made for the city again where we breakfasted. My handbag was still in Tom's flat, so I had to go to his workplace to get the key. I decided not to keep the modelling interview that had been arranged for me that morning and we agreed to spend the rest of the day together.

Killiney is to my mind the finest beach outside Dublin and I decided we should go there. After lunch we borrowed swimsuits from a friend in the city and took off. Now I'm a bit bovine when it comes to a sense of direction. First I took some misguided short cuts by foot and then hopped on the bus, only to find ourselves unloaded at Bray, the other end of the spectrum from Killiney. All those pebbles and stones, ice-cream shops and crowds precluded the idyllic day I'd planned. With no beautiful stretch of sand and no people-free sea we didn't go swimming, we just talked. I had a date that night with two under-graduates from Trinity who were taking me to the theatre, and I had to go home, wash and change and come back into town again. So we stayed by the sea for a few hours.

We talked about many things during those first twenty-four hours together. Later I came to realize that during that time he gratuitously told me facts about himself and certain of his attitudes towards life in general which many of his close friends did not know. It was a meas-ure of his intuitive trust in me to have shared so much, so soon.

There has been a lot of codswallop written about how Richard and I fell passionately and madly in love at first sight. I personally don't believe in that burnt-out, unrealistic cliché, 'love at first sight'. But there is such a thing as instant physical or chemical attraction, and it can sometimes be the first step towards a relationship that can con-tinue to grow into love for the remainder of one's life. This happened to us. I believe that love is something that both people must work at, and daily. We had to work at ours and like everybody else we had our highs and our lows.

Richard was planning to leave the following day for the Aran Islands in Galway Bay, in the west of Ireland, and would later return to Dublin for only one night. If I hadn't had those two broadcasts to entice me back to Dublin I would never have met him – and I would not be writing this book...

During our day together we discussed the pros and cons of the Edinburgh Festival and decided I should do it. As it turned out there were many unexpected benefits. Before we parted that evening we talked of my joining him in the west of Ireland after the stint in Edinburgh.

The week at the Festival proved to be yet another memorable chapter in that fabulous summer of 1955. My performances were so well received that I was invited back the following year to be guest star in a production in the official Edinburgh International Festival.

While in Edinburgh I became very friendly with some of the undergraduates from Oxford University, whom I was to meet again the following winter in Oxford with Richard. There was a lively, festive atmosphere in the city with entertainment of a high calibre at the theatres, followed by innumerable parties, whether thrown by undergraduate amateur actors or the more sophisticated. Sir Compton Mackenzie was a prominent figure in the social life of the city, but never more so than during the annual Festival. His generosity was legendary. Every evening for those three weeks in August and September the famous and the obscure flowed in and out of his elegant house in Drummond Place. He and the charming Hebridean, Chrissie MacSween, whom he later married after his wife's death, extended a warm Highland welcome to all who crossed the threshold. Most nights during that particular year Sir Compton was suffering from sciatica, and held court from his large four-poster bed, clad in bright orange pyjamas. Word of me and my work had got around and they invited me to one of their parties. Ulick O'Connor phoned and offered to take me there. I told him I wasn't keen on going and that I'd already accepted an invitation from one of the Oxford undergraduates to accompany him to a Dietrich Fischer-Dieskau concert.

As it happened, I changed my plans and went to the party with George Scott-Moncrieff, the Scottish playwright, who was, among other things, the theatre critic of the *Glasgow Herald*. He had presented himself backstage one evening and we had become friendly. After Richard's death he was to become my closest friend.

I was asked to sing at the party. I sang '*Eibhlin a Rún*' and everyone seemed very pleased. From that time on, Sir Compton interested himself in my career. When he invited me to be his house-guest for the remaining two weeks of the Festival, I explained that I had something to attend to in Ireland the following week. (The something was someone: Richard.) Sir Compton said that if I felt like it I could come back for the third and last week of the Festival. All I needed to do was send a telegram from Dublin.

I flew back that Sunday and spent a good deal of time on the journey home speculating about whether there would be the half-promised letter from Richard awaiting me or not. One minute I ardently hoped there would be a letter, the next I told myself I didn't care if there wasn't. On and on I vacillated until I reached the house, and there it was — the first of his sixty-two letters to me from that date until our engagement in February.

He opened by saying he intended to make it 'the longest letter I have ever written'. It was 2,729 words long:

> ... I have an inveterate, though now a long-restrained, propensity for romance; and I hope you will not be embarrassed by the fact that after less than twenty-four hours' acquaintance with you I wish to confide the details of my travels thus far as an expression of the warm affection I already feel for you. It satisfies some strong demand of my nature to have some one person to communicate with. You are the most likely candidate I have had in a long time. Taciturnity grows on me in proportion to a lack of love. To conclude this paragraph and to get on with my story, suffice it to say that I enjoyed your company very much...
>
> I must have lunch now and bring this to the post office before the *Dún Aengus* arrives. I shall be in Galway on Monday to await your wire and, I hope, your arrival.

The wire was sent off to Galway, and I followed it by train on Monday evening. I was wearing a flame-red cotton dress, which I thought was very fetching. As I came off the train, Richard's first disapproving words were, 'That's the colour the prostitutes in Amsterdam wear.' I ignored the remark. It was good to be together again. We spent the night at the Castle Hotel in the city. Next morning we hitchhiked to the summer house of Ernie O'Malley, the erstwhile revolutionary, a leader in Ireland's war of Independence and Civil War, and author of the book *On Another Man's Wound*. He had invited both of us there when he and Richard met on Inishere. Cormac was with his father as he had been on the Aran Islands.

We supped by candlelight – there was no electricity in the house – and next morning Ernie's method of getting us up was rather original, I thought. Without saying anything he handed a supine Richard a glass of sherry. Then he came into my room and proceeded to beat me playfully with a toy tiger. All this in friendly silence too.

After breakfast Ernie took me down to see their boat. Richard was elsewhere at the time. I was surprised and pleased to hear later on that, not being able to locate me, Richard got decidedly worried and had gone out on to the road asking local people if they'd seen a young girl in jeans with long hair and a man in his fifties. It was wonderful to realize that he cared that much.

Our next port of call was Achill Island. Richard had been told about Major Freyer, a delightfully eccentric old gentleman who ran a guest house at the foot of a mountain on the island. There was instant rapport between us and this retired English army officer. In no time we were being hosted in his own private sitting room. While we sipped drinks the major read his poems to us.

We were both fresh-air fiends and spent most of that week out of doors. There was little sun and lots of mist and the inevitable gentle rain, but the inclement weather couldn't keep us in. We found a lovely little beach where we swam every day, even in the rain. We had it all to ourselves and used to race up and down it and, on calmer days, we'd skim stones in the water and shout and leap in the waves. We climbed the mountain. One evening we even went to the pictures. The local cinema consisted of a village hall with a corrugated iron roof with wooden benches for the patrons. That night we had great fun. Sometimes in the evening, if it was fine enough, we'd sit on the front steps (we were the only people staying in the guest house) and I'd sing my songs to him – especially all my latest Elizabethan ones.

As we were travelling back to Dublin, Richard announced that he wished to meet my father who, home on leave from West Africa, was ill in a nursing home. On my return from Scotland, before catching the Galway train, I'd called in to find out how he was and to tell him I was joining Richard over in the west.

When Richard and I arrived, Father was sitting up in bed, which was strewn with volumes of his much-loved late-Victorian poets. So they met and I was glad. A salutary side-effect of that illness was that Father gave up smoking for good. Shortly afterwards he also gave up drinking and never looked back.

Before Richard returned to England we promised to keep in touch by letter and he asked me if I'd consider coming over to visit him. Term would begin very shortly and that meant he would be confined to Oxford. If we were to go on seeing each other I would have to be the mobile one.

I sent off my telegram to Sir Compton and booked a flight to Edinburgh. There followed yet another exotic week with Drummond Place as welcoming and brimful of celebrities as usual.

All the reviews of my performance during that first week of the Festival had been very favourable. Now there appeared a longish piece in *The Scotsman*. I wrote (my first) letter to Richard enclosing the clipping. His answer was immediate.

Magdalen College
Oxford
9th September 1955

Dear Mary,

To my delight I got your letter this morning and the clipping from *The Scotsman* of which I am very proud. I am happy to hear that you are comfortable at Sir Compton's and are able to rest after the rigours of our western travels It is hot here, too, and clear mostly, and Oxford looks lovely under the September light. I am staying in college temporarily until my flat is ready...

I spent most of the week writing what is for me a long poem and completed the first section of it yesterday, fifty-nine lines. I have begun to unravel somewhat, also. The first part, if not the whole thing, will be called 'The Coast'...

Listen, Mary, I think of you very often and miss your companionship keenly. And I want you to know that I am very fond of you and, knowing the sometimes ponderous fidelity of my own heart, will remain so. I'll send this letter special delivery for otherwise, this being Friday, you may not get it till Monday. Hoping to hear from you soon,

I am,

Your friend and affectionately,   Richard

Later on when he sent me a finished copy of 'The Coast' I marvelled that I had lived through that same week with prosaic eyes and here was the whole experience transformed through poetry.

Years later, when I was in the monastery, one particular line appealed so strongly to me that I had a calligrapher friend in the community scribe it for me on vellum. It was there daily before my eyes in my choir book – an impossible, yet perennial injunction, which one aspired to live each day. In the poem it was addressed directly to me:

> *Know that ... the one riddle the one great enterprise in this world is to learn how to love and keep loving.*

I did not know at the time, and indeed wasn't aware until I read about it in the press after his death in 1972, that Sir Compton had set the BBC wheels in motion where I was concerned.

A couple of days after my return to Edinburgh, the BBC TV people in Scotland phoned Sir Compton to ask me to appear on a programme later in the week. He gave me the message and kindly offered to listen in on the extension in his room to ensure that all would go smoothly. He said, 'When they get to the bit about fees, tell them you never get paid in anything other than guineas.'

It was well after Richard's death that I came to hear that Sir Compton had wanted me to play the lead, opposite Donald Sinden, in the film version of his novel, *Rockets Galore,* which he wrote as a sequel to *Whisky Galore.* One evening, in Sir Compton's library, the subject of that film came up in conversation and Donald Sinden asked, 'Tell me, I've always wondered why you made the heroine of *Rockets Galore* an Irish singer?' Quietly, Sir Compton pointed to me and said: 'There's the reason.'

Then he told me that the film company didn't want me because I wasn't 'a name'. Anyhow, I would certainly not have accepted the part, even if they had approached me.

I wanted to tell Richard the good news about the BBC television appearance and, since there was not enough time to write to him from Mackenzie's I sent a telegram giving details and ending with the word, 'Writing'. I never did get down to writing that letter and the omission provoked the following splenetic letter from Richard.

15th September 1955

Dear Mary,

I woke up laughing this morning at the intensely absurd notion we by now have about each other. I think of you as a neurotic young female throwing her weight about not knowing what she wants but enjoying for all their worth her new found, though ephemeral, powers. And you probably think of me as a romantic and vulnerable young man, looking for the impossible, much too intense and all too easy to kick. I'm afraid it needed that letter you didn't write to disabuse me of the former. I suspect omission is your habitual way of getting out of things.

However, if you can muster courage this time and try explaining yourself – all well and good. Otherwise, according to a proverb I made up today: Give word. No keep. New friendship dies easy.

Richard

The 'neurotic young female' was back in Dublin by then and deeply hurt by this letter. I think I was as much upset by *his* having been unintentionally hurt as by the well aimed barbs at myself. The injustice of being described as someone who 'kicked' was the unkindest cut of all.

During my week in Edinburgh, following our days together in Achill, I'd given our embryonic relationship some thought. While I undoubtedly wanted to be near him, I was wary. Nothing would have made me happier than to flit over to Oxford, but my pride would not allow me to do so. I would see him again only if something else occasioned my being in his part of the world. Nothing would induce me to adopt the role of pursuer. Let him do the chasing, I thought. Part of it also was that I was like all human beings, vulnerable, and besides it was all so early in our friendship. What if he changed his mind?

He had everything going for him. He could have had virtually any woman he wanted. I was schooling myself not to get involved. Who was to say that the whole thing might not end as abruptly as it had begun? Already I had seen how he could 'operate'. People were drawn to him as to a magnet. He had only to enter a room and all attention was focused on him. His charm was immense and could be turned on and off at will like a tap. But his general impact on people was beyond his control.

Young and inexperienced as I was, I could nevertheless see that Richard was a very special person. Naturally I was pleased that this twenty-five year old man so richly endowed, physically and intellectually, should be interested in me.

He knew his considerable power over others and, as I was to discover as our time together went by, his integrity was to match – understanding all these things about himself he was unusually aware of his responsibility not to abuse those powers, and certainly while I knew him he never did.

Still smarting, and very much affected by Richard's obvious pain I wrote a longish letter and sent it by special delivery. That night he phoned me from Oxford, and the troubled waters were calmed. His letter arrived a couple of days later.

18th September 1955

Mary dear,

I received both your letters this morning and, of course, was very much cheered by them. It is so long since I met anyone who prefers my kindness and respect to my ferocity that I am overwhelmed by the change the possibility of such a person existing can produce in my character. Showing my teeth and expecting to be at war with people at the slightest provocation, has become a habit that is hard to break. I hope you will forgive my last letter in which I exceeded myself in lack of gallantry. The reason I called you last night, if I may take credit for some sense, is that I couldn't believe that I had been wrong about you. The one thing I am seldom wrong about is people's character.

Richard

The phone call and the letter restored me to my usual happy self. I was beginning to understand the contrasts in his character, the outer aggressive, competitive side – Theodore Roethke used the word 'baracuda' in his piece on Richard in *Gemini*, written after he died – and the gentler traits which he didn't advertise to the world in general.

One morning I had a phone call from someone who had seen me on that BBC television programme from Edinburgh. He'd also heard some of my recorded songs on a commercial radio programme from Radio Éireann. He asked if I'd be prepared to make a test recording for the Decca Record Company in London. My fare and expenses would be paid for two to three days. I told them that I would be willing to have a go. Here was a golden opportunity to see Richard again, so the following extract was the major news in the second of the two letters he referred to.

... Along with your letter, I received permission from my draft board to stay overseas another year. I was rather worried about this since an American friend of mine, despite an appeal, has just been classified AI, which means he can be called up any day. He is also at Magdalen doing English and expected to finish at the end of this year. I think I've set the record for academic deferments, this being my sixth year. I hope by the time I'm ready they will have changed the selective service law, leaving me high dry and a civilian. My deferment is until September 1956, which is quite generous and means I will have next summer in Europe if I want it.

I am delighted to hear that your father has recovered so quickly.

I do very much hope you get this recording try-out, both for your sake and for the selfish reason that I would like to see you...

On Sunday I am having a drink with one of the directors of Faber and Faber, the publisher, at All Soul's College. He seems interested in my work...

Love,
Richard

In my insular fashion I knew nothing about draft boards till he mentioned it in this letter. As things developed, I am grateful to that institution for letting Richard stay on in Europe one more year.

Now he was settling peacefully into the new flat which I was soon to visit for the first time.

23rd September 1955

Dear Mary,
Thanks for your provincial letter.

I am writing this in the kitchen of my flat, a warm and most peaceful room. I moved in as scheduled two days ago on Wednesday. It is a more spacious place than I had remembered it, and I am already quite comfortable. (I was interrupted at this point by the arrival of my 'house-boy', the man who will do menial work for me. He seems agree-able and has had experience cleaning this flat before.)

As I had promised myself, I went to London on Monday afternoon. I stayed, as I usually do, with Alan and Joan Woodin, my research bio-chemist and his American wife. We all three met one another on the *Queen Elizabeth* coming over to Europe in October 1953.

The next morning, I went to the embassy and had my passport renewed. Stephen Spender took me out to lunch at Wheelers … I am having two pages in *Encounter* in November, about seventy-six lines; poems which, if he pays me the usual rate, means £20. You can buy *Encounter* in Grafton Street, Dublin.

The Faber man is interested but considers me Spender's property.

I hope you will soon be able to get to bed at a reasonable hour.

Love, Richard

Things were looking up for Richard. Top editors and publishers were showing interest in his poetry (at that time Stephen Spender was editor of *Encounter),* and there was a growing awareness of his gifts.

28th September 1955

Dear Mary,

It is a poor substitute for being with you, and I hope that will be remedied soon, but I shall attempt to do with my pen what my presence could do a thousand times better. I am writing to you today despite not having received anything but your Sunday note because it occurs to me that you are again in need of some assurance of my continued affection for you. It seems the burden at present lies with me to assure you of my feelings, rather than with you to assure me of yours. There are good reasons for this but they are of little comfort to one addicted to impatience and the expectation that he will always get his own way. I am by habit, custom and experience much better fitted for competition than for wooing. I think it has never really occurred to me that a well-balanced mixture of cruelty and tenderness, both administered with instinctive calculation, might be less effective than humility and forbearance. As you can see, though I talk of humility, the tone of this letter is one of pride. I speak of pride because I cannot repress the feelings that the tone of your letters has a certain flavour of a little girl's self-importance and of one who delights in the idea of a wooer but regards the fact in a slightly off-hand way.

I think I am being unduly critical because, having made the brave declaration of my feelings, I became frightened that it would not be given the respect and consideration my ego insists on. However, that is by the way. I am no longer particularly afraid one way or the other. Either you remember and know me well enough to continue to care, or you do not. All I can tell you is that I still like you very much and would be very pleased to see you again, and would appreciate it very much if you would let me know if you wish my interest in you to continue.

I am quite comfortably set up here in Oxford in a three-room flat. I live quietly and busily. If you care to visit me you will be very welcome.

Richard

Not only had I never had a personal relationship of this quality before, I was unaccustomed to having someone care for me who was so alive to my needs and feelings. His reference to the immature tone of my letters was fair. All of our life together, Richard, when he recognized the need to be so, was cruel with the relentlessness of the surgeon: he cut away so as to heal. But I think he was motivated by love. This emotional insecurity he points to was still all too present in my make-up.

I'd warned Richard many a time that I was a poor letter-writer. He wrote resignedly to say that he enjoyed writing to me, would continue to do so even though my letters to him were thin on the ground and would I let him hear from me when I didn't feel it was too much of a chore to write. He admitted to sometimes restraining himself with difficulty from phoning me. One of his letters ended with the reminder that his birthday was on 29th October and that though it would please him very much if I could get there around that time; if I couldn't he wouldn't be bitter, just sad.

An agent called Berlin had contacted me, and Richard's response to the news delighted me. He did indeed become my 'chevalier' and shielded me from the slings and arrows of outrageous agents and entrepreneurs in the two years ahead. He was so right about the insensitive and shady ways of many people in show business. For years I suffered from them; and alas, after Richard's death, I had nobody to act as buffer until Pat came along.

A passage in the same letter illustrates his philosophy of life – and contains a further reference to the impending birthday.

8th October 1955

Sweetest Mary,

... Duly I am impressed with the promptness of your reply, a very
pleasant one at that. Soon you will reach my standards of con-
scientiousness, I am sure. Anyway, thanks. I am pleased to hear the
concert went so well and that it in turn has paid dividends in other
engagements...

Apropos the letter from the agent and its ilk: not that I don't
know you can take care of yourself; please allow, however, an elderly
brotherly warning that there are a lot of unscrupulous people in show
business. But, yours truly, 'chevalier' lives only forty miles to the west
in Oxford and would always welcome an opportunity to defend his lady.

While I think of it, write this down in your address book: 38 Norham
Road, Oxford. Tel No. Oxford 57039.

As far as your getting 'grip' is concerned, and growing into a finer,
stronger, more disciplined being, I am all for it. That's what we're here
for: to make the attempt and with luck, faith and some help to keep
making it, success coming in part and pieces, the wonderful windfalls
of daily living; doing what one can when one can as often as one can.

I am sure you have the strength and goodness to do what you feel
you should and wish to do. As much as I may harbour reservations
about you, as a young woman, having independence, I am also sure
that you need and will make good use of that independence.

Since you asked me what I wanted for my birthday, I will be so bold
as to tell you what I am in need of at present and you can choose
between them. I need a long woollen scarf and I also need some underwear shorts (drawers to you). The ones I am wearing now acquire a
new hole for every stride I take. You asked me!

                                                    Love, Richard

The next few letters were as vivid and news-full as ever; one containing a lengthy dissertation on how to combat the common cold, to
which I was too often prone in those days. Another included an acid
dressing down for my use of red ink, exclamation marks and general
bad taste in letter writing. There was the news too of his myriad social
activities: entertaining in his flat and dining out; and an account of
the unintentional destruction of two squash rackets, one against his
opponent's calves during the course of his usual fiercely energetic playing of the game. He had also been invited to address the Spectator

Club on why he wrote poetry: 'I will attempt not to be facetious. There are some serious reasons, besides the basic ones of pleasure and the desire to excel.'

And there was the repeated question: when was I coming to visit him? A whole week went by without hearing from me.

… with difficulty I will restrain myself from telephoning you. I am worried, however and I hope your cold is better. If you haven't written already would you please answer this letter by return post?

Richard

23rd October 1955

Dear Mary:

… Thanks for using blue ink, refraining from the use of exclamation marks and from your usual clusters of nerve-wracking figures of speech. As for your ending your letters because they are so irritating, I can only suggest my ending mine if you find them too depressing…

You must forgive my annoyance at the fact that both your intention and your desire to see me have not at all been made clear by you. So far, all that I can gather from your plans is that a visit to me is contingent on a nebulous 'call to London' and an orchestral harp. I am sorry but I am too egotistical to be at all pleased by your considering me a matter of convenience. I don't wish to offer prayers for your call to London. I would be willing, however, to contribute to the cost of a visit to me if you wished to visit me. I am thus much annoyed because, if you recall, you accepted an invitation to come to Oxford and then left me for five days with nothing but a telegram telling me you had written and that you were going to be on TV at such and such an hour. Forgiveness comes easy to me when that which I am to forgive is not reinforced by subsequent events. I never forget a wrong, however, and this will probably scare you so I suggest that you exercise some tolerance. As the result of a good memory for both favours and wrongs, if you knew me or my friends, you would discover that my dealings are usually very fair. It is the legalist in my blood.

I hope you like the poem.

My moods vary but not my love,

Richard

Towards the end of October 1955, a call came to say that the plans to fly me to London and do the test recording were now complete. I phoned Richard from London Airport. When he heard my voice he seemed a bit stunned. After a pregnant pause he said, 'My God — where are you?' I told him, and added that I'd try to get down for his birthday two days later.

I recorded '*Eibhlin a Rún*', '*Ceól a' Phíobaire*', 'The Spinning Wheel' and 'The Spanish Lady'. All went well with the test recording and Decca got me to sign a contract with them there and then — which could have been a big mistake on my part if Decca, for any reason, did not want to go ahead and release the recording. I should have had an expert read through the document but, as it happened, things turned out OK.

The Decca people, having the test recordings in the can, so to speak, were dragging their feet about releasing the material. They still kept plying me with songs of a type that I found unacceptable. The unspoken hope, I think, was that I'd drop the Gaelic and perhaps the harp too and record instead the material they were sending me with instruments other than the harp accompanying me. But I stuck to my guns. It took my successful first appearance on Dutch TV in May 1956 to spur Decca on to test the waters, first releasing the material in Holland and then elsewhere. They were so pleased with the result, and realising that I was bankable as I was, full of good cheer, they asked me to record a long-playing album, which I called *Songs of Érin*.

Father had offered to travel to London with me. Business completed, he returned to Ireland with my harp. I trekked through London for a few hours seeking the perfect scarf as a birthday present for Richard. In the end I found it: the longest, softest cashmere scarf ever.

CHAPTER 5

Richard

The one riddle, the one great enterprise in this world is to learn how to love and keep loving.
RICHARD SELIG

WITH THE TEST-recording behind me and the Decca contract signed, I took the train from Paddington. Arriving in Oxford, there was no sign of Richard. There was no reply when I tried to phone him. Still in the kiosk, with the phone attached to my ear, someone tapped on the glass door behind me. It was he. Cool, and not exactly effusive, he said: 'Sorry I'm late. I was having an argument in the Bodleian with a friend of mine about prose styles.' In retrospect I wonder if it was an eye for an eye move: treating me in kind for my unpunctuality at The Bailey.

So began the first of my many visits to Oxford. Little detail stands out, but the overall memory is warm. Oxford and its ancientness I loved; and the long walks we took together through the meadows and by the river. Spring was even better. Anyone who has known Oxford in that season can never forget it. We punted and cycled a lot, I longed for spring and summer and the opportunity for tennis with Richard until one day in early summer we went out and bought tennis gear; from then on we played whenever we could.

Out for a walk one winter's day (we were throwing a ball to one another) I said wistfully: 'Richard, even if we don't get married, can I play tennis with you in the summer?' He thought for a few seconds and then said, 'No.' I didn't pursue the subject.

With each subsequent visit I met more of his friends, both English and American. Richard had told me quite a lot about himself during our time together in Ireland. Now I was regaled in greater detail. Excitement and success seemed to have attended him from childhood. His happy nature and zest for life is apparent even in the snapshots of him as a small baby in his pram. He had a radiant smile. Years after he'd left, he paid a casual visit to his old high school, and one of his former teachers said she recognized him instantly by his smile. An only child, he was born in New York City on Black Tuesday, the day of the stock market crash, an event that did not go un-noticed in his family since his father was a Wall Street lawyer. He grew up on Long Island and in his teens his family moved to Washington, DC. He did exceptionally well at his schools in all subjects. After leaving high school he started wandering. He studied psychology at the Occidental College in Los Angeles. It was his least favourite city. He said one could sometimes smell the evil in it. He had a gift for painting and had a scholarship to the Museum of Modern Art in New York City.

Drama and Greek at the Catholic University of America in Washington, DC, brought him into contact with Roman Catholicism for the first time as far as I know. While there he studied comparative religion. By the time we met he was considerably more informed about the church, her history and her doctrine, than I, a cradle Catholic. He once described himself to me as being 'fascinated by Christ'. This is borne out by several of his later poems. He spent a year studying French at the Sorbonne, a legacy of which was his elegant French accent sometimes commented on by his friends. He studied English at the University of Washington in Seattle from where he graduated in 1952. Later he held a teaching fellowship and taught English there for one year.

His peregrinations were not all on land; he'd slaved as a stoker on a merchant ship for at least one voyage (eight hours on, eight hours off). 'My first and I hope my last glimpse of purgatory.' He'd worked as an aeroplane mechanic, picture-frame maker and amateur actor – he'd been drawn to the stage at one point – so his background was both diffuse and extraordinary. He was an acutely aware man, benefiting in many ways from these diverse experiences. It was from the University of Washington in Seattle that he was awarded the Rhodes Scholarship in 1953. Vivid with life, he loved and relished its richness. People, arguing, art, literature, music, good food and wine were enjoyed to the full. He knew how to apply himself to hard work and

---

how to play: how and when to relax the tension of his probing, keen mind. He could be arrogant and overbearing, but not unconsciously. He was often moody, but if he felt he acted harshly, he was big enough to say he was sorry. He was a man of intense passion and commensurate tenderness. One morning he got very angry with me about something – it must have been a trivial matter because I don't even remember what it was about. I tried to hide my hurt, but in spite of myself tears came to my eyes. Then he went off to school and left me in comparative misery all day. That evening, when he got back to the flat, he gave me this poem he had written for me:

> Why the minnows' flash or last night's moon
> should so deflect my thought I cannot say;
> because your tears this morning fell so soon
> to humble me, I fear they marred the day.

He had a perception of his own worth and gifts that seemed uncanny in one so young. The night I met him he told me that he had never met anyone more intelligent than himself. I was taken aback by what seemed to me to be gross conceit. Later I mentioned the remark to Sister Mary Angela, my singing teacher, a gentle, thoughtful, intelligent woman in whom there is no guile – a true Israelite. Her response was very unexpected. 'It's probably true,' she said. While being genuinely serious about things that mattered, he had a delicious sense of fun; and a childlike playfulness that, I think, he seldom showed others. Some of his close friends later expressed surprise at how playful he could sometimes be with me.

I left Oxford knowing that my attachment to this vibrant personality was deepening and that my burgeoning love was indeed reciprocated.

Almost as soon as I got back to Dublin I learned that I was to sing in Claridge's at an International Press Conference on 12th December. Richard was thrilled. We both were. It meant we would see each other again. Richard wanted to know if I could go with him to Paris the week following the engagement to stay with the Jackson Matthews. He was working hard again and 'missing you very strongly. This time we spent together is very precious to me. It was very good of you to come.' The letters continued, with Richard bubbling with life and interest in it and his work. Term would end on December 4th and could I come to Oxford now *before* the 12th? From then on his letters to me were practically daily, his deepening affection more evident and matching my own feelings for him.

In a moment of misguided humour I'd sent a cryptic note from Belfast where I'd been taking part in a concert. To my shame and contrition, Richard had misconstrued the message and thought I was ill. Somehow he got hold of the telephone number of the private family I was staying with and phoned me. Confused by his unexpected concern all I could do to hide my embarrassment was laugh. This only compounded the situation. A very angry, hurt Richard wrote the next day.

Monday 7th November or Tuesday 8th

Mary,

When your laughing fit is over, do me a favour. I am enclosing a traveller's cheque for $10.00. Buy a white Aran ganzie, like mine if possible, and send it as a gift to: John Leyerle, Magdalen College Oxford.

He is a married friend of mine who needs to keep warm. If it isn't enough let me know, I'll reimburse you. *Also,* when you come to England next bring me tobacco, as much as customs allow: BALKAN SOBRAME preferably, or THREE NUNS. Pipe tobacco.

Thanks.
Richard

Then, the next day.

8th November 1955

Dearest Mary,

I have been angry with you all day.

First because of the fright, now ridiculous, that your note from Belfast gave me; second because you addressed me with no form of endearment; and third because of your infuriating laughter over the phone. Even if it was deserved, it was very frustrating.

It is my too well developed, too sensitive pride that gives me the courage to be angry with you but it also prevents me from expressing a feeling that is much deeper to me and more important, that is that I love you.

I do not wish our relationship to become a game of pride. I wish to love you and to give you the best that is in me with all the tenderness and respect of which I am capable.

If the seriousness of my feelings offends or frightens you, please let me assure you that I require nothing more of you than that you obey the inclinations of your own heart.

Richard

Next day the storm had completely blown over.

I bought the Aran ganzie for his friend. As a surprise I purchased the most spectacular one in the shop for Richard himself, plus a pair of socks. His exuberant gratitude was a tonic.

15th November 1955

Darling Mary,

Your gifts arrived this morning and are exceeding welcome. My ganzie is of a very superior ilk indeed! I like the design especially, the parallel paths of angles and arcs, diamonds and waves. I'm sure Mr Leyerle will be pleased with his: I won't show him mine. The stockings are a windfall, my feet having felt soggy, cold and wet for days now.

I don't think it at all strange that you should grow tired of certain of the songs you sing. I understand this very well: when one is young and/or of a romantic, emotional nature it is more for the sentiment that we love a thing than for its beauty and perfection as a work of art. Besides, most folk songs are extremely sentimental and in them there is little attempt to achieve the formalized sentiment of the art song...

Both your letters, the one of the 11th and the one of the 12th, arrived on Monday so I was unable to hear the re-broadcast.

I hope to hear from you soon,

All my love,
Richard

PS: If you take a flat don't sign a lease.

I did not agree with him about most folk songs being 'extremely sentimental'. At that time he was unfamiliar with the bulk of my repertoire and was later to change his mind when he came to see that many of the 'big' traditional Gaelic songs are, as has been pointed out elsewhere by Dr Percy Jones, Head of the Faculty of Music, Melbourne University, on a par with the best of *lied* and *chanson* and require considerable skill to sing them in a way that draws out the inherent beauty and excellence of the melodies.

Deciding now that I would be better off in a flat in the city, I'd found one in Lower Leeson Street. Perhaps I should have been sharper and read between the lines. Richard's advice against signing a lease was because he had plans of his own regarding my future living arrangements.

17th November 1955

Dearest Mary,
It occurred to me, during this morning's labours, that I was harbouring selfish feelings concerning you. And they are these: I resent your being so far away and your wish to live independently in Dublin. Then, a stronger feeling rose up to spite these ignominious ones. That was: I want you to do what is best for you. That, ultimately, is what is best for me also.

However, I expect you to make every reasonable effort to spend as much time with me as you can reasonably afford.

It is difficult to love someone and not want to have them near. But since meeting you, I have discovered stores of patience I did not know I had. I have such faith in your good sense, Mary, that I no longer feel I need to exert pressure on you to make you demonstrate that you care.

The play I have tickets for at Stratford is one of my favourites: Shakespeare's *King Lear.* I do hope you can come. December 3rd. During the week you have your engagements in London I shall be there also; if I may, I would like to be your chaperone at this 'all male' press conference concert at Claridge's.

Let me hear from you soon, .

All my love,
Richard

In the next day's letter Richard reported on the success of two of his Oxford enterprises, before continuing,

If you love 'hearing from me' you might encourage me by writing more often yourself. I'm at least as busy as you are so there's no excuse.

This child did *live. Mary aged about one with her sister Joan aged about five.*

Mary aged eighteen.

Takoradi, Gold Coast, 1954.

Mary had her first driving lesson in the Gold Coast and crashed her father's car into a ditch.

'Who's for tennis?'

Richard Selig, 1954.

Mary and Richard's Wedding day, 23rd July 1956.

Mary with Richard sound asleep on the Queen Elizabeth, September 1956.

Mary with Jean O'Leary,
John and Jeana, Westchester,
New York, October 1957,
a few days after Richard's
death.

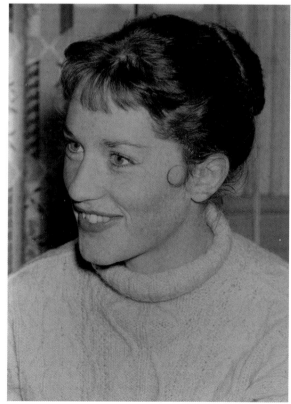

Mary during a press
interview on the
New Zealand tour,
Autumn 1959.

At the Irish launch of Mary's book The Scent of the Roses *in Dublin, 1980.*
Singer Frank Patterson and his wife Eily with Mary and Father Dermod McCarthy.

Photoshoot for
Mary's book
A Song For Ireland.

Pat on Rotnest Island, Australia after the 1986 concert tour.

After a concert during the Australia 1984 tour: Matthew Freeman, Mary, Sandra Peach and Pat.

Pat, Mary's father J.C. O'Hara, Mary and an old friend, Jenny Smith, at Rivendell on 8th August 1985, shortly before the wedding.

At Rivendell just days before leaving for their wedding in Canada on 17th September 1985.

*Mary in concert
at Carnegie Hall,
1983.*

*Pat and Mary at a
national press conference
in Melbourne, June 1986.*

By now we had both declared our love and I knew that if Richard asked me to marry him I would say yes. And if he didn't ask me I would never marry anyone else. He was the one I'd been waiting for.

26th November 1955

Dearest Mary,

Great quantities of thanks for your letter of Thursday night...

I love you too, Mary, and admire you deeply. It is a rare happiness to me to meet a woman with your dignity. I want to show you my favorite Grivelli's and Rembrandt's in the National Gallery and also the Constable landscapes in the Tate.

How was Segovia?

I've got two sets of Graves mythology. I'll give you volume two. Rex Warner gave me one set.

All my love,
Richard

27th November 1955

Dearest Mary,

... I want you to know what to expect when you see me again. For my part I have pursued our relationship with a great deal of energy but, because of my belief in the possibility of its success, with little sense of strain, I feel now, however, that if my feelings continue at their present pitch without the renewal and confidence that only your presence can give they could easily burn themselves out. This is a harsh but I think accurate estimate of romantic emotion. Without each other's company on some kind of day-to-day basis and real physical contact calmly discovered, I think love would not be the correct word to apply to our relationship. You must understand this quite clearly of me, moreover: I am a man who lives in his senses first. What I see is what I believe. I have a sixth sense also and I have a faith in it, also, though it is like hearing sounds from a great depth. When I love, I love with my body, thoughts, speech and all my senses. I don't love ideals and possibilities. I love real things, present things, all the thousand particular characteristics that compose a person. And when that person is away, I love the memory of those things as accurately as I can.

I want you to know that I am keeping faithful to you with little reluctance.

I want you to write me often because I want you to keep me on your mind until we can be in one another's arms: talking, walking and eating together.

I love you…

28th November 1955

Darling Mary,

This weekend was an acutely lonely one for me, full of childish love-aches. I am over the aches.

I've just re-read your spate of green letters and want very, very much to be able to talk with you. My long dissertation on the senses was just another, if infelicitous way of telling you I miss you and how nice it would be to have you in the vicinity. I am so unused to caring so much for someone else – being a veteran egotist – that it may make me a little uncomfortable at times. You will be patient, won't you?

I am just about to write to the tourist office of Obergurgel, a skiing village high up in the Austrian Alps. And also to Hochsholden for reservations. My budget won't allow plane travel. I hope you don't mind travelling third class by rail. When one is a student one must live as a student. Write to me often, dearest, and if suddenly you wish to come on Saturday, I'll keep your ticket.

All my love,
Richard

The prospect of a holiday together in Austria was exciting, and when I got this letter I started consulting some of my friends about ski clothes. Radio Éireann had sent me a contract for a broadcast on Christmas Day, but I told them I wouldn't be in Ireland on 25th December and cancelled it.

30th November 1955

Good morning!

… Talking to you last night made me very happy.

In about an hour I shall go to see the surgeon. I hope something is done quickly. However, don't worry, I shall keep you posted as to all the details. You'll probably have to learn some anatomical terms so that I can explain things properly. Although I have never had an operation, I have seen many: your fear of them is unnecessary. The body is full of spare parts and can take a great deal of punishment…

Afternoon

I met the surgeon; a brisk, imperious man with large hands very bulbous at the joints, an extraordinarily long middle finger. He seems trustworthy enough. I underwent examination, blood test and X-rays and was out by lunchtime. I had a very pretty radiologist who took a cool delight in shifting me into all kinds of ludicrous positions. The doctor said something about my going into hospital today or tomorrow for further tests. So far no word. It is now nearly four o'clock.

No word has come from the surgeon yet and it is now 6.00 pm so I guess I won't hear anything until tomorrow.

I think it would be foolish for you to come up to Oxford for the weekend because it would only be a gloomy one for you and that would not make me happy. Why don't you come up a day or so before your concert just for the day? It would be a pleasanter visit that way. I would hate to think of you hanging around Oxford just to look at a drooping Richard. If you come up on a day *excursion* on Wednesday, 14th December, the day after Claridge's, it would only cost 8 shillings.

Spender has arrived, I must to dinner. I'll post this now and write to you tomorrow.

All my love,
Richard

In retrospect it seems curious that I have no memory of what it was that caused Richard to seek medical attention. Perhaps it's because he made very light of the pain or whatever it was, only mentioning it *en passant* in conversation, in his debonair way. There is certainly no reference to it in letters up to then. Treat the matter lightly – even humorously – in his letters he most certainly did On the other hand, anyone who knew Richard then would understand that the idea of associating him with a fatal illness was preposterous. He was bursting with apparent good health, lively to a degree in spirit, mind and body; pulsating with life.

He was very wrong in thinking that I would not want to be there if I could while the investigations were going on. I was capable of a great deal more than he could have then guessed, and I didn't pare it down to a 'day excursion' but came for several days. Under this shadow, which was to grow, he continued to live life to the full, and his unending activities, social and academic, bubbled on unabated.

News followed about the imminent biopsy. He appeared unruffled. Due to uncertainty about the frequency of the tests and treatments, the plan for a holiday on the continent was cancelled. So I told Radio Éireann I would be available for the Christmas Day broadcast.

1st December 1955

Dearest Mary,

... Nothing to report about forthcoming operation. The surgeon managed to elude my GP all day. The surgeon has left me a message he will call tomorrow morning. The question at the moment is whether there is anything other than the jewel in the middle...

I have been keeping at work although somewhat desultorily. I'm going to see a French comedy now.

All my best, and every kind of love,
Richard

2nd December 1955

Dearest Mary,

... I can't tell how much happiness your last letter gave me. It is wonderful to have one's feelings reciprocated.

The surgeon phoned to say I must go into hospital as a private patient for a day or so to have a biopsy. A bed has to be found. I won't hear from him again until one is found.

I just saw Sean White on the street and told him to call you when he gets back to Dublin to tell you how robust I look. I thought I'd discipline his propensity for gossip by requesting him to be a bearer of kind news. I hope you don't mind. I'll close this now and mail it. I hope 'Imaginary Conversation' goes well.

If the timing is right, I may yet be able to meet you in London.

All my love,
Richard

Later that day:

2nd December 1955

Dearest Mary,

I shall be going into the Ackland Nursing Home on Tuesday afternoon 6th December...

3rd December 1955

Dearest Mary,

Thanks for your letter of the 1st. By now you will have received my letters. Mary, it is nice to have you worrying and praying, in so far as they are an expression of your care, but it would be much nicer still to know whether you would like to spend Christmas with me or me with you. I'm glad you got your Christmas engagement back. If I am on my feet I shall probably initiate yet another invasion of Ireland.

What do you want for Christmas?

All my love,
Richardus Seligonensus

An Imaginary Conversation had been performed at the Arts Club in Dublin. I had written to Richard and was inordinately puffed up by my little success as an actress. His response tinged with sarcasm was appropriate to the occasion.

5th December 1955

Dearest Mary,

I haven't heard of a performance to produce such an effect since Sarah Bernhardt. You must have been good. Congratulations! I hope Dublin has recovered. Thanks for writing.

All my love,
Richard

6th December 1955

Dearest Mary,

... In one of your letters of last week, you said that you would be free to leave Dublin Wednesday, 7th December. If this is still the case, then *come to Oxford forthwith.* I have no desire to be without you, either mobile or on my back, but merely suspected that you were a coward where illness is concerned and therefore suggested you should not come for any length of time.

I received a reply from Hochsholden in Austria which I shall discuss with you when you come.

I am in excellent spirits and am feeling very energetic, so the doctors can do their worst.

I'd rather have you than your letters.

All my love,
Richard

This was just what I wanted to hear: come to Oxford *quam primum*.
He wanted me to be there with him as much as I did. The Austrian
skiing plan was apparently taking shape. His report about feeling on
top of the world was very reassuring. He continued to convey this
impression of well-being over the next twelve months, and doubtless
this contributed towards my not grasping the gravity of the situation.

He went into hospital and surgery was performed. That same day
he got out of bed and phoned me, thus earning a severe reprimand
from the surgeon. Since the operation was the removal of a lymph
gland from his groin for analysis, this is understandable.

8th December 1955

Mary,

I just saw the surgeon. The earliest he will let me out is Saturday.
Therefore I cannot meet you in London as I had hoped. He was also
very annoyed with my having walked about today.

Please, please come to Oxford on arriving Saturday.

Richard

As usual I flew to London and took the train from Paddington. As
soon as I reached Oxford I made straight for the Ackland Nursing
Home, expecting to find him still in bed. Not so. He'd discharged
himself. I hurried down the road to his flat and rang the doorbell to
no avail. Not having any idea where else he might be I just waited
outside in the damp December twilight. Finally he turned up, looking his old self – and maybe a bit irritated that I'd not tried and discovered that the door was unlocked. (Many were the times when
Richard would throw up his hands and cry, 'Oh Mary you've got a
head, use it!') It was very good being together again after another long
lapse of about five weeks. Again, oddly enough, I have no recollection
of any discussions between us concerning the biopsy. Perhaps they had
told him nothing.

We travelled up to London together for the Claridge's engagement.
I had with me my own very first evening dress, designed and made
by a young Dublin dress designer, Sheila Russell. I knew exactly how
I wanted it: material, colour, design. White *broderie anglais*, sleeveless,

Princess line; buttons down the back (all the way to the floor) covered with *broderie anglais*; a scooped neckline in front forming a deep V at the back; a gentle bustle effect at the back of the skirt, achieved by the way the lavish underskirt was made. The making of it alone cost £20, which in those days was a sum to stop the breath.

This engagement was to be the first of many trips to London accompanied by my 'chevalier'. 'Escorting me among the sharks,' was Richard's expression. He revelled in it. He was more than a match for them. His strong, authoritative presence never failed to evoke either respect or fear among the wheelers and dealers. I think they sensed or recognized an all-perceiving shrewdness to match their own, in this handsome, cultured young man who was there with me at every meeting and consultation. He said little, but he always got things done.

That evening at Claridge's, Richard wore his evening suit. There was something regal in the air that night. I felt decidedly fairy princessish as we wandered hand in hand through the elegant rooms adjoining the ballroom where I was to sing. We spoke hardly at all. I try to avoid talking before any kind of a performance. I need the silence; because of the nervousness and to help me focus. Few people understand this need; far too many, well-intentioned to be sure, chatter away and crack jokes endeavouring to be light-hearted and amusing. It only makes things more difficult for me. Not a few misconstrue this quietness, which I find essential and interpret it as moodiness. Richard never did. An artist himself, intuitively he just knew.

That night we were sitting on a sofa together waiting for the signal telling me when I was to begin. It was to be an after dinner performance. As I was inwardly contending with my nervousness Richard leant tenderly towards me and said: 'Now you know what it's like when I don't get a letter from you.'

Everyone seemed very happy with the singing. We left Claridge's and Richard took me to an exclusive French restaurant, where he'd booked a table. We dined sumptuously by candlelight. That evening had a special cachet about it. The beautiful dress, the successful performance, the ambrosial meal and the elegant, stunning young man with whom I was by now deeply and irrevocably in love and he with me. Well, almost perfect.

The diagnosis was Hodgkin's disease. It is a cancer of the lymph glands. They called it 'the young man's disease'. The victims are generally young males. In those days it was incurable, but, thank God, it is no longer so. Then it could be arrested by radiation. The researchers were experimenting with new drugs all the time.

When his GP broke the news Richard asked, 'How long have I got?'

'Well, you'll probably live to my age,' was the reply. Losing no time, Richard sought out his tutor and asked him how old the GP was. 'About forty-five,' was the answer.

'Good, there's my essay for next week.'

And Richard proceeded with the business of living at his usual intense, overflowing pace.

Who could presume to attempt or dare to say what was going on in Richard's mind when he got this news and during the weeks, the twenty-two months that lay ahead. When he did speak to me about it at the beginning he seemed strangely matter of fact and objective concerning the disease. One of the things he said was, 'The sentence of death hangs over all of us.' I returned to Dublin and prepared for my Christmas Day radio engagement.

23rd December 1955

Dearest Mary,

Just got your letter of Tuesday. Delay is due to Christmas, I guess. I've sent you three letters c/o Dr R. Sorry to hear you are still stuck in 53. I wish I could go over and build a fire under Dr R. I know how to intimidate Dublin landlords.

George played me a lovely Haydn sonata (on the piano, not on a record-player) till the pubs opened; then we got thwacked on Irish whiskey and Guinness and finished the evening with a steak dinner. It was fine. Got up feeling slightly hung over but opened windows wide and did callisthenics.

Richard

Physical exercise is something I've always keenly enjoyed. In no time Richard became as enthusiastic as I was about it. Each morning would find him doing his push-ups or whatever. Often we would do our callisthenics together during the day. When I was in Oxford I used to sleep in Adrian and Maureen Mitchell's spare room in their little flat round the corner from Richard. After I came to actually live in Oxford, before we were married, my usual routine was to cycle to St Aloysius for eight o'clock Mass, go to Richard's flat for breakfast together, and use it as a base for the rest of the day.

In the end, we didn't spend Christmas together but Richard came across for the New Year.

24th December 1955

Dearest Mary,

Many thanks for your telephone call last night. It was very welcome indeed. I shall make every effort to come to Dublin if I can.

Keep after Dr R. or the place won't be ready on the 31st either.

No letter from you this morning but am not surprised.

Mary, it is impossible, or at least very difficult, to tell you over the phone that I love you but please remember that I do whether I say so or not.

More than anything else at the moment I would like to march down Grafton Street with you.

All my love,
Richard

The business of moving into my flat had been dragging on and on. For one reason or another it was never quite ready on the day I was supposed to take up residence. Grafton Street was the most fashionable street in Dublin. It was a source of wonder and delight to Richard that so many people who passed up and down it seemed to know each other. In those days when we walked down it together I could be greeted possibly a dozen times in one journey. It was one of the more endearing characteristics of Dublin that the city was still small enough for an area like Grafton Street to become a meeting place for friends.

Richard flew over to Dublin a couple of days before the 1st and saw to it that, despite the flat's not being ready, I was installed in Lower Leeson Street. I didn't sign a lease as he'd advised me against it; this turned out to be good advice as, early in April, I moved out of the flat and went to live in Oxford.

Although Richard hadn't asked me to marry him we both knew it was in the air and since I was a Catholic and he was not, with the possibility of children there arose the potential problem of their religious upbringing. I recall a long walk through the New Year rain talking about it. Richard's view was that children should grow up and make their own choice and not have a particular religion foisted on them from the cradle. But the ruling of the Catholic Church at that time was that all children of a mixed marriage should be brought up as Catholics. The non-Catholic party had to promise to agree to this and see that it was implemented. This ruling has since been modified.

Richard came from a completely non-religious background. Neither of his parents adhered to religious beliefs of any kind. In his late teens, he'd examined the tenets of various faiths and found them all more or less wanting. But his attraction to Roman Catholicism was strong and became increasingly so the further he investigated. He was familiar with the writings of some of the great theologians and mystics, such as Thomas Aquinas, Augustine of Hippo and John of the Cross, before I became acquainted with the teachings of these and other spiritual giants.

It sometimes irritated him that I was so patently ill-informed about the history of my own church – the result of inattention during Church history classes. He soon gave up trying to provoke me with taunts about ecclesiastical scandals over the centuries. There was nothing I could say and, when I failed to rise to the challenge, in exasperation he would defend the Church himself, saying that it was members of the Church from the Pope downwards and not the Church herself who could be and often were corrupt and immoral. We never argued about religion. I have never been one for debate about my beliefs.

We'd been invited to a dance at the Arts Club on New Year's Eve. We seemed to be one of the very few couples who were not middle-aged or over and despite the fact that Richard was far from being a good dancer we enjoyed it all. He left for England on 3rd January.

3rd January 1956

Darling,

… I caught the plane at noon, the train from Birmingham at three and was in Oxford before five this afternoon.

Mary, come to Oxford on the fourteenth if possible. I suggest that you book your flight now since it is a Saturday. See if you can come by way of Birmingham. Have you written Mrs Rowlands about practising? I will make inquiries about practice rooms and harps.

Richard

Mrs Rowlands was the only person we could find in Oxford who had a concert harp and it was hoped I could be allowed to practise on it. An arrangement was made with her.

Geographical separation once again showed up my dilatoriness in letter writing. The number of letters I wrote was chronically insufficient to his demand.

5th January 1956

Dearest Mary,

Good morning from Magdalen College Library! It is below freezing in Oxford and the fog has crystallized into tiny spears, the better to penetrate the skin of pedestrians.

If you must sign a lease of a year with Dr R, make sure you have the right to sub-let. It would seem more practical to me that instead of spending so much of your money living in the grand manner you might better spend it on a decent wardrobe of which you are in great need... In your trade, mobility is essential: are you sure you want to support a flat for a year?

I have been dutifully doing my exercises morning and night and am beginning to feel more like a prize fighter than a student.

I look forward to seeing you and before that to hearing from you.

> All my love,
> Richard

7th January 1956

Dearest Mary,

No letter from you again this morning. I hope it is the fog that has delayed letters you *have* written rather than that under cover of some mental fog of your own you have omitted to write. I shall continue to write you as often as possible under the assumption (I hope it isn't a delusion) that you want to hear from me.

Last night I went to a Twelfth Night celebration at the Leyerle's. Mulled claret and all kinds of goodies were served. It was very pleasant. They did an excellent job of serving and of seeing that people got acquainted with one another.

I am working hard: writing letters, reading and school work; am doing my exercises; and am looking forward to seeing you again.

If nothing comes on the noon post I shall send you a wire,

> All my love,
> Richard

PS. I just phoned the post office to find out whether there has been a delay in the mail from Dublin. There has been none. Mary, don't you believe in me or my love enough to write to me before you hear from me?

Richard

The wire of consummate brevity arrived that evening. It read:

PHONE ME NOW.
Richard

During our last time in London together we'd been to see people at Decca, at their suggestion, regarding future recording possibilities. In this next letter Richard touches on Decca's concern with the commercial side of my singing. During my entire career the conflict, however unavoidable, between the music and the money nexus has been a constant irritant. My music and my performance of it are what matter to me; the box-office returns tend to outweigh other considerations in the minds of those on the organizing side.

10th January 1956

Most beloved Mary,

A windfall arrived this morning: two letters from you. Warmest thanks for them. I was deeply touched and delighted that you reserved your first phone call on your new phone for me. It was lovely to talk with you, Darling. I am more grateful for your love than for any of the favours that have ever been bestowed on me, and more honoured too.

As for S., an idea occurred to me, one of many, last night, that may be of use to you. I suspect that they are building up to do some popular recordings *comme ci:* 'Jo Gooch and his Orchestra introducing Mary O'Hara on her Irish Harp'. He will probably dazzle you with an introduction to Joe Gooch himself and to his famous vocalist, Marilyn Muck. You know, the girl who made a hit with 'Stagnant Whirlpool' and 'I loved you in Old Shoes'. After meeting these bright stars, he will treat you to anything you want at a restaurant in Soho and expect you to be fawningly impressed and grateful. This is my idea for what it's worth. If you can get enthusiastic about some folk songs in English, some lively or poignant American ones, perhaps, to which you can give your own inimitable Irish flavour, you might turn the tables on him.

One of the reasons he is acting the way he is is that the first recording you made was rather effete and probably not very saleable. He is
trying to get you to do something which is saleable in his own clumsy
way. You feel that he wants you to go too far in the opposite direction,
that to sing things like 'Croce de Oro' would be merely making a fool
of yourself. You're probably right. Since you've been so passive about
your repertoire, he is taking the initiative. Find some songs that are
new and interesting to yourself before you see him and when you do
see him: if you can, wax enthusiastic about them and ask to play them
to him and Mr Lee. If you don't sell what sort of thing you want to do
to them, they will try to make you do something in accordance with
their own crude notions. Try Carl Sandberg's 'American Songbook' and
some of Allen Lomax's collections. You may find them in the National
Library.

All my love,
Richard

I've always liked beards – the smaller, neat variety. Although they
were fairly rare in those days – the mid and late fifties – some of my
friends sported them. To please me Richard grew one, and he looked
even more strikingly handsome, if that were possible, than before.
Being a six-footer already marked him out from most others. Like his
head of brown hair, his beard was luxuriant, with reddish areas. There
was one particular tie of a soft olive colour which he sometimes wore
which emphasized his unusual green eyes. He had a black corduroy
suit which the President of Magdalen used teasingly to refer to as his
'Hamlet suit'.

A few days later I arrived in England for an engagement. By now I'd
started flying to Birmingham rather than to London. It was a shorter
flight and Oxford was conveniently mid-way between the two cities.
Richard Afton, the BBC TV producer, was including me in his Variety
Programme, 'More Contrary'. This time Richard didn't travel up with
me – term had begun again, and he was confined to Oxford. Sydney
MacEwan sent me a good-luck telegram. I was very pleased. Richard
phoned me after the TV programme, which was live. Everyone was
happy and I was signed on for the two remaining programmes.

Next day, after lunching with Decca people, I travelled back to
Oxford and Richard.

We had a glorious two weeks together this time, having tea with friends, going to the Film Society, sometimes lunching or dining out, and going for long walks. And Richard was initiating me into the mysteries of the culinary art. He had an innate gift for cooking and he did it creatively. Over the years, and in different countries, he'd picked up some fairly simple but very appetising dishes to which he added his own inventive touches. Meals cooked by him were always succulent. Now I was to discover that cooking could be as exciting as the finished product was enjoyable.

Towards the end of that spell we travelled to London together, where I had my eye on an elegant black coat I'd seen in the shop where I'd bought the evening dress for my first BBC 'More Contrary' programme. I emerged from the shop clad in the same coat but of a colour I would never have dreamt of choosing for myself, but which Richard had decided on. A very difficult colour to describe: a pinkish coral is the nearest I can get. It was the most successful purchase I'd ever made. People passed remarks about it's being a most flattering colour for me.

Next day, before leaving for Dublin, I bought some dresses in Oxford to team up with the new coat. Richard approved.

Together, we had a meeting with Richard Afton.

Back in merry England Richard was not only immersed in his studies and the usual social whirl, but also finding time to try to straighten out my career, and see to it that I would find the right agent 'with good taste, integrity and who lacks the overbearing attitude of self-aggrandisement which seems to possess many of them'. A task that wasn't all that simple.

31st January 1956

Dearest Mary,

The second of your letters to be written 'every single day' arrived this morning. Thank you. It was dated the 28th so I gather the weather in the Irish Sea is unpropitious for the postal services. I hope my yesterday's letter reaches you soon. I wish to keep you informed of professional matters...

I think you can carry sympathy too far.* Also I think you can overestimate your power to do good. There is an insidious element of pride in thinking that you can bestow love and affection on those weaker or more afflicted than yourself. It makes you feel very strong and generous when you make such a bestowal but beware that the cur that you honour with comfort and consolation does not repay you with laughter and destruction. You must be a saint, indeed, to bear the enmity of those to whom you are most kind. Those who need the most kindness are often the least capable of gratitude. Those who *ask* for your sympathy often have an insatiable hunger for which sympathy is insufficient food. They want more and more of you, more than mere sympathy can satisfy. It is noble to feel compassion. It is nobler still to know when and where love and affection will be gladly received and to be able to bestow them in a truly generous spirit. Compassion can also be an excuse to yourself. In its name you do for others what does them no good. In its name you do what you want to do anyway.

Darling, forgive this sermon but it has been stewing in me for a long time. I don't expect that you will agree with all of it or perhaps any of it. Please believe that it is not based on the distrust I have often accused myself of. I do not love people the less for what I have seen in their hearts or in my own heart for that matter, but rather I attempt to love more efficiently, with fewer delusions and self-deceptions, to expect less and to give more. Human nature needs constant correction and attitudes toward it need constant revision.

Mary, I study to love you better and better, to love what is truly you, to love what is best in you because that increases my respect and admiration for you and to love what is at fault in you because in that, too, I know you – and knowing and loving you is what I desire and need to do more than anything else in the world.

Richard

My domestic arrangements in Dublin continued to cause Richard some small concern and he was as usual ever ready to come to my rescue and straighten things out.

* This was occasioned by an incident with an acquaintance in Oxford that prompted Richard to launch into the above reflections about indiscriminately bestowing and accepting friendships. He may also have had in mind the world of entertainment where people are so often 'used' by others under the guise of helping them.

1st February 1956

Dearest Mary,

Your letter of Monday the 30th is gratefully received. Remind me to buy you a gallon of blue or black ink. I do think it is rather a drain on one always to be writing in one's blood.

Dearest, I can't tell you how good it was for me to talk to you last night. As you have probably surmised I miss you very much.

As for signing a lease, if the question arises, explain that you cannot sign one until your next birthday. As for paying your rent you need not do so in person. Send him a cheque to the amount of a month's rent. Don't under any circumstances get yourself under obligation to him, keep the relationship business-like.

Though it is still contingent on a number of things, I think the best time for you to move to England would be during the spring, in early April. I could help you to move at that time. Also, even a short trip with you during my spring vacation, after moving you here, would be highly desirable. However, all of this must be discussed at greater length. I look forward to hearing from you.

> I remain devoted to you with all my love,
> Richard

2nd February 1956

Dearest Mary,

Darlingest Mary, I'm full of love for you this morning and wish with all my might I could be telling it to you in person.

There was no letter from you this morning but I am hoping for one on the noon post.

I'm down to my final revisions on my poem, a sonnet, on Antarctica. I finished reading Scott's last journal on Tuesday with tears in my eyes. It is the first time in a long time that a book has so affected me.

Yesterday evening I was with George Pitcher and Sir John Gielgud. Sir John is one of that rare, amazing ilk, the pure artist. I've known only two others to equal him, Mark Tobey, the painter, and Roethke. The surge of their thoughts is an experience I have long missed, especially in this effete, self-conscious and too-sophisticated community. And, darling, believe it or not, his intelligent simplicity reminded me of you.

I haven't told you this before. But I find the trueness of your reactions to things, and your clear, beautiful company most invaluable to me.

I'll wait to see if there's a letter from you before I mail this.

Sweetheart, I just got your letter of Tuesday. Infinite thanks! I love
you too with all my heart.

Richard

Richard asked Sir John Gielgud for advice about 'a friend of his'
who was at a sort of crossroads in her career. He explained that
several persons were trying to act as her agent and she needed friendly
professional advice. Sir John recommended Joyce Grenfell. An introduction was arranged and she was subsequently to become my good
friend.

Later I knew that Richard had battled with himself over the problem of his own prospects and mine. He wanted us to be together
always but should he ask me to marry him or not? In those days the
odds against a young man stricken with Hodgkin's disease living a
normal life span were virtually nil.

3rd February 1956

Darling Mary,

I have a two-berth cabin, No. A7 on the *Queen Elizabeth* sailing from
Southampton to New York on the 6th of September. Would you like
to come along?

When you arrive in Birmingham eat lightly for I have two large
steaks waiting for us.

With all my prayers that you will be able to come Sunday.

I remain,
Your devoted
Richard

This was the first open acknowledgement that we should still be
together when he had finished at Oxford. I felt that this meant he was
now on the brink of actually asking me to marry him. This move
was supreme Richard. A two-berth cabin on a ship to America with
me, un-consulted, as the second passenger was sheer presumption. He,
when he sent the letter and I when I received it, both knew I would
want to accept.

Two days later I arrived in Oxford. On the morning of 10th
February, in the kitchen of his flat in Norham Road, Richard proposed.
Without a moment's hesitation I said yes. After lunch we walked out
into the cold February day and looked in the window of Davis the

jewellers on the High Street. There was an antique ring there that caught our eyes, but when we got inside the shop we saw the perfect one. It was a late Victorian antique ring with four amethysts and one diamond surrounded by rose diamonds. It fitted me beautifully.

I swelled with secret pride when friends and strangers in shops remarked on my beautiful engagement ring.

CHAPTER 6

Marriage

W E WOULD HAVE liked to marry at once but, being a Rhodes Scholar, Richard was not free to do so. In those days Rhodes Scholars in residence were not allowed to marry. Some went ahead anyway and got married secretly. We toyed with the idea of marrying on the quiet during the Easter vacation, and in some obscure part of the continent. But since it was to be a mixed marriage between a Catholic and a non-baptized person, we were going to need a whacking great dispensation for that alone. Marrying somewhere other than in my parish would have meant seeking yet another dispensation. So we decided not to complicate things, but wait until Richard's exams were over sometime in the summer.

At St Aloysius Presbytery Richard received the usual instruction meted out to the non-Catholic party. He learned nothing that he did not already know; and he spoke to me with gentle humour of the unnecessarily (for Richard) elementary nature and method of the teaching he received from the good parish priest. When the appropriate time came, he promised that any children of the marriage would be brought up as Catholics. It meant much to him that I grow in the faith and be as diligently practising a Catholic as I could possibly be. It was never an issue with us. Countless times he opted to come to Mass with me on Sundays: never did I suggest or even hint that he might do so. He was a man who knew himself, and his own mind, and who acted with immense integrity.

Thinking the coast would be clear by mid June and exams well out of the way, with the parish priest's concurrence we set the date for June 14. I was able to spend seven weeks in England: most of February and March. It was packed with happenings, great and small.

By now, Sydney Lipton was acting as my agent, although I'd not signed any contract. He procured a five-week tour for me with Harold Fielding's 'Music for the Millions'. Although it was a summer tour I did my first of these concerts at Eastbourne in April. Sometimes Rawicz and Landuer headed the bill; other times it was Terry Thomas or Eartha Kitt or Elsie and Doris Waters. I would be next on the bill, singing about half a dozen songs, with comedians following and occasionally two male dancers, Flak and Lucas, and a singing couple.

That February I had my first photographic session with John Baron. Richard came with me to London on all these excursions and excitement was never lacking. As arranged, I appeared on the last two 'More Contrary' BBC TV shows and afterwards Maurice Wiggan of *The Sunday Times* wrote some unexpectedly kind things about my work The performances went out live in March and April 1956. When it came to writing my TV scripts, Richard's help was invaluable.

In February I had my first fifteen minutes on Children's Hour television. Sir John Gielgud had alerted Joyce Grenfell beforehand and she'd agreed to watch my performance. Afterwards she invited me round to her flat in the King's Road for tea. She was gracious, kind, strongly encouraging and helpful in many ways – including giving me tips as to what outfits looked better on television and what to avoid.

As best I could (it was rather complicated by then) I acquainted her with the situation regarding the agents and prospective managers who were making approaches to me at the time. She advised me to opt for Sydney Lipton – 'the gentleman among the lot', as far as she could judge.

More often than not, Richard and I lunched or dined in Wheelers during our London jaunts. It was the fashionable place to eat. Wheeler's presented its cliental with *Wheeler's Review* a quarterly magazine devoted to food, personalities and fashion. On one occasion that summer of 1956, we were tickled to find it contained a Baron photograph of me, with an accompanying blurb. Earlier on, John Baron, had featured me in his widely read weekly column entitled 'Baron Profiles' in the *Evening Standard*. The blurb in the Review read:

THE QUARTER'S MUSE – BY BARON

For this Quarter of musical festivity we call upon Music's own Muse – Euterpe: here interpreted by MARY O'HARA, with her Irish harp.

Born 21 years ago in Sligo, she made her first broadcast on Radio Éireann, at the age of 16. Her appearance this year on BBC Television in her own series of traditional songs of Ireland and Scotland was a lasting delight. She appears this summer at the Edinburgh Festival, before leaving for the U.S.A. in September.

It was not, however, exclusively in the interests of Music that we called on this Irish Muse. No less than four of our contributors to this issue have derived undoubted inspiration from their compatriot: Sir Shane Leslie, Spike Hughes, P.I. Mannock and our Racing Correspondent, Bernard Walsh.

Deciding that I needed to brush up on my harmony, and since doing so in Dublin was now out of the question, an undergraduate friend of Richard's, reading Music at Magdalen, came to our flat a couple of mornings each week to give me harmony lessons. We got on like a house on fire. His name was Dudley Moore. Years later when I was in Stanbrook I picked up *The Times* one day and read a fascinating profile of Dudley. I'd no idea that, in the meantime, he had become an international entertainer. He and Peter Cook had become household names. To my joy I saw him for the first time since those Oxford mornings on the Michael Parkinson television show in 1978. He hadn't changed an iota. Dudley Dorian Gray Moore. Since then we've had dinner together.

I flew back to Dublin for one week to see Seán Óg and learn some new songs, have singing lessons from Sister Angela, orchestral harp lessons from Mercedes, see people in Radio Éireann and contact friends. I returned to England for a Harold Fielding concert and the beginning of the television series.

It was the Easter vacation by now. Clad in jeans and duffle coats, Richard and I hitchhiked to Birmingham airport. BBC-TV in London had decided to follow up the successful guest appearances I had made with them on the series 'More Contrary' and gave me a prime-time Saturday Night series of my own called 'The Starlight Series'. Richard Afton was the producer of the first couple, and Frederick Knapman produced the remainder.

Now I was in a bit of a quandary: I had already done one programme and there were three more to come. This required a lot of harp practice. As the Easter vacation was the only time Richard had free and as we had planned to spend the holiday cycling around Connemara in the West of Ireland, I came up with a solution. My bright idea was to borrow one of the little Brian Boru knee-harps from Sion Hill, strap it on my back and get my practice in at the end of each day's cycling. After all, I reasoned, that's how the harpers of old travelled, give or take a horse or two instead of a bicycle. Richard was duly despatched to Sion Hill and picked up the harp. But that was about as far as my daft idea got. Common sense intervened and we jettisoned the romantic, if highly impracticable idea. The West of Ireland is all hills and as Flann O'Brien points out in his novel *The Poor Mouth*, 'rain and Connemara are inextricably linked'.

We took the train from Dublin to our old haunt, Galway. There we hired bicycles and, for the next few days, rode through the Connemara rain enjoying every minute of it. Whenever the rain let up it was cause for celebration but, rain or clear skies, the Connemara magic is potent. I know of nowhere else apart from the Aran Islands themselves to match the stark independent beauty of the treeless landscape. We both thought it was the most beautiful part of the world and later seriously thought of some day buying property there. We returned the bikes to Galway and got a lift back to Dublin by car. Before we left for the airport I evacuated the Leeson Street flat.

The following Saturday, around 10.15 pm, I had my second programme of the television series, and again on the following two weeks. I did some more children's television and flew to Holland for a television appearance there. I sang two songs: '*Eibhlín a Rún*', one of the most beautiful of our big Gaelic love songs, and 'The Spanish Lady'.

The repercussions of that appearance reverberate to this day. Holland continues to be one of the non-English speaking countries where my records have gone on selling steadily.

The contract I'd signed with Decca was for five years. There was no obligation on the part of the record company to release any of my material. They were holding on to the four songs I'd sung for the test recording in October 1955 and showed no signs of bringing them out – hoping I would record 'pop-folk' songs instead of the traditional songs for which I understood I had been contracted. Little did they know that the sort of material I was singing was to become so popular in the sixties.

Richard had entered the fray and now proceeded to take measures to get things moving. A correspondence commenced between him and the record company which made interesting reading. It was clear from his letters that while his objective was to persuade them to release the recordings I'd already made, he thoroughly enjoyed the sparring. He helped me write a letter, one sentence of which was: 'My primary aim is not to make money.'

I was safely so far removed from this controlled warfare that I knew little about the detailed moves. Somehow, from somewhere, Richard sought expert advice that resulted in Decca's releasing the original material as an EP: two songs a side. Decca was stunned by the public's response. They called us to their office to tell us that in Holland alone they'd sold two thousand copies in the first few days. Now they did a *volte face*. Would I record a long-playing album of songs of my own choosing?

My initial reaction was one of apprehension. Among other things, I thought I didn't have enough material. (In those days one recorded eighteen songs on an album.) This was also how I'd greeted the BBC's proposal that I have my own television series. On both occasions, Richard quietly but firmly banished that mistaken fear and very quickly let me find out for myself that I had more than enough songs. In fact, within fifteen months, I'd cut three twelve-inch long-playing records: *Songs of Érin*, *Love Songs of Ireland* and *Songs of Ireland*. A new recording contract with Decca was drawn up. An additional clause, which Richard, his advisors and Sydney Lipton had Decca insert into the agreement, stated that my work must not be coupled with that of others on a recording without my express written permission.

Richard decided not to speak of his illness to anyone. Apart from the medical people and myself, only his tutor and the warden of Rhodes House knew about it. We didn't tell his mother or my father. Why? Richard was such a wise man that there didn't seem to me to be a need to question such a highly personal decision. Compassionate towards others, he was also a man in whom there was no shred of self-pity.

At a party one spring evening in Oxford, in the midst of a light-hearted conversation, an undergraduate banteringly asked Richard if he was going bald on the chin. Richard laughed it off, but when we got back to his flat we examined his beard. Sure enough, there was an area underneath one side of his jaw where the hair was thinning. The lymph glands in his neck were acting up. Sadly, we said farewell to the beard.

Spring passed into summer and we were both fully occupied. Richard's final examinations were on the horizon. I was working on my first long-playing record and about to begin the summer tour. We spent what time we could on the tennis court or on the river. We went about on bicycles. There were end of term parties and picnic lunches on the lawn at Magdalen. I snatched five days in Dublin filled with the usual singing and harp lessons and sessions with Seán Óg. Then back to Oxford again.

For some reason not recorded, the date of our wedding had to be postponed. The new date was 23rd July.

While I toured, Richard stayed on in Oxford preparing for his *viva,* but he usually managed to come and join me on weekends, whether it was Llandudno, Bournemouth, Torquay or elsewhere. I did a week in Aberdeen and was grateful that the following week in Bristol was cancelled. This left me with eight days free before our wedding.

Together we'd shopped for the wedding dress and finally found just the thing in Knightsbridge. The shop assistants were horrified to discover that Richard was my fiancé. We'd never heard of the superstition that the groom ought not to see the bride's dress before the wedding. Richard and I laughed about it. The dress was very simple; ballet length and made of white lace. We bought the ring in Davis' in Oxford where we'd got the engagement ring. This, too, was antique; a thin band of gold with delicate tracery edged all around.

When Richard heard that his *viva* was on 24th July, the day after our wedding, he made every possible effort to have the date shifted. His attempts were futile. So the unheard of had to happen. We got married on 23rd July, and the exam was on the following day.

Richard's mother was in Washington, DC and my father in West Africa. Most of our other friends were on vacation. We'd planned a very small, quiet wedding anyway, and I was most anxious that it be kept out of the newspapers. No photographers were invited. Peter

Levi, the poet, was to be Best Man; my brother-in-law, Frank Barry, was to give me away and my sister Joan was to be the Matron of Honour. At the eleventh hour Frank became involved in a court case which necessitated his being in Dublin on the morning of the 23rd.

Alan and Joan Woodin had been invited, so Joan took my sister's place and Richard's tutor, Jack Bennett, gave me away. Jack and his wife Gwyneth were very good friends of Richard's. I spent the night of the 22nd at their home in Ferry Hinksey and in the morning Gwyneth drove me to eight o'clock Mass at St Aloysius. Back at their house we had strawberries for breakfast. Then off again in the convertible for the wedding ceremony at 10 am. I arrived to find that Richard's great friend, Peter Levi, was not after all to be our Best Man. Alan Woodin had stepped into the breach.

Later that day I heard the story. Peter was a Jesuit scholastic at the time. It had been arranged well in advance that he would be Richard's Best Man and no dissenting voice was raised. But when Richard arrived at St Aloysius Church – about ten minutes before me – he was greeted by a very nervous parish priest who said he'd decided that Peter, being a Jesuit ought not to be involved in a mixed marriage ceremony. If that fact got bruited about it might look bad, and so on. 'But', he hastily added, 'I've asked another Rhodes Scholar to be Best Man instead.' Cold with fury, in deadly quiet tones Richard pointed out that he had not invited any Rhodes Scholar to his wedding. Who could he possibly mean? Taking him into the church, the poor parish priest, now all of a tremble, pointed to the Warden of Rhodes House himself, Bill Williams! Time has erased (if I ever did know) the memory of any further exchange between the irate groom and the Jesuit. We ended up with charming Alan Woodin being Best Man. It was indeed a mixed marriage. The non-Catholics outweighed the Catholics that sunny morning. Neither the groom, the Best Man, the Matron of Honour nor the Giver-Away were Catholics. Some weren't even Christian.

There was no nuptial Mass. There was no Mass at all. The ceremony was very simple. We both stood outside the sanctuary and exchanged vows. Peter acted as acolyte and handed the celebrant the ring. There were about a dozen people present. Afterwards we repaired to the New Rooms at Magdalen for our reception. Everyone drank champagne except the bride. Since we couldn't leave Oxford because of the *viva* the following morning, someone suggested we have lunch on the Isis. It was a brilliantly hot sunny day. We piled into some punts and for the next few hours lazed about on the river talking, eating and relaxing in the glorious sunshine.

In the late afternoon we left the punts and dispersed. Richard and I got a taxi back to Norham Road where he got on with his studies for the following morning while I slipped over to the Mitchells' place and did some ironing. That night we dined in our favourite restaurant outside Oxford, and spent the night in an hotel further down the road.

After the exams next day we flew to Dublin. We'd tried to book in at the Shelbourne, beautifully situated on Stephen's Green, but it was full. We had to be content with the Gresham. Next morning after a gargantuan breakfast we headed for the west.

Hitchhiking as usual we spent the night in Galway intending to travel to the Aran Islands next day on the *Dún Aengus*. We discovered it was laid up for repairs. The locals told us that our best bet was to travel into Connemara and take a turf boat from there to the islands.

On our way through Connemara we stopped at a pub out in the middle of nowhere so that Richard could buy a glass of beer. He stood at the counter ordering his drink while I sat by myself in a corner, incognito as I thought, in my duffle coat and jeans with my hair in plaits. The pub was filled with local men. To my consternation one of them asked me in Gaelic if I would sing for them. I did so. Here I was singing a Gaelic song at the source so to speak, so their response meant as much to me as would that of a sophisticated concert hall audience.

We reached Carraroe, but once more we were stymied. The mainlanders who rented the boat were on some sort of a strike. But it was thought that one man in the neighbourhood was going to break the strike and set off early in the morning. We booked in for the night in the only guest-house in the area.

Strolling down to the sea after supper, we clearly heard a piper playing. The thin, sweet sound filled the silent summer evening. We searched around but never found where the strange plaintive music was coming from.

Around midnight when we were both asleep the door suddenly opened and a man walked in holding a lighted lantern above his head, talking in a fairly loud voice. Leaping naked from the bed Richard grabbed hold of his hawthorn stick and with arm upraised advanced on the stunned intruder. The latter backed out in terrified confusion. The explanation was simple. There was no double room vacant that night in the guest-house. The man's wife had put us up in the children's room and had forgotten to tell her husband. He'd looked in, as usual, to see if his children were safe and sound.

In the morning the rumour about the strike-breaker was confirmed, so after breakfast at eight o'clock we presented ourselves on the quay. We came to a financial agreement with the owner of the 'hooker' (the turf boat), climbed aboard and set off for Inishere. The sea was calm and the sun shone hotly down on us. At mid-morning the sailors shared their thick bread and jam and sweet tea with us – and it was delicious.

Inishere is the smallest of the three Aran Islands and in those days it had no pier. The currachs came out to meet the boats, and the cargo, human or otherwise, was transferred and rowed ashore. There were three men in our currach. I overheard their conversation, which was in Gaelic, and realized that they thought we were not married, so I displayed my rings and told them we were husband and wife. They looked a bit embarrassed and kept quiet after that.

Richard received a warm welcome from the Conneelys with whom he'd stayed the previous summer. When he was leaving they had expressed the hope that he would return another time, Richard's reply had been 'I'll be back this time next year with my wife.' Once more our bedroom arrangements were not idyllic. Our double-bedded room led onto a single one that was occupied by another guest. To reach his room he had to go through ours. Late that night he climbed upstairs, tramped through our room and proceeded noisily to attend to the necessities of nature. Richard swore in the darkness and wondered out loud why he couldn't have gone outside and done it.

It rained a lot that week and we were the only ones who ventured into the thrashing seas. Richard was a very strong swimmer. At that time, I was not. Too timid I think – I missed the reassurance of being able to touch the bottom. With Richard, however, I gained more and more confidence.

The day came for us to head off for Achill Island and our *sui generis* friend Major Freyer. We were rowed out to the *Dún Aengus* that was anchored in the bay. Soon after we'd climbed aboard, I was approached by a man who asked me if I'd sing something on tape for a German group who were in Ireland recording songs. I refused and the man persisted in his request. To silence him I explained that I was under contract to the Decca Record Company and was therefore not free to record for anyone else. I thought no more about the matter. The deck was thronged with people and some of the islanders prevailed upon me to sing for them before I left. So a few minutes before the boat weighed anchor a crowd of us went down below to the saloon. People seated themselves or stood around the edge of the room. One corner was partitioned off, hiding the bar from sight. When everyone had grown silent I began to sing. Richard sat next to me with a large mug of beer in his hand. As I neared the end of the first verse of 'Eibhlín a Rún' out of the corner of my eye, I noticed a movement of something at the top of the partition. I nudged Richard and continued singing. Richard now saw the furtive microphone – and so did everyone else. By now I was beginning verse three. Richard rose from his seat and tiptoed noiselessly across to the partition. Reaching up, he coolly emptied the contents of his glass into the offending apparatus. No one budged, and I finished my song.

We sailed to Galway and, from there, headed for Achill Island and Major Freyer for a few days. Though we'd written to warn him of our coming, we had no way of knowing that he was expecting us. We'd heard it said that he never opened his letters – one of his charming but awkward eccentricities. Whether he expected us or not he welcomed us warmly.

After a few days we returned to England and I finished the tour with one week in Torquay.

Earlier that year I'd agreed to appear as guest artist in the official Edinburgh Festival production 'Pleasure of Scotland' written by George Scott-Moncrieff. Before we went north I recorded in London *Songs of Érin* – my first LP for the Decca Record Company.

Calum Maclean, with whom I'd kept up a correspondence, kindly offered us the use of his flat in Edinburgh for the two weeks we were to be in the city for the Festival.

It was a lamentably cold and very wet fortnight. Alistair and Rena Maclean were all set to have us stay a few days with them on South Uist after the Festival engagement – I was longing to introduce Richard to the Hebrides – but the weather was too miserable and Richard had a cold so we opted to return to London earlier. It was a special joy introducing Richard to George Scott-Moncrieff and his family, Sir Monty and Chrissie and all my other Scottish friends. We promised to be back again soon – all being well, the following summer.

September 10th was fast approaching and our excitement was mounting at the thought of our five-day voyage aboard the *Queen Elizabeth*. We talked about it for weeks in advance. Richard would be returning to his homeland after a three years' absence, during which a multitude of things had happened to him. I would be arriving in the United States for the first time in my life.

We climbed aboard the ship with me carrying a Briggs' harp in each hand. One of the things we most looked forward to was playing deck tennis. After we'd deposited our things in our cabin we lost no time in seeking out the person in charge of games. It was a very windy day. I could hardly contain myself with delight – which was my undoing. The combination of excitement and the strong wind resulted in my tossing at least six rings into Southampton waters, in the space of half an hour. The man said: 'Madame you may not have any more rings, nor play this game again on the voyage.' So we had to content ourselves from then on with shuffle-board. It was all very static but better than nothing.

In no time we were sailing up the Hudson River with Richard showing me the Statue of Liberty. We were there.

CHAPTER 7

Light and Shade

W E WERE MET at the docks in New York by my mother-in-law Florence and her sister Elsie, both of whom I liked instantly. Richard used to say with amusement: 'You get on better with my relatives than I do myself!' They drove us to the apartment they'd found for us as a stop-gap while we hunted for somewhere ourselves. It was out on Long Island and not far from Elsie's home.

Richard had decided while in England that he'd had enough of the academic world for a while and would try to get a job in industry. Through various contacts he had several interviews lined up. The morning after we arrived, as Richard was leaving for an interview, he handed me $15 and told me to buy food for the coming week. The only assistance he gave me was to explain that $3 was roughly the equivalent of £1 sterling. So there I was thrown in at the deep end. There was nothing for it but to accept the challenge and shop. I found the nearest supermarket (something I'd never seen before but only heard about) and started purchasing the necessary provisions, going round from item to item frantically dividing by three. Months later I was still able to buy our weekly groceries for $15 (it was the latter half of the fifties) with a little money to spare for wine, and Richard admitted his astonishment that I could do it. In fact I began to enjoy housekeeping. It was all new to me and I found budgeting quite exciting and satisfying. I would buy in the supermarkets only the 'specials' that really interested me. As the weeks went by, I discovered particular small shopkeepers who sold certain foods at a lower price than in the supermarkets. For instance I'd buy all my chickens from one butcher, all the lamb chops from another, and so on.

A young American couple at our wedding had scribed a delicious recipe for brown bread made with, among other ingredients, honey, buttermilk and sunflower oil. After a couple of abortive attempts (it tasted scrumptious but wouldn't rise and felt like lead), I succeeded in baking whole wheat bread and from then on I never bought a loaf.

At first we looked for a place in Greenwich Village but nothing suitable turned up. After some more searching, one day out on Long Island we saw a notice in a real estate agent's office window. It was unusual in that it was advertising for a *young* couple. Intrigued, we went to see the place and found that the apartment below the empty one was occupied by the landlord's young daughter and her medical student husband with two very small children. Below them again, on the ground floor and in the basement, lived the landlord and his wife. We were taken with the amount of light in the apartment – there were windows back and front – and decided to rent it. We both liked lots of light and air. So many of the places we'd seen up to then were dark, often with rooms within rooms and decidedly depressing.

The apartment was unfurnished. Aunt Elsie was both very wealthy and extremely generous. In her beautiful house on Long Island she had a basement full of good furniture which she no longer used. She told us we could take all we wanted, which we did. We also discovered a cleaner's where unclaimed carpets were sold at a very low price. The beds we bought from the Salvation Army. And Richard made a handsome dinner table with wrought-iron legs, with a coffee table to match, and bookshelves.

We soon settled in and I felt very much at home. Richard had taken a job as a public relations consultant with Bell Telephone and was enjoying his work. I was more than busy being an exceedingly happy housewife and practising my singing and playing each day, building up my repertoire, and both of us enjoying my growing skill at cooking. The only time during our life together that I was totally miserable was when Richard, exasperated with me about something or other, stalked out of the apartment without telling me where he was going. It was as though the bottom had dropped out of my world. I felt utterly devastated. Time passed and no sign of him. I walked over to Aunt Elsie's hoping he'd be there. She knew nothing. Even when I returned home he still hadn't come back. When he did, he told me he'd gone for a walk and then to a movie and 'it was no good without you'.

Shortly after we arrived in the States, the Decca people invited us out to lunch. We were taken to an excellent restaurant where I proceeded to concentrate on the food, leaving Richard to talk over business. A couple of days later Richard received a charming letter from the Decca representative, who ended his letter thus: 'And I hope you'll come and have lunch again soon, if only to watch Mary eat.'

Occasionally we went out to dinner to friends and also entertained in our apartment. At first I found the latter a strain, since as a child I'd had no experience of this – my parents' drinking and constant dissension precluded any socializing while I was growing up. But Richard was there to get me over the hurdles and I was learning. We sometimes wandered round Greenwich Village at weekends in the winter, visited galleries, went to the odd film, concert or play, and indulged our liking for Chinese food.

Frequently during the week after supper we would take a walk over to Aunt Elsie's, about three miles away. Her welcome was unfailingly warm and we often watched TV there.

In November 1956 we travelled to Washington, DC to spend Thanksgiving (Richard's favourite Festival) with my mother-in-law Florence. Before we'd left England, Richard's friend and tutor Professor Jack Bennett had given us an introduction to a friend of his, Anne Moray in Washington DC. We had drinks with her and her Spanish husband one evening and she kindly brought us along the next day to meet Elmira Beer the procurator of the Phillips Gallery, with a view to arranging a recital some time later. She was enthusiastic and 10th February was set up. As this was our engagement anniversary, it augured well.

Richard was getting a lot of writing done in the evenings and at weekends. Shortly after we moved into the apartment on Long Island he arrived home jubilant one day about his great purchase of a handsome roll-top desk. It was of such generous proportions that to get it up the stairs into the apartment we had to take the door off its hinges.

From about the time that Richard started earning we began to save. Like every young married couple we had enjoyment and satisfaction from this. I told Richard I didn't want to know how our savings were mounting up. Sometimes he would come home with a huge smile and say, 'Guess how much I put in this month?' or 'Guess how much we have in the bank *now*?' and I'd get all excited and say, 'No, no don't tell me – keep it a surprise until the end of next year!'

Christmas came and Father flew from West Africa to spend two weeks with us. My mother-in-law travelled up from Washington, DC and he and she got on tremendously well. Early in January he flew to Aden to take up his new appointment as a Technical Expert with the Food and Agricultural Organization of the United Nations.

It was my practice to go to daily Mass. We would set out together and at a certain point go our own separate ways: Richard to the city by subway and I to the local church. We would kiss each other good-bye at the corner, sometimes to the accompaniment of cat-calls from the passing garbage collectors. He'd whisper things to me like: 'I wish I could take you with me in my briefcase.' Since I took Communion at Mass, and in those days, one had to be fasting from the previous midnight, this meant that on weekdays I didn't eat breakfast with Richard (while he ate I prepared sandwiches for his lunch). One day I decided that sharing this first meal of the day with him was important and consequently I forfeited going to Communion during the week. After a while, noticing this, Richard remarked, 'Why aren't you going to Communion?' From the way he said it, I knew he wanted me to go on receiving the Eucharist during the week – so without any discussion I happily went back to the original routine.

Richard's doctor in England had referred him to a doctor in New York City. After the first couple of visits Richard became increasingly uneasy. This man kept boasting that the longest he'd ever kept a Hodgkin's disease patient alive was five years. He used the X-ray machine on Richard with appalling carelessness, not bothering to shield the rest of his body properly while the affected area was being treated. Richard told me that even the paintings in the Waiting Room were disturbing. When, through sheer negligence he gave Richard a third degree burn on his jaw, that was the last straw. As a result he had an ugly purple patch there for several weeks.

Richard had struck up a warm and humour-filled friendship with a splendid man called Michael O'Leary, who worked for the Bell Telephone Company. Michael was a Catholic, and one day Richard took him into his confidence and told him his medical history and that he was being treated by a very unbalanced New York doctor. Could he recommend someone else? At first Michael took it all as a huge joke. Here was this singularly healthy-looking young man bursting with vitality, spilling over *with joie de vivre,* his vigorous mind teeming with ideas telling him he was suffering from a killer disease. When Michael was finally convinced he was stunned, as he wrote to Peter Levi:

> As to Richard's health, I must confess that I completely ignored the first oblique allusions that he made to this subject. I did not understand them and I put them down to a flair for self-dramatization perhaps. I just could not believe that this vital young man was anything but bursting with health.
>
> Now and then he would remark to me, 'O'Leary, I haven't got much time,' to which I would not pay the slightest attention. I was always suspicious that he was ribbing me. Another time he said to me with a chuckle, 'You know I have a strange affliction that seems to attack young men and kill them in their prime.' I inquired acidly whether his was one of the commoner social diseases or one of the more odious afflictions found in the Orient. He chuckled as if over some secret joke and said, 'You wouldn't believe me if I told you. But don't worry, I do not believe it's very catching.'
>
> Once the course of his conversation led to his posing this question to me. 'Don't you think it's blind inefficiency on God's part to let a man of immense talent die before he has a chance to do anything with that talent?'
>
> 'Why? What does his talent have to do with it?'
>
> 'Well, if he writes a great play or a novel, why that's to the honour and glory of God.'
>
> One afternoon, when he seemed quite calm, he stopped by my office and dropped into a chair. 'O'Leary, I can't stand this progressive doctor I'm going to. Your brother-in-law is a doctor, isn't he?'
>
> 'Yes.'
>
> 'Will you ask him for me if he can recommend a man who specializes in Hodgkin's Disease? Now, besides Mary and the warden at Oxford, you are the only person in the world who knows what's the matter with me.' With that he got up and walked out.

In no time through his brother-in-law, a doctor, Michael introduced Richard to Dr Rottino, then head of the Research Department on Hodgkin's Disease at St Vincent's Hospital, New York City.

Joyce Grenfell had kindly written to Ed Sullivan telling him I was coming to New York. I did an audition for him at his apartment and he told me that he'd be delighted to have me on his programme on 17th March 1957. The William Morris Agency was acting on my behalf and they set up an audition for the Gary Moore TV Show. That, too, went well and I was booked for an appearance in February. When the time came I sang a couple of songs which were well received.

Within a few days of the Gary Moore Show we found ourselves once more in Washington, DC, for the recital at the Phillips Gallery. This was my first solo recital anywhere and it was a great success. Richard, as usual, wrote my script and helped me compile the programme of traditional Irish and Scottish songs. The reviews in both *The Washington Post* (Paul Hume) and *The Washington Evening News* (Frank Campbell) were magnificent.

When 17th March came round I was all set for the Ed Sullivan Show. It was a Sunday. The night before, Sullivan phoned me to say that Bob Briscoe, the very popular Jewish Lord Mayor of Dublin, would also be appearing on the show. Would I, with my Irish harp, be prepared to be part of the background while the Lord Mayor was on stage? I had no objection to being on stage with Bob Briscoe, a man much loved in Ireland and especially in Dublin, my adopted home town. In fact he and my father were good friends, and later after I'd become a Benedictine and Bob Briscoe's daughter a Carmelite nun, our respective parents used to meet in Grafton Street and console one another that their entry into heaven was more or less guaranteed because of their daughters! But I objected to being part of any background, especially what I suspected might be an embarrassing stage-Irish one. But at this point there was nothing I could do but agree. Richard was seething about this. He instinctively felt that Sullivan had deliberately waited until Saturday night before asking me to do this – a time when it was impossible for me to consult with my agent.

We arrived for rehearsals and saw that I was advantageously positioned on the bill. That allayed Richard's fears somewhat. But as the afternoon wore on, they kept shifting me around on the programme. To my horror I saw them carrying on two giant cut-out shamrocks and placing them at the back of the stage. I was dumbfounded when I was asked to sit with my harp in one of them while Bob Briscoe was on stage. I envied the beautiful Irish wolfhound standing in the other shamrock, seemingly impervious to the indignity of it all. There's nothing wrong with the shamrock as such, but when it is perennially associated with leprechauns, shillelaghs, green beer and Delaney's donkeys, I feel it is prostituting the true image of our beautiful country and of its ancient culture. It smacks of stage-Irishism. It has echoes of *Punch's* earlier racist caricatures of the Irish as capering troglodites and simian-faced morons. Celtic Ireland has a wealth of art treasures of rare beauty and craftsmanship, much better suited for representing a nation than the kitsch emblems of pub-culture.

When the programme went on the air and I found myself perched up in the cardboard shamrock monstrosity, I was so incensed that instead of sitting facing out towards the cameras, at the last minute I deliberately sat as near to having my back to the audience as possible.

When the show was drawing to a close, the stage manager came to me in the wings and said, 'Miss O'Hara, I'm afraid it looks as though there won't be time for your songs after all.' It was supposed to be a St Patrick's Day, ergo, Irish programme. Apart from Mayor Briscoe – and the charming wolfhound – my songs were the only other contribution that was genuinely Irish.

After this I remained silent. Richard was by my side, livid, but powerless all day to alter the inexorable course of events. Suddenly a stagehand rushed up to me: 'Quick, there's time.' Unceremoniously I was shoved across the vast stage, had a stool pushed under me and was told, 'You're on.' Good accommodating Irishwoman that I was, I took a deep breath and launched into 'O Danny Boy, the pipes, the pipes are calling...' It was Sullivan's own choice of song. But before I could even finish one verse, I felt his patronising hand descending on my head and heard him saying to the viewers something like: 'That's it for tonight, folks.' Off the air, he had the temerity to ask me to 'sing a little song now for the studio audience...'

That winter and spring found us still living our lives in our customary top gear. But as summer approached, Richard became subject to more frequent attacks of the disease. These were characterized by severe exhaustion and accompanied by cold sweats. He would sometimes come home from work washed-out and deathly pale. His face was getting thinner but not his body. His appetite, which was always superlative, now waxed and waned. After these bouts he would be his old scintillating euphoric self, vivid with life.

Richard had read every book about Hodgkin's disease that he could lay his hands on. He knew every form it could take. The radiation treatment to arrest the disease continued at St Vincent's Hospital and all the time they were trying out new drugs. He would phone me some mornings and report that the most recent drug seemed to be showing good results. But our elation was always short-lived. They would find that it wasn't as effective as they'd thought it was, and start experimenting with something new again.

Although we were planning not to start our family before getting back to Ireland, sometime in the middle of that summer I thought I was pregnant. I don't recall having strong feelings about the business of child-bearing one way or another. We searched around for names. Richard asked me for my prayer book (the Missal) and read through the list of saints in the Canon of the Mass. We both liked the name Clement, and Charity was the girl's name we were happiest with. But it turned out to be a false alarm. I wasn't disappointed. With Richard I had everything; besides there was lots of time. Afterwards Richard said that he had sensed that I wasn't pregnant but had said nothing. And I'm certain that being the highly intuitive person he was, he would indeed have known if I was pregnant, even before I'd told him, perhaps even before I knew myself.

We were both realistic enough to appreciate the seriousness of the illness, but we lived, I'm sure like any other young couple in a similar situation would have done: full of hope. After Richard's death, many people assumed that we had married *knowing* that he had little time to live – that he was doomed to an early death. That's not the way it was. Such a thought was not something that influenced our lives or future plans. Richard's lifespan, as far as we were concerned, was going to be as normal as any other. We were going to grow old together. However, earlier that summer, Richard had taken the precaution of having our bank account in both our names.

From the time we married I was concerned that his writing might stop. But I need not have worried. When he'd got settled in at his new job and into the apartment, he began writing regularly. I am not a great reader of poetry. I was even less so when I first met Richard. There are still some early poems of his that I do not understand. But after our marriage I understood each new poem he wrote. That is to say, I saw meaning in his poems. He used to try out new ones on me and ask, 'What do I mean?' I would say, 'Well this is what *I* think you mean.' One day he said, 'Mary, I want to write poetry now for people like you,' meaning, I suppose, the person of average intelligence who doesn't often read poetry. For instance, when he wrote 'A Small Request', I could tell him what I thought it was all about with ease. There is so much in that poem with echoes of our life together. The opening four lines clearly refer to my spirituality of that period when I had a strong sense of penance. The 'suffering is a sign of grace' alludes to the occasions when we would talk about the mystery of suffering, especially in relation to Richard himself. I had been taught that suffering, far from being a sign of divine disapproval (a decidedly Old Testament view) is often in some mysterious way an indication of God's love. Scripture is dotted with such allusions. 'Gently falls the rain' is a reference to Ireland where we'd been so often together in the ubiquitous rain. The 'small garden and a hearth' is about our decision to return to Ireland after about a year in the States, settle down there, preferably the Aran Islands or Connemara and raise a family. County Galway was the spot in the world we loved most. We would have supported ourselves by Richard's writing, my royalties and the occasional concert.

After Richard died, Stephen Spender read Richard's last poems and considered 'A Small Request' to be his best.

> You who feel the instructive hand of God
> Raise boils and welts upon your chosen skin,

Whose self-affliction quells the offended rod
And gets you up the hillside out of sin,

You whose suffering is a sign of grace
You whose privilege is to feel more pain
Whose hope is Heaven and to see God's face
Please recall how gently falls the rain;

And when, if you remember me, you pray,
Pray thus for me: 'Though he loves the earth
Too much, do not send his soul away:
Give him a small garden and a hearth.'

'A Small Request' was written a few months before his death and
was therefore in a sense his last request.

Some of his last poems appeal to me even more. The delicate love-
liness of 'Reflection' unfailingly leaves me in a state of great inner stillness. It deals with the Greek myth of the beautiful youth Narcissus,
who fell in love with his own image in the water.

'From the 16th Floor' was actually composed from his 16th-floor
office at Bell Telephone, on Broadway. His eyrie afforded him a
particular perspective of his surroundings, a perspective also affected,
no doubt, by the knowledge of his own illness, which must have hung
like the sword of Damocles over his life.

Pardoning this borough for its evil,
I look past the tops of buildings, to where
The sky is. Remembering that man's malice,
This man's fate: the former's cunning,
The latter's jeopardy – seeing the sky,
Placid in spite of soot and heartache,
I am reminded to pray. Redemption,
Like our janitor, comes as we go home:
A stooped man turning out the lights.

These three poems were among his finest and last.* One day in the
summer of 1957, our second and last summer together, he phoned me
to try out his latest prose poem. It was about a unicorn and he'd called

* When 9/11 happened an American friend wrote to me saying how uncannily apposite
this poem still was. She herself had narrowly missed being involved, having reported in
sick that morning.

it 'My Friends: A Fable' I was enchanted by it, for I have an insatiable appetite for faerie and myth. Thus through Richard I was introduced to that mythological creature, a medieval symbol of Christ: the unicorn. Since then, my interest in this mythical beast has grown and whenever I can, I visit the Cloisters in New York to look at the Flemish Unicorn Tapestries there.

After we'd become engaged Richard said to me: 'One of the lovely things about our marriage will be watching you grow.' Something of supreme importance had already begun to grow from the time Richard and I became friends: my faith. Although it was never spoken in so many words, I knew that Richard wanted me to be a thinking, full-blooded Catholic or nothing. It was as though, with his uncanny insight into people's characters, he perceived that I would have to give myself fully when it came to any matter of lasting importance.

I'd had the usual convent education where the practice of one's religion was taken for granted. Up to the time I'd met Richard I'd felt no urge to delve any deeper into the beliefs I had inherited. It had never occurred to me not to go to Mass on Sundays; sometimes I went to daily Mass, too. But it could never be said that I was fired by my belief in God and by the truths of the Christian religion. I was what might be called a routine Catholic. My faith, as it were, lay dormant. With Richard's dynamic entry into my life it was awakened. I had never met anyone who probed like this before. He was instrumental in helping me examine and be ever more committed to Christianity. He was by my side shaping my perceptions and attitudes towards life.

There came a day when I saw with astonishing clarity that I was undergoing a conversion: the kind that I now believe every cradle Catholic must, at some time or another, experience. I had never heard or read about such a thing. It was happening to me and I was aware of it. And I was able to share it with Richard and tell him that it was taking place in me through our relationship. It was a realization that brought with it immense happiness and although Richard did not speak, he smiled and I knew he shared my joy.

I also discovered that the more I loved my husband the more I loved God and vice versa. I had come to perceive that love is one, yet many faceted. That too was a joyous discovery. And how grateful I was and am that I was aware of it at the time and not just in retrospect. So there was great light and shade in our life together; cause for rejoicing and celebration over against the distant threatening cloud of the illness touching the horizon of our daily lives. There were times in the midst of gaiety when we were arrested in our tracks by some casual word or insignificant happening: sobering reminders of the reality of Richard's incurable condition.

It was our ever deepening love for each other and the growing realization of the fatality of his illness that made us together more and more dependent on and rooted in God. We were also conscious of how singularly blessed we were in having each other and were deeply grateful. As things became more difficult, together we had learnt how to abandon ourselves to the Almighty. Different people have remarked on the pronounced element of playfulness discernible in our relationship, at a time when these people had no idea that Richard was mortally ill – in fact only weeks before he died. The situation was always bearable in the knowledge that we were in God's care and mysteriously upheld by Him. Like T.S. Eliot's 'Lady of silences' we were '... calm and distressed/torn and most whole'.

There is one weekend that summer which stands out in my memory. Richard phoned me excitedly on the Friday to say he'd bought me a rucksack (a smaller version of his own), and sleeping bags and a tent for both of us: we were going to Fire Island for the weekend. I was thrilled. We started off on Saturday morning and all went well until we finally landed on the island and tramped happily across the sands for about a mile or two. By now it was evening and we decided to eat supper. Richard lit a fire on the beach and cooked some chops. After we'd finished eating Richard became violently ill. He was so bad I feared he would die. He recovered enough to prepare for bed. We got into our bags and lay half in and half out of our tent. Richard, as was his wont, mercifully fell promptly asleep. I lay there serenaded for hours by bullfrogs. They got so vocal and sounded so close that I was convinced we would be invaded at any moment. To add to the drama, lightning began to flash across the summer night sky. The storm didn't reach us and by morning Richard seemed restored.

I was anxious to work, largely so that I could support Richard. He needed rest. Apart from the exhaustion brought on by the radiation treatment, the journey each day to and from work was taking its own toll. He came to dread that twice daily subway ride. He was beginning to look haggard and drawn, and suffered from a dry cough: he'd given up cigarettes for a pipe after he met me, but with the advent of the cough, thinking it was due to the tobacco, he eventually gave that up, too.

As that summer wore on, the attacks of nausea and severe sweats increased. There were nights when his side of the bed (although it looked like one large double bed, there were actually two separate mattresses) would get so soaked with perspiration that Richard would leave it and lie on the spare bed in the study. When that in turn became uncomfortably wet he would use the sofa in the sitting room. Not having air-conditioning didn't help. And being the top storey of the house, by evening the rooms often became uncomfortably hot.

One day, during the course of conversation Richard said: 'If anything happens to me, I want you to marry again. It's not right for you to be alone.' I remained silent. How could I tell him that I could never marry anyone else, for I could not bear to belong that totally to any other; that if he died my sole desire would be to devote my life exclusively to God? The religious life and monasticism in the Church was not something we ever had occasion to discuss together. I wasn't sure that Richard would understand this course of action for me. Perhaps I was wrong? Anyway it was a very painful moment and didn't seem to be the right time to bring it up just then. I let the opportunity go – it never presented itself again. I still believed that Richard would recover.

From time to time we prayed briefly and spontaneously together. It was always a strengthening and peaceful experience. We knew ourselves to be in God's care. When at night, before we went to sleep we said 'God bless you' to each other, it was deeply meant. A favourite prayer of Richard's was 'Lord, give us the wisdom to know your divine will, the grace to accept it and the strength to fulfil it.'

People sometimes conclude that it was the knowledge of Richard's fatal illness that made us turn in desperation to God and commit ourselves and the situation to Him. That is not wholly true. The process had begun long before Richard was struck down by the disease. On the contrary, it could be said that it was happiness that drew us to the

Almighty; it was the joy in our mutual love and the ever-deepening gratitude for the gift of each other that quickened in us the awareness of the Giver of life and all good things who is everywhere and whose right hand holds us fast. Some years later my Dominican friend, Anselm Moynihan, expressed this more eloquently when he wrote in a letter to me: 'I think your experience has taught you a lesson which many people are slow to learn; it is that joy, received as God's gift, brings us closer to Him than suffering. Suffering, rightly borne, has the power to increase our capacity for happiness, but in itself it is happiness that lifts up the heart directly to Him.'

Looking back I suspected later there were many times during weekdays throughout that summer when Richard was running a fever, knew it and kept the knowledge to himself, forcing himself to keep going. I recall weekends when he would ask me to give him alcohol rubs, and in a state of exhaustion he would sleep for hours. Sometimes the exhaustion was so extreme that he slept with his eyes open. At other times he was his usual energetic and happy self. We both felt that he needed more rest as the doctors had warned he must not get over-tired.

About that time I wrote to Sydney MacEwan in Scotland, to enlist his help in getting some singing engagements. I made this approach on the strength of his having volunteered, back in 1954, to help me get work in America, if I so desired. At that time I was not interested. Now, whether I wanted to or not, I badly *needed* to work so that I could support both of us and so that Richard could have the rest that was so crucial. Father Sydney's reply was so unexpected and his interpretation of my request so wide of the mark that I was too disappointed and hurt to write back and explain. (And anyway, how could I since our policy was to keep the knowledge of Richard's illness strictly to ourselves.) Mistakenly, he'd thought that my wanting to work was motivated by ambition, and felt that I was putting my marriage in jeopardy. No doubt Father Sydney had my best interests at heart when he wrote that letter. How was he to know the truth of the matter?

That avenue closed, we discussed the possibility of my taking a job locally as a doctor's or a dentist's receptionist. But first the new record had to be got out of the way.

Armed with the fat cheque my father had given us for a wedding present, we had gone out and bought a double action Erard concert harp from John Morley in London. He put me in touch with Lucien Thompson, a harp teacher in New York City. That summer I had several lessons from him which I found enormously helpful. He was a good teacher and introduced me to a different finger-technique from the one I'd learned in Dublin, which I adopted and have used ever since. He kindly gave us what was to become our favourite LP, *The Art of Marcel Grandjany* (he'd been a pupil of the great French harpist). This incited us to buy our first record player and we played the Grandjany record till it was virtually worn out. But not before it had furnished us with countless hours of untold pleasure.

July came and it was time to make my second album for the Decca Record Company. Much as we would have liked to go to London and record it there, the record company chose to send their man to the USA instead. I decided to record after 6 pm so that Richard could be there, and chose the evening before our wedding anniversary and the one following it, hoping to get sixteen songs done in that time. We kept July 23rd free to celebrate our anniversary. We didn't realize it but it was to be our only one together. Richard was far from well but insisted, despite my protestations, on our dining out as planned, to spare me. He gave me one perfect red rose which lasted for weeks as I put it nightly in the refrigerator.

The album was recorded in the Carl Fisher Hall and later entitled *Love Songs of Ireland.*

In those days the Clancy Brothers had not yet become famous. They had started their own record company, Tradition, and wanted me to make a long-playing record for them. Being under contract to Decca, whose records in the USA were issued under the 'London' label, I felt I could not do so. But when they persisted, Richard approached Decca and persuaded them to allow me to make the one album for Tradition. By the time I came to make this record, *Songs of Ireland,* Richard had been dead a few weeks. I intended it to be my last album as my interest in singing had died with him.

But I anticipate. That summer Paddy Clancy told us that Al Grossman, later to become a key figure in the Folk revival, was very interested in my work and wished to get in touch with me. Grossman was to become wealthy as Bob Dylan's manager. Now he approached me with an offer of a season at the Gate of Horn in Chicago, soon to become a starting point for people like Odetta *et al.* I'd never met the legendary Grossman. Our conversations had always been over the telephone. At first this offer seemed like a good idea: an opportunity we'd been hoping for. However, to leave Richard alone in New York and go off by myself to Chicago was out of the question. The fee for the engagement was not sufficient to keep us both, so that was the end of the Gate of Horn. In fact I didn't get to meet Grossman for another four years, when I was returning to Europe via the USA after a concert tour of Australia and New Zealand.

August in New York City is a bad month: the merciless heat is oppressive. Weekend trips to Rockaway Beach and the anticipation of our impending holiday sustained us through those stifling four weeks. Earlier on we'd toyed with the idea of a trip to Seattle, a part of the United States of which Richard thought very highly, and where he'd spent some of the most stimulating of his – always colourful – academic years and a place to which he was keen to introduce me. But it was a long and expensive trip and we decided to postpone it until some later date. It was to be the early 1980s before I eventually got to Seattle – to give a concert. Instead Richard and I took a flight to Nantucket Island for two weeks in early September. We seemed unerringly drawn to islands.

As soon as we arrived we hired bicycles, which were our mode of conveyance to and from our seaside cottage five miles outside Nantucket. A few hundred yards from the cottage there was a freshwater lake and a boat for our use. The first evening we ventured forth equipped with Richard's fishing gear recently purchased in New York. There followed a dramatic episode out in the middle of the lake when one of the rowlocks broke and Richard was hard put to get us ashore on one oar, contending as he had to with a stiff wind. It was frightening for me, but Richard made light of the situation. However, the ordeal was quickly forgotten in the excitement of cooking a wholesome supper of our freshly caught fish.

We spent the next week lazing, reading and swimming, cycling, and exploring the village and its fish restaurants. Some days before we were due to leave, Richard's health worsened and he slept a lot. By day, he slept outside, wrapped in a rug. The night before we left Nantucket I found it well nigh impossible to sleep and the sight of hordes of mosquitoes pressing blackly against the window attracted by the light inside added a macabre touch to the night.

Time came for us to return to New York. We sauntered into the airport on that Sunday morning with plenty of time to spare. We hadn't known about the ruling that passengers must re-confirm their booking twenty-four hours before departure. This regulation had come into force while we were on holiday so it was irritating to find that our seats had been given away. The clerk, however, assured us that we would undoubtedly get a seat on the next flight at 7.30 pm. We resigned ourselves to a long drawn-out delay of several hours. During the wait we struck up a conversation with a charming American woman, an official at the airport. It turned out that she was a keen radio ham and was occasionally in communication with another ardent ham radio operator in the west of Ireland with whom I was slightly acquainted.

In the meantime the clerk approached us and volunteered the information that we were certain of getting seats on the next flight. From his experience he felt sure that as fog was forecast at Boston Airport, where the plane was due to land first, some passengers would cancel their booking and go by sea instead, to ensure their being back in time for work on Monday morning.

As the late afternoon wore on, we had ample time to observe the leisurely arrival of various passengers for the evening flight. Being such a very small airport (there weren't even refreshment facilities), people could be studied at fairly close quarters. It was a motley little crowd. Because of what was about to happen I remember some of their faces to this day. An intense-looking bespectacled young man carrying paintings under his arm was in earnest conversation with a couple of middle-aged Eleanor Roosevelt-type ladies. Another couple were being ruled by their dog. There were family groups, and so on. Shortly before the first announcement about the flight was made a young man of compelling good-looks swept into the terminal accompanied by a middle-aged man and his daughter. The casual dress of the father and daughter implied that they were just seeing the young man off. He was a six-footer, darkly beautiful, quite flawlessly proportioned, deeply suntanned and with an air of great self-assurance about him. I noticed he had no socks on inside his 'Gene Kelly' shoes. While he talked with the man at the counter, he kept looking repeatedly in our direction.

Now the fact that he was looking so directly and frequently at Richard was nothing unusual, but it seemed odd to me that he was looking at both of us. A few minutes later, at about 7.20 pm the instruction to proceed to the gate for the flight departure came over the public-address system. After the announcement, the clerk called us over and said: 'Mr Selig, I'm in the embarrassing position of being able to offer you only one seat. Because of the fog at the other end, they have had to take on extra fuel and so reduce the number of passengers. Which of you will travel?'

Leaving the decision to Richard I waited for him to answer. Naturally my preference was to stay with him on or off the plane. But he might deem it best to travel himself, so as to be home in time for work, leaving me to catch the next available flight. Or he might decide it wiser for me to go ahead of him. Whatever his decision I would go along with it. To my relief his unhesitating reply was that we would not be separated, but would leave together on a later plane. Naturally we were disappointed, and Richard was inwardly fuming over this further development. Could it be that this elegant young man, whoever he was, was known to the airline people and had somehow used his influence to obtain one of our seats? In any case there was nothing we could do about it. So once again we were left behind, while the last passenger boarded the aircraft and took off for Boston. The clerk, now displaying signs of nervousness at Richard's unspoken anger, timidly informed us that there was another small plane leaving Nantucket at 11 pm. Another wait lay ahead of us.

About three-quarters of an hour later, our new-found radio ham acquaintance of that afternoon walked briskly into the terminal with a surprisingly business-like air about her for 8 pm on a Sunday night. She headed straight for her office. When Richard made some comment to her about working so late, she kept on going and remarked that she had some work to catch up on, and left it at that. Minutes later, a local man came into the building, enquiring in a loud voice: 'Has it caught fire yet?' In no time the horrific truth was out. Poor visibility due to fog had caused the 7.30 pm plane to crash into a swamp close to Boston Airport and it had eventually caught fire. There were no survivors. Our ham radio enthusiast had, by chance, picked up the distress signal on her set and had come in at once to deal with the insurance papers.

Now of course there was no question of the 11 pm flight taking off, so we were driven back to Nantucket for the night and given a meal, which we ate before the restaurant public TV set. The current programme was interrupted every now and then with news of further developments on the air disaster.

Next morning we flew back to New York City. During the flight Richard put his arm around me and said: 'I wouldn't have minded if we'd both been on the flight together.' I felt exactly the same way.

That was not the end of it. A couple of months later, after Richard's death, I was discussing with Professor Jonathan and Mary Gray Hughes the possibility of setting up a Poetry Award in Richard's name at Oxford. This was something he once told me he would like to see happen. The Hugheses thought it a good idea and began to tell me about a talented young painter they'd heard a lot about from a mutual painter friend. His parents were very wealthy and had disowned their son when he decided to earn his living by painting. After he was killed in an air crash they were stricken with remorse and decided to establish a bursary for needy painters – all this to assuage their consciences and perpetuate his memory. The Hugheses went on to describe, among other things, his unusual good looks. Suddenly, something alerted my mind and, startled, I enquired further about the circumstances of his death. He was one of the victims of the recent Nantucket to Boston air crash in September.

His name was Eli Schless. *He* must have been the young man who jumped the queue and ironically thereby saved our lives.

John Hughes had been a Rhodes Scholar at Oxford with Richard and they were great friends. Mary Gray was up at Oxford at the same time. They had married clandestinely at Oxford just before Mary Gray left for the States one year ahead of John. The secrecy was because of the Cecil Rhodes' ridiculous regulations against married scholars.

A few nights after we'd returned from Nantucket, we had dinner with John and Mary Gray Hughes at their apartment in the city. This was to be our last social engagement together. During the meal Richard broke out into one of his enervating ice-cold sweats so badly that he was forced to leave the table. John, not knowing what the real trouble was, followed him out of the room and suggested a hot shower. After that Richard seemed to recover. They drove us back to Long Island and John recalls that Richard and I were restored to our usual

high spirits, and on the way there was a certain amount of what John
described as boisterous playfulness between us in the back seat.

Towards the end of that same week Richard became so ill that
Rottino had him admitted to St Vincent's Hospital in New York City.
We travelled in by subway but by the time we reached the hospital
Richard was so exhausted that they put him in a wheelchair. While
we were together in the waiting room the gravity of the situation was
borne in on us. We talked quietly together, our voices low and fully
under control, but with tears streaming down our faces, oblivious of
all the other people in the waiting-room. With my hand in his Richard
said: 'Mary, I'll come out of here either cured or dead.'

From my heart I said: 'Richard, I only want what God wants.'

'So do I,' he said.

Smiling through the tears I said: 'Richard, you're a brick.'

As if seeing ahead he warned: 'It's easy enough to say that now, but
things will get harder.'

Then we travelled in the lift up to his ward and joined the three
other patients in his room.

At first Richard seemed to pick up wonderfully. By the time I
reached the apartment on Long Island the phone was ringing. It was
Richard on the line to tell me he was feeling *lots* better, had eaten some
food, which he reassuringly described, and I was not to worry. He
sounded very cheerful. More intensely than ever, I commended
Richard and myself to God and slept soundly that night. It seems
extraordinary to me that from then until Richard died I, who am a
light sleeper, went to bed each evening and slept peacefully through
the night until morning. Nor did my appetite wane.

During the final few days Paddy Clancy most kindly offered me a
spare bed in their Greenwich Village apartment, a few blocks away
from the hospital.

The visiting hours were very strict: one hour each evening. Whenever
I tried to slip in unnoticed ahead of time I was invariably stopped. If
I lingered on after the hour the attendant came and rooted me out.
Except for the last few nights before Richard died. Then the attendant
turned a kindly blind eye. The hospital authorities had by then waived
the rules in my case and I was allowed to arrive and leave at any time.

Mine is in some ways a very simple faith. I do not argue with God.
The certainty of the existence of a personal, infinitely loving Being

who is omnipotent, omnipresent and omniscient has always been part
of the very fabric of my mind. I like to have the knowledge that the
science of theology provides. My intellect needs to be fed with truth;
needs to know. But not my heart – in the sense that it does not question God's providence. I have always, despite the pain it sometimes
involves, been content to let God go ahead and 'write straight with
crooked lines'. I feel profoundly convinced that he is at the helm of
the ship that is our life and that in the words of Julian of Norwich,
the great English mystic: 'all shall be well, and thou shalt see that all
manner of things shall be well.'

So at Mass every day for the three weeks Richard was in hospital,
I opened my heart and with all my being asked God to perform a miracle and cure Richard or else give him the grace of a happy death.

During those one-hour visits each day we talked quietly together.
But not all that much. Richard seemed to be taken up with his own
thoughts. He never again showed the insouciant side of his character.
There was a gravity about him which I was careful to respect and it
was enough to just sit there by his bedside, sometimes holding hands.

Richard's sense of humour had by no means deserted him in his
illness. Michael O'Leary came on one of his visits a few nights before
Richard died. Richard's condition had greatly deteriorated. The
curtains of his cubicle were drawn, to give him more privacy and hide
the drip erected by his bed. He seemed to be asleep. Towards the end,
whenever I arrived and Richard was lying there with his eyes closed,
I could never be sure whether he was asleep or in a coma, and didn't
like to disturb him. But hardly had Michael entered when Richard
opened one eye, moved his head slightly in the direction of the
bottle of glucose and said to Michael: 'Tell the nurse to change the
flavour!' The very night before he died when he was having blood
transfusions, Michael again called to see him. Minutes before his
arrival the nurse had removed the blood and replaced it with a bottle
of glucose. Once again Richard quipped at his own expense: 'You've
just missed the meat course.'

It is not easy to watch someone you love suffering intensely and know
that there is little or nothing you or the medical profession can do to
alleviate things. Richard was rapidly losing weight. Somewhere I came

across a powdered food rather like Complan, which I would mix for him in the ward, hoping to give him extra nourishment. I used to bring him those delicious Italian tomatoes which I knew he liked so much, but either he couldn't eat them or, if he did, more often than not they came up again. Richard appreciated these pathetic efforts and generally made some kindly remark.

When he was admitted to hospital, the medical examination revealed that the persistent dry, hacking cough was caused by nodes all down his oesophagus. So the disease was spreading. Within a few days his spleen had also become affected. Preparations were being made to have the spleen removed and then without explanation the idea was abandoned. The only disfigurement evident was in his feet, which swelled up.

In the final days he had to have frequent recourse to an oxygen mask. It was very distressing to come on a visit and find him thus enmasked and unable to speak. One such day (on weekends the visiting hour was in the afternoon), feeling the need for the oxygen mask, Richard had put it on himself. He either indicated to me that he'd like the window by his bed opened, or else I decided myself that it should be. I called to a passing nurse to please get the long pole to open the window. This fat girl proceeded to walk off down the ward with such infuriating slowness that I couldn't stand it any longer. I dashed past her imparting a dirty look as I did so, and ran to the general cupboard to get the thing myself. At times they seemed to be short-staffed and there was a poignant comfort in being able to attend to Richard's bedpan needs. When he asked me to 'campaign for an enema' I felt I was doing something positive. Richard was astonishingly calm about everything when he wasn't suffering acutely. There were times when he tossed incessantly from side to side and whispered: 'Oh God, please help me.'

He frequently asked me for a report on how the Tradition album was coming along. During that period while Richard was in hospital I spent most of each day working on the songs for the record. I think some of my best arrangements were done during those sad days. It is said that suffering is creative. I have often found this to be true in my own life.

These were not days for smiling. I must have given an impression of great gravity and quietness. One day I arrived to find a friend visiting Richard. The visitor had brought a little portable radio as a gift and – one of his better days – Richard was smiling and enjoying getting the different stations on the set. He must have said something facetious, for I laughed and smiled, and in doing so happened to glance at the patient in the next bed, a middle-aged man. He had never addressed me before but now he called out. 'What a beautiful smile you've got. I wish you'd use it more often!'

A couple of days before that a very moving incident had occurred. John and Mary Gray Hughes were at Richard's bedside. A patch of afternoon sunlight came through the window. Richard was very weak and exhausted and barely able to talk but he said: 'I want to feel the sun.' John lifted Richard in his arms and helped him into a chair. 'It was like lifting a child,' John said later.

I was stilled by the unspoken affection evident between these two friends. Though he had lost so much weight Richard's mind remained unclouded and completely alert. He was still able to see the funny side of dying to the extent of making rather macabre jokes to John about the moribund patient in the bed next to him. 'I would rather feel pain than nothing,' he told John Hughes, rejecting injections and analgesics. Probably the reason why he kept drugs to a minimum was so as to be able to keep in touch with reality as long as possible.

About two or three days before Richard died, I asked him if he would like his mother to come and see him. He agreed that I should phone her. I did so and told her for the first time about the incurable disease. She took a train to New York and spent a couple of hours with her only son. We talked about the three of us going on a holiday together, somewhere in the sun, as soon as Richard was out of hospital. Florida maybe. Florence would treat us. She left shortly afterwards and returned to Washington, DC.

One evening after I'd kissed Richard goodbye, I turned just as I was leaving his cubicle and said: 'Richard, don't worry about anything.'

Richard quietly said: 'I don't worry. I'm completely in God's hands.' I felt profoundly comforted.

Months before going into hospital Richard had spoken to me about his desire to talk things over with a 'wise man'. He said he didn't mean a priest or a psychiatrist – just some 'wise man.' With Richard's condition apparently not improving I phoned Michael O'Leary. Apart from the fact that he and Richard were such very good friends and Richard had confided in him about his illness, Michael was the only thinking, theologically informed and practising Catholic among our friends. Sadly, Michael, while understanding what sort of person it was that Richard was seeking, couldn't recommend anyone. All he could suggest was getting in touch with an old classmate of his who was a priest. This was unfortunate. I pointed out that Richard didn't want a priest. But Michael thought his friend would be better than nothing.

In the light of my own monastic experience later, I realise more fully – though I did dimly even then – what sort of person it was that Richard wanted. Someone (preferably old) wise in the ways of God and human nature; a listener, a sifter, a gentle counsellor, a man of the Spirit, a staretz. For his own best reasons God decided to deny Richard, and by extension, myself, this solace. Perhaps so that Richard would have to rely in faith, totally, without human intermediary, on God's infinite loving mercy.

Michael's friend was willing to come to the hospital, but had to officiate at a funeral. In his place he sent along a priest colleague. It was a disaster as far as I was concerned. The priest, for whatever reason, behaved throughout in a singularly unsympathetic and unpastoral manner.

When the situation became unbearable I made for the telephone and called Michael. I asked the priest to wait. As Michael's office was only a few blocks away, he was with me in a matter of minutes. Briefly I described the horror of my predicament and told him I simply could not handle the problem. This man was definitely not what Richard wanted. All he had succeeded in doing was to cause me deep distress. Leaving me, Michael took the man aside. Eventually the priest left.

Michael returned to me and said: 'Everything is OK now. I explained all that was necessary and the priest said: "From what you've told me, there was no need to come. This man has baptism of desire."'

This statement was to be gratuitously made yet again. After enormous difficulty I succeeded in getting permission to spend the night by Richard's bed. The nurse had come by and given him an injection (he seemed to be doing his level best not to allow it to work) and a large armchair had been wheeled in for me for the night. Suddenly one of the Sisters of Charity (they were in charge of the hospital), called to me from the doorway. When I got outside she said gently to me: 'Mrs Selig, I thought you might like to know that the Chaplain says that your husband has baptism of desire.' Words can't describe what her message meant to me. It was like manna from heaven. That night I returned to Richard's bedside and he said to me: 'Did she tell you I was resisting the injection?' I shook my head.

Seeing the armchair by his bed, with me settling into it for the night, Richard quietly told me that since he wanted me to have a proper sleep, I must go to Paddy's flat. Without demur I left the hospital that night. My personal desire was to remain by Richard's side. Only *his* wish that I go would budge me. I never questioned the wisdom of his decisions in my regard. They were made with love and I carried them out in the same spirit. It was his last night on earth.

The problem of whether or not a doctor should tell his patient that he is dying is a perennially difficult one. Surely, it must depend on the patient. An experienced and intelligent medical practitioner should be able to tell whether a particular patient can 'take' the truth about his being terminally ill or not.

The morning of his death Richard's doctor visited him. I was there. Minutes before, this same man had sent for me to tell me that it would be a miracle if Richard lived through the coming night. (He'd shyly informed me that there was a chapel in the hospital. I'd found it long before.) Now he was bending over Richard telling him that he had an ulcer in his stomach (to explain to Richard why he was passing blood) and 'You are getting better Mr Selig.' Richard received this information calmly, consciously, with closed lids. The doctor went away. Richard made no comment to me nor I to him.

As the morning wore on Richard's mind wandered. He told me he longed to go for a walk. He struggled to get out of bed. I tried to reassure him that we'd go walking together after he'd had some more rest. Eventually he sank back on his pillows, mute with exhaustion. The early autumnal afternoon sun shone brightly across the bed and on his face. But Richard's senses were already fading.

'It's getting very dark, Mary,' he said.

'Yes,' I whispered, 'it's getting late,' and I used our secret mutual pet name.

This was it: the crisis Richard was destined not to get through. I could no longer hold back the tears. Soundlessly and openly I began to weep. It was like a fountain within. Just then the nurse came by to change, yet again, the soaking wet sheets. Together we lifted Richard and I helped her with her task. My voice steady as a rock, but with tears coursing down my face, I murmured tender comforting things to Richard as I held him momentarily in my arms – for the last time.

I phoned Michael. By the time he arrived I was on my knees praying aloud with great intensity of spirit. My whole being was concentrated in one burning desire: that Richard would see God face to face. It is truly a tremendous privilege to be physically with the one you love with all your heart, more than any other person on earth, at his or her moment of truth. To be near, when in death he reaches the remotest outposts of time and space; experiences with the totality of his being the mystery of God and makes his final and definitive decision about his eternal destiny.

Michael O'Leary wrote:

A young nurse spotted the end coming. She hurried out and fetched back a young intern who fussed over Richard with the oxygen mask. Two more young internees hurried in. There were muttered words, an injection. The last desperate measures to hold life. The medicos stopped muttering, stood there a moment. Two of them walked out quietly. The last, who had been the first to come in, stood, still holding Richard's wrist, feeling where the pulse had failed. I whispered to him.

'It's over?'

'It's over.'

'He's dead?'

'Yes. He's dead.'

The young doctor looked like a disappointed little boy as he walked out. He was not yet used to his job, I thought. Behind Mary, kneeling close to the head of Richard's bed, praying aloud oblivious to all about her, two nurses knelt for a moment and joined her. The patients in the other beds lay still and silent.

I had no wish to leave the cubicle. My instinct and desire was to stay on silently praying. Whereas clinical death can be recorded, no one can say for certain when relative death has occurred. But above all, the moment of absolute death cannot be determined. I deliberately refrain from using the expression 'the separation of the soul from the body'. This originally Platonic idea, later taken up by Thomas Aquinas, is an incomplete definition, and gives an inadequate explanation of what really takes place in the mysterious process of death. Can anyone really know? Medicine and metaphysics view death differently. So, I wanted to 'stand by' and 'help' Richard, if at all possible, at the impossible-to-pin-down moment when he would be swept into the splendour that is the unveiled presence of Almighty God, to make his final decision in a completely personal act, totally alone.

But now Michael was bending gently over me telling me that the doctor wanted to have a word with me. Very tenderly I kissed Richard's forehead. I knew it was no longer Richard, but his dead body, his remains. I turned and left the cubicle, drained, but at the same time charged with the indescribable conviction that Richard was safe.

Downstairs I signed a paper giving permission for an autopsy to be performed on the body in the cause of research into Hodgkin's disease. Richard once told me he wished to leave his body to medicine and had joked: 'At least I'll make an interesting corpse!'

With Michael by my side I walked out into the fading light of the gentle autumn evening, wrapped up in the thought of the inconceivable bliss in which, with every fibre of my being I trusted Richard was now rejoicing, and in which in some inexplicable way, a part of me was somehow sharing.

> Who have gone before me,
> Stronger by the breath they give,
> I recall the men of my race,
> Grave ghosts in whom I live.
> I receive their many blessings
> For a journey from flesh and bone,
> Questioning their shadows, saying:
> Fathers, were you alone?
>
> RICHARD SELIG

CHAPTER 8

Transit

You go out on a terrible wide sea
You go and you keep going, till there are storms
Where all except you get smashed up;
And in the morning of the next day the sun shines.

From 'The Way I See You'
by RICHARD SELIG

I
T NEVER OCCURRED to me not to return to the apartment on
Long Island, but as we left St Vincent's Hospital Michael insisted
that I spend the night with him and Jean at their home in
Westchester. From there I phoned my mother-in-law in Washington
and sent telegrams to my father, Peter Levi and Sister Mary Angela
my Dominican friend and singing teacher. The O'Learys and I talked
about Richard for hours and I confided my decision, crystalized that
very evening, to go into a monastery. They were very startled and their
immediate reaction was to tell me to wait and think it over. Surely,
they argued, this was not the moment to make such a major decision.
Perhaps, they said, it was a reaction to the traumatic experience I'd
undergone, best to let time pass and review things later on. I had made
up my mind, but in deference to their evident, and very caring concern I said I'd not do anything immediately. Michael strongly advised
me to go and visit my father in Arabia, volunteering to handle the
entire business of the funeral. Their advice was very wise. With
Richard's death, life here on earth for me had lost all meaning and
purpose and had I been an atheist I would have committed suicide.

Next morning I went shopping alone, in New York City, for a black
dress. In the store where I bought it the assistant asked me why on earth

a young girl like me should be buying a *black* dress. When I told her
my husband had died the evening before, she broke down and wept.

The night before the funeral, a few friends and some relatives of
Richard's gathered at the funeral parlour. It would never have entered
my head to arrange this funeral parlour ritual myself, but Michael
advised that it should be, so I went along with the convention for the
sake of others. Moreover, he arranged everything, relieving me of
yet another difficult chore, and I was grateful. Had Richard been a
Catholic, the coffin would have rested in church the night before the
burial. Instead here was the a-religious version of that meaningful
vigil. The whole thing smacked of Evelyn Waugh's *The Loved One*.
Artificiality and, in some instances, ersatz emotion were the keynotes.
There was an unreal, 'padded', sort of hush-hush and airless atmosphere in the building. When I looked into the coffin marked 'Richard
Selig' what lay there bore a very faint resemblance to my husband.
The most ludicrous thing about it all was the way the face had been
literally *painted*. After that initial glance, I ignored the coffin and
greeted the people who had come along.

I think John Hughes was right when he later said to me that
Richard would have relished the macabre confusion in the funeral
parlour. There were several 'slumber' rooms connected by a long
corridor, but there were no instructions saying which corpse was in
which room. It was left to the mourners to find out for themselves.
So John peered into coffin after coffin and was finally hailed by me in
the correct room. John looked miserably at the open coffin and I said:
'Don't bother about that, that is not Richard. It's only a painted shell.'
And the irony didn't end there. Next morning the cortege going to
Ferncliff cemetery in Westchester travelled at a spanking sixty miles
per hour. That too would have provoked chuckling from Richard. His
grave is in a high and quiet spot marked by a simple brass name-plate
on the ground.

Back on Long Island I continued working on the third album.
Though I had no wish to go on singing, I felt strongly that Richard
would want me to finish the work I'd begun. He'd always been like
that. Anything that was worthwhile to begin was worthwhile to
finish. I felt no need of human comfort. If people came to see me I
welcomed them, but I did not allow anyone to 'distract' me. I had my
work to do, letters to write and to answer, packing to get on with and

above all I needed to be alone for reflection. Now I reached for the books on theology and the spiritual writers on Richard's bookshelf. St Thomas Aquinas in an abbreviated form, St Teresa of Avila, of whom he'd spoken to me with admiration; St John of the Cross; St Augustine; Martin d'Arcy *et al.* I knew that he'd wanted to read Augustine's *City of God* and I had planned to buy it for his twenty-eighth birthday two weeks later, on 29th October.

I cancelled a concert I was to give in Georgia and told the William Morris Agency that I didn't wish them to represent me as my agents any more. As the days following Richard's funeral went by, time and time again I was stirred to the depths by the letters of sympathy written to me by Richard's friends when they'd heard the news. His impact on the lives of his friends was as marked, if, for obvious reasons, not as profound, as it had been on mine and the affection, respect and admiration he'd engendered was fresh cause for yet further expressions of gratitude for his life. Anthony Levi, Adrian and Maureen Mitchell, Stephen Spender (who had done more than anyone else in England and America to have Richard's work published) and Jonathan Bennett were among those whose words touched me. Tom Boase, President of Magdalen College, remembered Richard's wonderful courage, while fellow American and Rhodes Scholar Brock Brower recalled, 'No art could ever have substituted for the passion he had in living...' George Scott-Moncrieff's empathy was exceeded by no one. (Our incipient friendship dating from the Edinburgh Festival days was to burgeon months later after my return from Arabia.)

A couple of days after I'd sent the telegram to Peter Levi I sat down and wrote him a long letter from the heart. I knew no one who would better understand the depth and the glory, the pain and the peace of what I was experiencing. His letter in reply was perfect.

One of the most eloquent and understanding letters came from the poetess, Elizabeth Jennings:

Dear Mary,

I don't know if you'll remember me, but I remember Richard and you so vividly and happily that I wanted to write at once when I heard about Richard's wonderful courage and death...

He was a beautiful person and I think the most startling thing about him was his deep innocence and childlike simplicity. Everything was direct and open with him. He was a very true person...

I am a Catholic and I feel, as I know you must, that all is very well with Richard. He was such a *naturally* religious person. I feel utterly inarticulate when I think about your great loss and yet there is joy, too, in a death like Richard's. To go to God when one is young and beautiful, and full of talent and honesty is something tremendous...

'And yet there is joy, too, in a death like Richard's' – how I totally concurred with that sentiment. Elizabeth had expressed for me, as it were, a vital part of what I'd been feeling.

Both Jack (Richard's tutor and friend) and Gwyneth Bennett wrote separately. Gwyneth's letter contained the following memorable observation: 'Happiness is not measurable in terms of time and Richard clearly found with you all that he had been seeking.' Jack's letter said what a shock the news had been to them both. He'd heard through the president.

The Times published Richard's obituary. 'Cut is the branch that would have grown full straight,' quoted the writer, before continuing: 'But his last poems, reflecting in their increasing mastery of form a hard-won serenity, will be a meet memorial.'

Besides spending time with Michael and Jean O'Leary, I stayed on and off with John and Mary Gray Hughes. Michael and John had known Richard well in their own different ways and at different times in his life. It was an immense joy for me to talk with them about the Richard *they* knew. I think in the end John began to understand what I meant when I told him that far from seeing Richard's life as tragically short, I had a very definite sense of his life having come full circle. I had known something of his genuine, sincere inner searching. I knew that together we had found something irreplaceably precious in our spiritual lives that had welded us together, forged us in a common, shared reaching out to God. And in my own case I had a sense of having lived *my* life. I felt there was a relatively fleeting interim period before my moment of truth would come and we would be together for all eternity.

About a month after Richard's death, I was ready to leave the Long Island apartment. Before doing so I burnt all my letters to Richard.

It was more convenient for me to stay in the city while I was recording *Songs of Ireland*, and the Hugheses kindly invited me to use their place. Once the recording was finished my plans were to leave America, spend one week in Dublin and another week in Oxford before flying out, for an indefinite period, to my father who was with the FAO in Aden.

It seemed only right that I should visit my mother-in-law before I left the States. Almost immediately after the recording was over, I took a train to Washington, DC. I was incredibly tired, emotionally and physically, and was looking forward to a very simple, ultra quiet couple of days alone with Florence. It wasn't until I got there that I discovered she had planned the first evening otherwise and had invited a couple of friends to dinner, who would 'understand'. My heart sank and I braced myself to be sociable.

I was lying down when the guests arrived, and was anything but attracted to the voice and attitude of whomever it was who was holding forth almost non-stop in the living room next door, from the moment she entered the apartment. I put in an appearance in time for supper. The voluble lady, who must have been in her seventies, later turned out to be a minister in some esoteric spiritualistic sect. I was prejudiced against her from the start. Firstly I wanted to be alone with my mother-in-law and the last thing I needed was to be burdened with an opinionated chatterbox, who behaved as if she had come to 'cure' me of my bereavement. She was a tough hard-faced old girl, by no means endowed with a sympathetic nature. I think she sensed my dislike. I was reluctant to be drawn into the conversation, which mainly centred on herself and the importance she attached to her connections. She announced that a close relative had been the architect of some famous church or other known as 'The Church on the Corner'. Innocently I asked: 'Which corner?' She took this to be flippancy on my part. Later on she took exception to some sharp retort I made which gave her the excuse to fly into a towering rage. Jumping up from the table she retreated to a corner of the room declaring that she'd been insulted and wouldn't stand for it. I've forgotten exactly what I said, but her next outburst touched a sensitive nerve: 'A-ha, now we know why Richard was taken.' With that I burst out crying,

left the table and ran out of the room into the night. As I was leaving I heard her shout: 'Pay no attention to her, she's only acting.'

For some time I kept running, still crying. I wandered forlornly
along the suburban roads. It must have been up to an hour before
I composed myself sufficiently to return to the apartment. It was now
empty save for the leaflets judiciously sprinkled round the living room,
for my benefit no doubt. Beneath her picture, in bold print, the leaflets
declared that my erstwhile antagonist was, among other things, 'in
direct contact with the Divine'. I could have guessed! Could it be that
I had spoiled the opportunity for a good séance and lost for the
Reverend X a potential client?

When Florence returned I apologized for upsetting the dinner party.
Later I discovered that Florence had been going through a bad patch
and had temporarily fallen into the clutches of this charlatan, who had
guaranteed to put her into contact with her deceased relatives. The
painful episode was never referred to again.

After all the business connected with the *Songs of Ireland* album was
finished, there was no further reason for me to linger in America. John
Hughes saw me off at the airport, and I arrived in Dublin on a cold
and dull November day.

Up to that time my connection with Deirdre Flynn (as she then was)
was fairly tenuous. She had written with typical warmth and concern
when she'd heard from me the news of Richard's death. Now she came
to meet me after my flight from New York. This meeting was to be
the start of what was to develop into one of the deepest friendships of
my life. Looking back, I'm inclined to think that before Richard's entry
into my life I had many acquaintances and pals. But there were no
real friendships as I now understand the word to mean. It was under
the subtle tutelage of Richard's influence that the latent ability to
form friendships began to grow. This is Deirdre's recollection of that
meeting:

> My personal memory jumps back to meeting you at the Aer Lingus
> terminal when you came back to Dublin after Richard's death. We had
> always been in some contact, even though the lines of communication
> were sometimes long ones, and we had corresponded after Richard's
> death. You phoned from the airport to say you had just landed and

your voice sounded the same. But grief had so changed your appearance that I did not, in fact, recognise you when you stepped off the airport bus. I had settled myself to wait for the next bus when I saw someone wearing a familiar heather-coloured tweed coat. Before you went to Sion Hill, I phoned Sister Angela to warn her that, though you had come to terms with what had happened, your personal grief was unbelievable – and all the more so for being so rigidly controlled.

I stayed in a hotel selected by Déirdre and from there visited my sister Joan and Sion Hill, where I spent quite a lot of time with Sister Angela and Mother Ambrose. The latter introduced me to the work of C.S. Lewis, one of her favourite writers, and urged me to try and find his book, *The Great Divorce,* but I was unsuccessful. From her I heard for the first time that wonderful Portuguese proverb, 'God writes straight with crooked lines', which she inscribed in a little copy she gave me of Francis Thompson's *The Hound of Heaven.*

Dublin was followed by a week in Oxford staying with Jack and Gwyneth Bennett, from whose home on the outskirts of the city I visited Peter Levi and other friends.

I flew to southern Arabia five days before Christmas. My father had advised me to fly to Aden via Cairo, and I booked my passage accordingly. His work in connection with irrigation and water resources took him to various areas all over the desert. So he had impressed upon me the importance of his knowing the date and hour of my arrival to give him a chance of getting back from the desert to meet me. Transport for him was varied and sometimes rather colourful, ranging from Land-Rover to camel, none of which tended to work to a predictable timetable, least of all the camel. At the last minute my plane had to be re-routed to Aden via Athens and Asmara, too late to let my father know of the change beforehand. It was a very long, tiring flight. We landed in Aden in the late afternoon and I recall the hilarity among the Arab customs officials when they read the description of my occupation as 'housewife'. I'm still not quite sure why they found it so funny, though if one takes the word literally one can understand their being tickled by it.

There was no one to meet me. A high-ranking Arab official took me under his paternal wing and took me off to lunch with him and his daughter – my first experience of Arab hospitality. In the meantime, my father had been contacted and a few hours later I was collected and driven by a French woman to his quarters outside Aden. This friend of my father's invited us to a Christmas party at the European Club but I was not anxious to go. My father was very understanding when I systematically declined all subsequent invitations from his many friends and acquaintances to dine or attend parties. I had to make it clear to him from the beginning that for me all socializing was out. Mine was to be a retreat into the desert with time given over to reading, reflection and prayer.

I felt the need and desire to be alone as much as possible and in that quietness perhaps make out what was God's *specific* will for me for the future. Naturally I confided in my father my conviction that through the events of the past year or so God was calling me to serve him in some special way. As it happened, my father's lifestyle fitted the bill admirably for this Pauline-like sojourn.

When he was not away in the desert my father lived in Marshag, among the barren hills of Aden. The dwelling was pitched on the side of a hill well above a lighthouse. It was part of a complex formerly used as an artillery battery station and was situated six or seven miles from Steamer Point, the passenger entry port for Aden through the town of Crater (Crater is actually built on the edge of an extinct volcano). It commanded a magnificent view of the Indian Ocean, with almost no one to be seen apart from the occasional Arab fisherman, jogging down to the town with his early morning catch. This often consisted of a single fish, a tuna or a barracuda about ten feet long, cut in two and suspended from a stick across his shoulders.

The nearest church, a few miles away down in Crater, was served by Italian Franciscans. In the mornings I was driven down by Land-Rover for six o'clock Mass and back again. More often than not I walked the distance there and back for Benediction in the evening. When my father was away in Yemen or elsewhere in the desert, I enjoyed doing both journeys by foot. The walk along the coast road was bracing, with the Indian Ocean crashing against the low wall just a few yards away. Coming back in the pitch black could be quite awesome. With the turbulent sea on my left and the leaping firelight of the crematorium stark against the forbidding hills on the right, if one were easily frightened, then scared one would assuredly be. From the look of incredulity on the faces of Europeans who, stopping their cars and offering me a lift, found I preferred to go on walking alone, I gathered that it was not common practice in those parts. But I never felt unsafe – except for one night. Returning in the pitch dark (I never thought of carrying a light) – a night so black that I could barely see the light-coloured cotton dress I was wearing – I heard the unfamiliar patter of bare feet following me. I kept going. I could hear the steps quickening till they finally broke into a decided trot. My instinct was to bolt, but I refused to allow myself to alter my pace. I prayed passionately within for protection – making massive acts of trust in God. The sound of bare feet was almost beside me when suddenly the runner veered off to the right, obviously heading for the crematorium. Relief, relief.

Another memory is of the strange, haunting singing of the Arab night watchman at the foot of Marshag, just after dawn. Was he recreating? Or perhaps worshipping? It sounded curiously not un-like the traditional Gaelic singing one used to hear in places like Connemara on the west coast of Ireland.

Much to my joy and amazement, I was able to find in Aden a copy of C.S. Lewis' *The Great Divorce*. I became an instant devourer of as much C.S. Lewis as I could lay my hands on. A cliff-top house overlooking the Indian Ocean was as good a place as any to be introduced to his work.

In Aden in those days there was ample scope for doing charitable works. Although I'd never before felt attracted towards the active apostolate of alleviating the physical sufferings of the needy, now I regretted that Richard hadn't lived long enough for us to do something of that nature together. Here in Aden, every time I went into the town with my father to the market or to the library, I could not help but notice the cripples and beggars everywhere. People gave various reasons for this abundance of maimed humanity in a Moslem town, but the explanations were of little concern to me at the time. I felt a deep urge to be of some practical consolation to these people, but there was so little I could do. It was at this time that I started to visit the local hospital. I spoke no Arabic and the patients had no English, so we smiled quietly at one another and exchanged salutations. Whether or not the patients derived any benefit from my visits is hard to judge, but I have my doubts. They preferred the cigarettes to my Western-style sandwiches, however lovingly prepared. Nor was I ever sure that the ice-cream they so graciously accepted was all that welcome to their palates. It was difficult to know how they regarded this European Christian girl wandering about in their midst. I'll always remember the naked joy on the face of the little Arab boy when I gave him a toy racing car. He's probably driving a real *babur* by now. However, I gradually made friends in the men's and children's wards, and there were smiles of recognition whenever I appeared on the scene. I don't remember seeing a women's ward.

My stay in Arabia coincided with both the Christian Lent and the Moslem Ramadan, the penitential seasons of the two great religions. There is a basic difference between Moslem and Christian fasting. From sunrise to sunset the Moslem tastes neither food nor drink but can feast unrestrainedly after sunset. The Catholic fast was different. It consisted of one full meal and two tiny snacks per day. There was no food at night. It's hard to gauge which fast is more difficult, but I can still recall the voracity with which I fell upon that one full meal. I kept a very rigorous fast.

I was still deeply affected by Richard's death. Swimming and playing tennis and enjoying myself generally was something I had no mind for without Richard to share it with. I avoided the inviting tennis courts, swimming pools and even the sea. A wealthy Persian friend of my father's, who had a holiday house on Marshag, offered to teach me to ride on one of his many Arab horses. But that, too, I declined. I once overheard him remark to my father: 'She's behaving just like my mother did when my father died. She spent all her time touring all the local mosques.' When I eventually turned down his invitation to go horse-riding his only remark was: 'I thought you would.' I was talked into attending dinner at his house (on one rare occasion) in honour of the young sultan of Lahej, but I was absolutely bored. The fault was probably mine. Apart from visiting the sick I limited my social contacts to the bare minimum. Only twice did I venture into the desert with my father in the Land Rover.

April came to an end and my father and I decided it would be better for me to leave the Middle East before the dry season set in. I still held fast to my resolve to go into a monastery but where, or which Religious Order, was not yet clear to me. I didn't worry. I knew the way would be shown me. After Easter I left for Europe. I was physically underweight but spiritually buoyed up and charged with confident expectation.

CHAPTER 9

Rootless

As LIFE ON EARTH had ceased to have any meaning for me, the United States, Arabia, England, Ireland – anywhere – these places had lost their significance at this stage of my life. I was not unhappy but at the same time felt I had no roots. I was very aware of being a pilgrim. I remember remarking to Joyce Grenfell some time later, 'I am rootless.'

'What!' she exclaimed in a horrified voice. She thought I'd said 'ruthless'. She gently pointed out that I shouldn't think that way; that Richard wouldn't want me to live out of a suitcase for the rest of my life. At that stage, I hadn't yet shared my plans with her.

At any rate, I was back in Dublin and had to anchor somewhere, however temporarily. Sion Hill, my old Alma Mater, put me in touch with a person who had been recently widowed and had a spare room. For the next three years I stayed with the Morrison family as a paying guest. It was a happy arrangement and without doubt what I needed at that time.

Having established a temporary base at the Morrisons', I set about earning a living again. I contacted my former agent Sydney Lipton in London to inform him that I was available for work and prepared to take on selective engagements. It seemed only right that while I waited for guidance about my call to the monastic life I should carry on singing.

Finances, thank God, had never been a worry for me. I had a steady income from my three albums. Two months before Richard died I'd received my first royalty cheque from Decca. It amounted to £8. Then the very day after his death a substantial three-figure cheque arrived. It meant nothing to me then. All it evoked was a shadow of sadness that it had come, so to speak, too late. On the same day a fat cheque arrived for Richard. This was for poems of his that were to be published in *Botteghe Oscura,* edited at that time by Princess Caetani. From then on the amount in royalties progressively increased as the sales of my records multiplied.

I had already appeared on Dutch television, and now they asked me back to Holland to do more radio and television. On the way to Amsterdam I spent one night in London. That afternoon I called to see Sydney Lipton in the West End and from there took a taxi back to my hotel. As I wasn't the one paying for the taxi I was in my room before realizing, to my horror, that I'd left my small clutch handbag in the vehicle. Passport, travellers' cheques, air-ticket – all were lost. It was 6.30 pm and as my plane was to take off at 9 am it was impossible to find replacements in time. In a controlled panic I eventually got through to my agent, who called the police. He also alerted all the radio cabs in London. The police sent out a call to all their stations. I tried to get through to the Dutch Embassy but got no further than the bureaucratic doorman. I rang the Irish ambassador at his home and could get little sense out of the *au pair* girl who answered. The family was out. When the hotel receptionist went off duty the switchboard extension to my room was left open, in case the police called with any information. At five o'clock the following morning the message came that the handbag had just been handed in to a police station somewhere on the outskirts of London. Sighs of relief all round. I got the handbag but precious little sleep.

With plans for going into a monastery firmly established in my mind, I decided to record a few more long-playing albums before finally giving up singing forever. My repertoire of Irish songs in English and in Gaelic was comparatively large and I hoped, if possible, to make one album of Scottish songs because of my attachment to that country.

By now a regular correspondence was underway between myself and George Scott-Moncrieff in Edinburgh, known to his friends as Scomo. This name was arrived at by combining the first three letters of 'Scott' with the first two of 'Moncrieff'.

Scomo's reiterated invitation to stay with him and his family in Edinburgh eventually resulted in my bestirring myself and flying to

Scotland. It was a happy reunion and the beginning of countless visits to stay with Scomo, who was to become, during that period of my life, my closest friend and confidant.

Scomo was a remarkably fine character. Endowed with a tremendous love of life, he had rare gifts of the heart. By nature a sort of bohemian, his income was forever slender and by some standards he was indeed poor, but the quality of life in that household was of a high order. I have never come across anyone so unswervingly kind. Open house, open heart. If ever there was anyone who gave the lie to the impression that religion is gloomy, it was Scomo. After his first wife died, he had gone to live on the Hebridean island of Eigg. There single-handedly, with insight and energy, he combined the difficult role of father and mother and successfully raised his three small children. Shortly after his marriage he and his wife had become Roman Catholics. He was my first close contact with a convert and I found in him a commitment and a spiritual fire that I had not so far encountered in anyone else. His intellect, and not just his heart, was totally involved in striving to live the Christian life. He had taken the trouble to inform himself theologically about his convictions and up to that time he was one of the few lay people with whom I could discuss religion comfortably. Those next three years of intermittent visits to Edinburgh, during which our incipient friendship budded and blossomed, were an education.

I have always maintained that he was a man of whom not only I, but countless others, could say: 'He was my closest friend.' Not physically handsome, but of a noble and endearing countenance, he had immense charm and one of the things that distinguished him from others was his unabated gaiety.

The duration of my visits became longer and longer. I would arrive intending to stay for one or two weeks but Scomo would press me to stay on. This frequently led to urgent requests to my father, now back in Dublin, to go to my wardrobe and send necessary items of clothing. For instance, late summer sojourns would imperceptibly drift into autumn and I'd need an overcoat and so on. One such occasion resulted in a customs declaration form being hurriedly filled in by my father. I'd asked for a specific fine wool black sweater that my mother-in-law had bought for me. It was a bit on the small side. The little green customs form hurriedly completed in my father's handwriting stated: 'Old black woollen lady's vest.' Beside the word 'value' appeared not the usual 'no commercial value' but 'useless'. On receipt of the garment we all fell about the place laughing at the idea of an old black woollen lady.

While no one could accuse Scomo of being musical, he had a great appreciation of the arts in general with a keen awareness of and high regard for beauty in any form whether visual or aural. He agreed that it would be a splendid idea for me to make a long-playing record of traditional Scottish songs. His encouragement and help in research on individual lowland Scottish songs was prodigious. He introduced me to David Murison, then editor of the Scottish National Dictionary. I regularly visited David in his rooms at the School of Scottish Studies in George Square in Edinburgh, where together we painstakingly went over every syllable of each word. David would pronounce the word and whenever I had an initial difficulty I would write it down phonetically. It was astonishing how this gentle, learned man could say with authority how a particular word was pronounced in such and such a century and in a particular district.

For the Scots Gaelic songs I turned to my very dear friend Calum Maclean, also based at the School of Scottish Studies. After he heard about Richard's death he typed a very affectionate letter to me with a PS at the end: 'I'm recovering from the loss of my arm.' Cancer had struck. A year or two before that he'd had a kidney removed. He died, peacefully, in his mid-forties in South Uist very shortly before I entered the monastery and before I could implement my plan to visit him in a Hebridean nursing home. Calum had become a Roman Catholic some time before I'd met him. His family was staunchly Presbyterian and once, in his flat in Edinburgh when he was teaching me some Gaelic songs on a Sunday morning, his mother kept trying to dissuade him from doing so. Finally, in her beautiful Hebridean accent, she threatened: 'If you don't stop singing, I'll hit you with the poker.' I believe she meant it too.

It was while I was staying with Scomo that I met his great friend Father Jock Dalrymple, the well-known spiritual writer, who came to dinner a few times while I was there. He was to play a most important role in my life years later. Scomo's friends were legion.

Besides being a playwright, Scomo was the author of a number of novels and prose-works including some dealing with spiritual matters. In one of these works he wrote that 'happiness is a duty' and no one discharged that duty more regularly and whole-heartedly than Scomo.

Back in Ireland once more, my agent Sydney Lipton telephoned me about an eight-week concert tour of Australia. It was to be a charity tour to raise money for the homes and hospitals run by the Vincentian Fathers and Sisters of Charity. I wasn't enthusiastic about the prospect, as my primary concern at this stage was to seek for guidance about a monastic future. However, as I was still unable to see my way ahead very clearly, I consented to do the tour. While talking to my father on the telephone he happened to mention that he was going to Australia and had in fact already booked a passage by sea to Sydney. It was to be a business-cum-holiday trip. 'What a happy coincidence,' I said. 'I'll probably see you there.' We decided that the sensible thing would be to travel together, so my agent arranged a passage for my father on the same ship.

The Australian tour was to start in early July 1959 so we set sail from Southampton on the *Southern Cross* at the end of May.

The voyage took five weeks and I thought the rest would do me good. However, despite the comforts of first-class travel, I found five weeks cooped up in the one place a bit much. We went ashore at Las Palmas in the Canary Islands and again in Cape Town and Durban, South Africa and these were welcome respites. But generally I was to find the voyage tedious. I was in no mood for joining in the social activities on board ship. I played some deck-tennis and tombola and saw a few films. But what I enjoyed most was playing table-tennis and reading.

Twenty-seven days out of Southampton we docked in Cape Town. Sion Hill must have sent word that I was coming because the Dominican sisters waylaid me and brought me to their convent. They gave me a very warm welcome. I remember we laughed a lot. They were a very happy group of people in that place, a fact that struck me about every Dominican priory and convent I had ever had occasion to visit. That evening in Cape Town I tried to sing a certain humorous Irish song, but with all the laughing we were doing I don't believe I ever finished it.

About an hour before our arrival in Sydney I learned that I was to give a press reception in my cabin as soon as we docked. 'Impossible,' said my father. 'You couldn't swing a cat in that place.' Though I was moved into a larger cabin, the reception eventually took place in the ship's lounge.

Just after dawn (or so it seemed to me) a representative from the promoter's office came aboard with the pilot. She briefed me about the day's events and every moment seemed to have been accounted for. I was to start with TV, radio and press interviews, which I found difficult enough, but what I was not prepared for was the giant green shamrock that confronted me at the foot of the gangway. Shades of the Ed Sullivan Show … This is my least favourite representation of Ireland. It was supported by two little girls dressed in matching green and gold Irish dancing costumes. Smiling as warmly as I could, I descended the steps to pose for the cameras in the shade of the towering shamrock. I discovered later that all this was being televised for a 'News of the Day' programme. Mercifully I was quickly plucked away and taken to meet Cardinal Gilroy, who was patron of the charitable organization that benefited from the concert tour.

From there I was whisked off to the Town Hall to lunch and a civic reception given by the Lord Mayor of Sydney. The packed day ended with an appearance on a popular, live TV programme where I sang a couple of songs on my own. But I simply *could not* bring myself to join in the spirit of the dancing to the song 'If You're Irish Come Into the Parlour' which concluded the programme.

The eight-week concert tour opened with one week at the Assembly Hall in Sydney. The critics were unanimously kind, and the audiences very warm, all of which contributed towards sending me on my way for the next seven weeks full of encouragement. The promoters were not altogether sure how a diet of voice and harp alone would go down with the Australian audiences, so they added a dash of Irish tenor in the person of a young man with a pleasing voice called Terence Finnegan, who was accompanied on the piano. He started off the concert with a group of songs for about twenty minutes, after which I took over for the rest of the evening. As far as I know, attendance at the Sydney concerts was good, but I preferred not to ask. To the end of my singing career I preferred not to know how a concert was selling. All I wanted was to get it over with.

As this tour was in aid of a charity, I was receiving a very modest fixed fee, with expenses paid, per week. The rest of the proceeds went to the charity. The organizers were professionals but as time went on I could see that they relied heavily on the support of the local clergy to promote the concerts. Occasionally, somewhere along the ecclesiastical line, communications broke down, (perhaps a parish priest was sick and didn't open his mail for a while) and I recall going to some smaller towns where even the parish clergy did not know of the concert until my arrival there, which meant publicity was nil. There were no posters or flyers to announce the concerts. The charity itself spent nothing on publicity or promotion, quite understandably leaving it to the professional organisers. One night I found myself singing to an audience of one...

When I first arrived in Sydney, Joyce Grenfell was in the midst of a season at the Phillips Street Gallery. (Needless to say she was a thundering success.) She came to one of my concerts and was very enthusiastic, but concerned about the way things were being handled. I remember how, backstage afterwards, she complimented me lovingly, and then graciously but firmly – in a way that could offend no one – she made some remark to the organizers to the effect that she felt I wasn't being looked after properly. It was a genuine caring on her part. All through the subsequent phases of my career we kept in touch.

After the opening week in Sydney, I recorded a series of seven fifteen-minute programmes for ABC Radio before travelling throughout New South Wales giving concerts in different towns. Joyce invited me to spend one free weekend with her in her flat at Maclay Regis overlooking Sydney Harbour. She told me that she closed her eyes to the decor and furniture, but selected the flat because of the breathstopping view it commanded.

This is how Joyce described our relationship in her autobiography:

Mary O'Hara ... first came into my life in the mid-1950s when John Gielgud asked me if I would advise a young and very talented Dublin girl, not yet known in Britain, about getting an agent to look after her concert and recording work ... I've no idea what I advised, but we made friends, and she sent me a copy of her first recordings, sung in a clear early morning soprano, very musical and very appealing...

I lost touch with her for a while, but when she arrived in Sydney, to do charity concerts for some Roman Catholic 'good cause', she came to stay with me in my flat. It was a difficult time for her. She was still numbed by sorrow...

Mary was an easy guest; quiet and orderly – the kind that leaves her room and bathroom tidier than she found it. She was only with me for four days. Breakfast was our meeting time. We had plenty to talk about. I see her now sitting opposite me on a sunny morning, wearing a white polo-necked sweater and holding in her hand a scarlet apple. She was twenty-four years old and a radiant beauty. She said she had something important to tell me. Her life was over. Her marriage had been perfect. The world no longer had any flavour for her. She believed she had a calling and to follow it was the only way she would find peace. She had decided to enter a religious order...

Joyce was an unfussy hostess and her patience un-ruffable. One night, knowing I'd be back later than she would be from the theatre, Joyce had given me a key. Coming up in the lift at about 3 am I clumsily dropped the key down the lift shaft. Nothing for it but to ring her door-bell. A sleepy, but exceptionally sweet-tempered Joyce, came to the door, her long brown hair in a plait down her back. My profuse apologies were all received with a dreamy, genuinely kindly smile and a reassuring shake of the head which meant 'It's nothing, don't worry.' Not a word of disapproval was forthcoming.

In a letter to her friend Virginia Graham she wrote as follows:

(24th July 1959) I've got Mary O'Hara, Irish folk singer, in the spare room. In a burst of enthusiasm I offered it to her and here she is. She's a nice creature – practically a nun really. She's just off to Saturday mass at 12.10 with nothing but a drop of coffee in her stomach. She is deeply involved with her Church and is doing her tour to raise funds for a home for old people. No one is doing anything, so she arrives in small towns unheralded, unknown, and plays to empty halls. Such a waste. She is a superb artist and had a terrific time here where the publicity was good.

She is an easy guest and very quiet, so no complaints except that I really like it best when I'm here on me own...

On Sunday I went to my Church. Mary O'Hara took a tennis racquet to hers in the hope of a tussle with a Holy Father after Mass!

Bill came to tea and Mary sang 'She Moved Through the Fair' for us unaccompanied, and it was so remarkable and touching that we were both quite cold with wonder.*

Australian winters in New South Wales can be bitterly cold. Sometimes the theatres and concert halls were badly heated (backstage at any rate) and the lavatories like refrigerators. There was one place that didn't have a loo at all. At least I never found it. I recall opening the only door in sight to find nothing but some steps leading directly onto a huge mound of coal. My need must have been particularly dire, for it was there, on that poleaxingly cold antipodean night, that I attended to the necessities of nature.

After the bitter cold of New South Wales the warmth of the weather in Queensland was heavenly and welcome. The night I sang in Brisbane coincided with a public visit by Princess Alexandra. Just down the road from the theatre where I was performing someone was playing the bagpipes loudly – and I'm sure devotedly – in the Princess' honour, out on the street, as part of a ceremonial welcome. After my road manager heard the cacophonic non-duet between the offending bagpipes and an unaccompanied song of mine, he promptly scampered down the road and paid the piper handsomely to stop, at least until the concert ended. I doubt if the Princess ever noticed and even if she had, she'd be too gracious to comment. I met her face to face two decades later after one of my Royal Command appearances in London where she told me how much she enjoyed an album of mine someone had given her.

By now the organizers were happy with the way the concerts were going, so they extended the tour to a further six weeks in New Zealand. Early in September, with no break, I flew to Auckland. I was pretty tired by then. The plane was droning along nicely. I reflected that if the New Zealand audiences were as warm and enthusiastic as the Australian ones, all would be well. Comforted by this prospect I dozed off and didn't wake until the plane touched down.

As one of the first to descend to the tarmac, I couldn't help but notice a sizeable group of people – some clutching bouquets of

* In Pleasant Places, Joyce Grenfell, 1979, Macmillan, London, pp72-5; and Joyce & Ginnie: The Letters of Joyce Grenfell & Virginia Graham, edited by Janie Hampton, Hodder, 1997 pp.247-50.

flowers – standing with an air of hushed expectancy and gazing in my direction. 'Good gracious', I thought, 'how touching.'

Beaming broadly, I advanced towards the throng, radiating suitable appreciation and permitting myself modest gestures of acknowledgement. As the space between us diminished I noticed no smile to meet my own. Undaunted I pressed on; after all, they might all be short-sighted. Suddenly they burst into life. I responded with my most engaging smile. I was quite close now. However not a single beatific gaze was directed my way. I stole a quick glance over my shoulder. The Russian Ballet Company was descending from the plane.

The New Zealand tour was more skilfully organized than the Australian one. Here, too, the reviews were most generous, the audiences enthusiastic and appreciative. It was in Auckland that I met Father David Sheerin, a Dominican of the Irish Province, a brilliant young man, who was then chaplain at Auckland University. He came backstage after the first concert in the Town Hall (I gave two concerts in each of the major cities in both the North Island and South Island) and introduced himself. Father David and I visited the zoo together next day. It was there that I confided in him my determination to enter a monastery. He was very sympathetic and said he knew the person: his former novice master Father Anselm Moynihan, now Prior of St Dominic's in Drogheda, Ireland. David felt sure that Father Anselm would be the right person for me. He was, he told me, sensitive, wise and discerning.

When the six weeks' tour was over I flew back to Sydney. My agent had offers of television work for me in Melbourne, so I decided to stay on in Australia for a while longer. Within days of my arrival, I was contacted by Dr Percy Jones, a Catholic priest and head of the Faculty of Music at Melbourne University: he was also one of the foremost liturgists in the English-speaking world. Dr Jones, an Australian, had studied in Rome and Ireland and while a student in Dublin had acquired a love for Irish music and culture. He was eager to organize a concert for me. Eventually I did give a concert – in a hall where the temperature was 95° – which was so successful that I was prevailed upon to give another one a couple of weeks later. I say prevailed upon because I was expected to present a completely different programme and I wasn't sure if I could do justice to it at such short notice, especially as I already had ample work in hand in connection with the TV programmes. Soon after that the seven live weekly TV programmes that had brought me to Melbourne in the first place had finished, so I decided to return to Sydney.

With the help of friends my father and I rented a bungalow on the beach outside Sydney where we spent Christmas. It was my first experience of eating Christmas turkey with the sun blazing down.

When I returned from Melbourne my agent had another offer of a recorded series of thirteen fifteen-minute television programmes for ATN Channel 7 in Sydney. So I was to remain in Australia for a further few months, preparing for and recording the series. We know from correspondence that this series went out after I left Australia but as far as I know I never got paid. By then I had lost any slight interest I'd ever had in matters financial. I had set my sights elsewhere.

May came and I felt it was time to close the Australian chapter. I turned down the offer of more concerts in Sydney. I had worked hard and made lots of new friends but now it was time to fly back to Europe and sort out the monastic business.

CHAPTER 10

Into the Unknown

I RETURNED TO Dublin after a year's absence with one thing uppermost in my mind: to find a monastery. Following up David Sheerin's advice I wrote to Father Anselm Moynihan explaining who I was and why I wanted to see him. He sent a cautious reply, graciously inviting me to Drogheda to meet him at my convenience. So in late summer 1960 I set off on the two hour bus journey to Drogheda. I found him to be a man in his fifties, of great spiritual strength and matching gentleness. At times he had about him an air of severity, but his delicious sense of fun and humour was ever ready to break through to the surface. He had a flexibility of spirit that combined, in a happy blend, respect for tradition and openness of mind and was forever hearkening to what the Holy Spirit is saying to the Church today. His reputation as a sound theologian meant that he was in great demand as a giver of retreats. He was knowledgeable about the ways of contemplative communities and was the official *visitor* appointed by the Vatican to the Contemplative Houses of women in Ireland.

From the start I trusted him wholeheartedly and spoke very freely to him about myself, my failings and my aspirations. I felt that, guided by him, I would, sooner or later, be shown what I must do. He had to see me a number of times in order to assess whether or not I had a real vocation to the contemplative life – which I believed I had.

After many visits and prayerful reflection on both sides Father Anselm concluded that I did indeed have a genuine call to the monastic life. We drew up a list of the major Contemplative Orders for women in the Church and systematically set out to examine what

differentiates one Order from another, something that Father Anselm
was well versed in. In his estimation we should look for a Religious
Order where there was some emphasis on study. He felt that I was the
type of person whose mind needed to be nurtured on a substantive
diet of theology if I was to lead a balanced spiritual life. This elim-
inated some Orders. When I mentioned that it was in the Poor Clares'
favour that they did not sing the liturgy but spoke it, he dismissed
the remark with a wry 'That would be an easy way out.' And that
was that. I was strongly attracted to the Cistercians because of their
perpetual silence and austere way of life, though Father Anselm was
doubtful about my ability to endure such physical hardship. He also
made the observation that my inclination was to practise charity
vertically rather than horizontally and that living in a community that
did not include in its timetable regular verbal communication with
others might only accentuate that tendency.

The next step was to visit the individual establishments of the
various Religious Orders. Travelling in connection with my work
facilitated this part of my quest. Whenever I had occasion to be in
England or Scotland I made a point of visiting whatever monastery
in that area we had singled out. It sometimes involved lengthy train
journeys. I always wrote beforehand asking for permission to come
and talk to the Superior and over a period of nine months I visited six
monasteries.

The first House I visited was in Ireland, where I was quite well
known to the community. But since what I sought was relative
obscurity, for that reason it was unsuitable. My meeting with the
Prioress there led to a friendship that lasted for years. The next place
was in Scotland. Like most of the other Superiors I came into contact
with, the Prioress of this House was a remarkable woman. She struck
me as having a single, shining passion – the service and love of the
Lord. She explained to me the particular way the enclosed life was
lived in her community and I came away feeling encouraged and
impressed by the warmth and evident happiness of this dedicated
woman.

The following two visits were not so successful but the next
encounter was an experience I still look back on with affection. The
setting was a most attractive medieval house in a picturesque part of
rural England. I warmed immediately to the Bavarian-born Prioress

who welcomed me – a stranger – like an old friend. She had a vivacity of spirit that belied her years and she radiated joy and love. She seemed genuinely disappointed that I wasn't staying overnight and personally showed me around. Because this was an historic building the community was in receipt of a government grant which obliged them to open the house to tourists during the summer months. This effected a modification of the strict rule of enclosure and wouldn't do for me. I wanted the whole or nothing; I couldn't be content with half measures.

These ventures into the unknown took place at intervals during my engagements. I was doing a series of thirteen programmes for Scottish Television which kept me in Scotland for a few months. I divided my time between Edinburgh and Glasgow, staying with the Scott-Moncrieffs in Edinburgh and with my good friend Hannah Keane and her family in Glasgow. It took two days; I taped the programmes in the morning for transmission that evening and next day I was back in Edinburgh. Scomo helped me with the STV scripts.

Scomo was the only one who knew that this might possibly be my last appearance ever on TV. Therefore he was very angry when he discovered that STV, as was customary then, had erased the tapes after each programme went out.

It's not difficult to find Irish and Scottish traditional songs that contain a reference to God, however obliquely, and I made a point of including one such song in each programme. The make-up girl told me that during one of the programmes someone in the control room was overheard muttering: 'What the hell does she think this is, the Vatican Radio?'

Because of my interest in the Cistercians I visited Nunraw, the Cistercian monastery outside Edinburgh, to talk to the Abbot, Father Columban Mulcahy. He was away when I called so he came to see me later at Scomo's. A small man, he had a huge presence.

One afternoon Father Columban arrived for tea at Scomo's flat bringing along a book on the Cistercians called *La Trappe* in English. After we'd spoken for some time he suddenly leaned forward urgently in his chair and said: 'I know the place for you – Stanbrook.' Puzzled, I asked, 'Where and what is Stanbrook?' He explained that it was a Benedictine monastery in the Midlands. When I asked him why he was enthusiastic about the Benedictines and not his own Order, he said, 'It's a hunch.' He added that it seemed to him that the singing gift I had was such that if I didn't use it an important part of me would not go on developing. When he said that there was a strong tradition of plainchant at this Stanbrook Abbey I threw my eyes up to heaven, thinking: 'Here we go again!' While I enjoy listening to singing when it's properly done, I have never been attracted to the Gregorian Chant, sometimes called plainsong, plainchant or simply the Chant. Mary Gray Hughes had given me an album of plainsong by the monks of Gethsemani Abbey in Kentucky, which had left me quite unmoved, even rather bored. It is too much of a coincidence to expect that a group of disparate individuals called to live together in monastic community should each be endowed with the gift of song. I suspected that Father Columban had not much of an ear for music. And listening to him later singing the Divine Office confirmed my suspicions. He was quite tone deaf.

When the TV series was over, I stayed on in Edinburgh continuing work on the material for the three long-playing records that I hoped to make before entering the monastery. I read *In A Great Tradition,* the book about Stanbrook Abbey which Father Columban had lent me. The book was no great help but on Father Columban's advice I visited Stanbrook. There I spoke to the Abbess, who later on was to become not only my Superior, but also a close friend and confidant. The Novice Mistress joined us after a while and then departed. As in the other monasteries I visited, I was separated from the nuns by a wooden counter, on top of which was a double iron grille reaching to the ceiling. There was also a black veil which obscured everything beyond the grille and to see Lady Abbess I had to open this curtain. All this seclusion appealed greatly to me. As I was leaving the Abbess extended her hand through the grille and gave me one of her trans-formingly lovely smiles. It was about 3pm and the community was in church reciting *None,* so on the Abbess's suggestion I stopped in the Extern Chapel to listen on my way out. My feelings about monastic choirs remained unchanged.

Some time after I got back to Ireland at the completion of the STV series, I went to see Father Anselm to discuss my monastic peregrinations. I had a strong feeling either for or against each place I had visited, except Stanbrook. We discussed this at length and went our separate ways to pray about it; and eventually we both agreed that Stanbrook should be the place for me. I then wrote to each of the five other monasteries I had visited to tell them of my decision. Interestingly enough, the three who answered wrote to say how happy they were and that they felt my choice had been a wise one.

Stanbrook sent me a questionnaire. My father happened to be in the room when I was completing it. I was absent-mindedly reading the questions aloud and when I came to 'Reasons for wanting to enter the monastery' my father piped up, 'Trouble at home!'

The year before, when Father Anselm was first sure I had a monastic vocation he gave me what he called a small test. He asked me not to wear mascara (which, along with lipstick, was the only make-up I used) between then and the time I would enter a monastery. That was no small test for me, because ever since I'd finished school I'd darkened my eyebrows and eyelashes with mascara. I am very fair and without mascara I feel quite naked. When I asked if I could continue to keep my eyebrows tidy, plucking them to give them shape, after some hesitation, he said yes, as that was like 'brushing one's hair'. Yes, of course, I could wear mascara and other eye make-up in connection with my work. Denying myself these female vanities was quite a trial, especially as I had to travel so much during those days. I must admit that I gave the dispensation 'in connection with my work' a wide interpretation. During this period my sister Joan often remarked: 'Oh Mel, why don't you go back to wearing mascara? It's so depressing when you don't.' But she was not party to my secret plan.

In the autumn of 1961 I took my father for a holiday to the Hebridean island of Barra. I thought it would be the last holiday, for I expected to be in the monastery before the following summer. I'd written to a friend on Barra who arranged accommodation for us in one of the local houses. We flew from Glasgow in a very small plane that landed on the beach. For some reason it circled the strand for ages before it touched down and I felt exceedingly air-sick. As I staggered from the plane the friend who was meeting us remarked: 'There is no doubt about which country you come from – your face is green.'

The holiday was quiet, as it was meant to be, and there were plenty of lovely long, windswept walks. Walking has always been a favourite exercise of mine and I still manage to do a few miles on most days even when I'm staying in a city. Indeed, often if I'd been too busy during the day, I still enjoyed walking through the fields alone at night; and many visiting friends had sometimes found themselves press-ganged into Wellingtons and marched out into the darkness. They learnt to enjoy it – at least our friendships don't seem to have suffered.

Barra was also ideal for cycling, so I hired a bike and cycled contentedly along the island roads. It was October and there was very little sun, but one day I braved the elements and went for a swim in Seal Bay. It was not a misnomer. My father was sitting on a sandbank reading a book while I disported myself in a large sheltered natural swimming pool. Suddenly I heard him shout – I turned around and there looking into my eyes a few yards away was a large inquisitive brown seal. I'm sure it meant no harm, but I didn't wait to find out.

Another time I had cycled out alone to a different part of Seal Bay and, walking along the deserted strand, I was thinking about a story I'd read of someone who had attracted seals with her singing. I had a good look round first to ensure that no one was watching and thinking I was dotty. Standing at the edge of the sea I began to sing 'Bella Signora' – a vocal exercise which consists of a rising arpeggio on the first four syllables with a descending scale on to the second last syllable. The phrase is repeated a note higher each time. After the first phrase I waited expectantly. After a few seconds a head appeared in the water. I tried a note higher. Another head bobbed up. I continued until I could go no higher and counted in all twelve pairs of eyes staring soulfully at me. So the singing worked. I think a seal has a beautiful head. And oh, those eyes! If I were to have a fishy pet it would be a seal.

Back in Dublin I recorded a number of programmes for Radio Éireann. Since my return from Australia I had received numerous concert offers but I declined them all. I also had an offer from Al Grossman, telling me he could arrange another appearance for me on the Ed Sullivan Show. However, when I replied that in the light of my earlier experience (1957) on the show I'd be loathe to go on the programme ever again, he replied as follows:

You can be sure that none of the things you mentioned in your letter will occur when you appear this time. The songs that you do will be selected from your repertoire and I am sure that this appearance will be a more pleasant one.

If you are planning staying in NY I would like to arrange a small recital at the Carnegie Recital Hall which seats 299 people. It would not be possible for you to receive your normal fee in such a small hall but I do not believe it would be possible in such a short time to promote a larger concert...

Please let me know when you plan to arrive, how long you plan to stay and if you would like me to make hotel accommodations for you.

So I travelled to New York once more to make an appearance on the Ed Sullivan Show. My friends the Clancy Brothers were appearing on the programme, too, as was Brendan O'Dowd, whom I was meeting for the first time. Mr Grossman was attentive and took me to different folk clubs of note in Greenwich Village. He had a large collection of interesting records in his apartment and it was there that I heard for the first time the glorious voice and artistry of Joan Baez. It was her first album, just out, and she was nineteen. I'd never heard anything to match it and I was instantly hooked. Magic. For years afterwards, I raved about her to everyone I met. It wasn't until December 1977, after one of her sell-out concerts in London, that I met her briefly backstage.

During that visit to Mr Grossman's apartment Odetta walked in, very surprised to find me there. She said: 'Oh ... I, oh ... oh you're beautiful ... er, I mean your *record* is beautiful.' She was referring to *Songs of Ireland* which had become well known in the United States by then.

Mr Grossman was disappointed in what seemed to him to be my lack of ambition. I just wasn't interested in getting further work. After seeing me sprint up the steps to his apartment he remarked wistfully: 'Won't you even let me make you into a star *athlete*?' I just laughed. All this combined with occasional remarks I made in conversation, must have led him to believe that I was planning something special or 'taking that last mystical step' as he referred to it in the taxi on the way to the airport.

Towards the end of 1961 Ireland was preparing to set up its own television station, which opened on 31st December. I was asked to take part. So, I recorded my contribution beforehand because I was to be in Africa on opening night visiting my brother Dermot and his family. My father was travelling with me and we had planned to stop off in Rome for a couple of days. The Prior at the Irish Dominican House of San Clemente knew we were coming and had arranged a surprise private audience for us with Pope John XXIII. Unfortunately, because our plane was late we missed the audience. Eventually we reached Lagos.

It was a pleasant few weeks in West Africa. I hadn't told my brother anything about my future plans, and didn't see him again until 1978 when he walked into the television studio for 'This is Your Life'. By then he was living in Alberta, Canada.

I now had enough material ready for a final three albums and I wanted the recording over and done with, before entering Stanbrook. I felt that, as far as I was concerned, I had come to the end of an era with that type of song. I went into the studio, nervous yes, but with a distinct sense of satisfaction and joy that a definite chapter in my musical career had come to its natural close. In the end one gets tired of doing the same thing over and over again. I had that experience with 'The Quiet Land of Érin' because, at one time, I was forever being asked to sing it. The recording took place in the basement of a house in Lower Mount Street in a small studio owned by Prionsias MacAonghusa, a well-known Dublin journalist and broadcaster. Some time in March I recorded fifty-four songs, eighteen of them Scottish and the remainder Irish, for what were eventually to be released as *Mary O'Hara's Ireland*; *Mary O'Hara's Scotland* and *Mary O'Hara's Monday, Tuesday – Songs for Children*. Material for the latter album was chosen with children in mind, but the songs are by no means children's songs. Since there was no immediate plan for making records from these tapes, I left them in the care of MacAonghusa, a decision that later led to untold confusion when the studio changed hands. The 'Mount Street Master Tapes', as we labelled them, cost £183.14 and it took only a matter of days to do the recording.

The recording over, I now felt free to enter Stanbrook. I thought that a good time to enter would be during Lent, since penance was a sizeable ingredient in my vocation but, Easter Week of that April, I was told, would be more convenient for the Benedictines.

My last public performance was on St Patrick's Night, March 17th 1962 taking part in the annual broadcast concert with the Radio Éireann Symphony Orchestra, singing three songs: 'My Lagan Love', '*Róisín Dubh*' and '*Cucúín a Chuaichín*'.

I entered Stanbrook on 23rd April 1962 to begin the final chapter in my life — or so I thought at the time. It was at the same time to be the definitive end of a singing career and I had absolutely no regrets; in fact I felt relieved.

As it turned out, the 'Mount Street Master Tapes' were the only part of the 'outside world' that followed me into Stanbrook.

CHAPTER 11

Stanbrook

DON'T TALK TO ME about packing. Even the anticipation of it, trying to decide what to put in and what to leave behind, wearies me; I generally end up taking more than is necessary and leaving some essential things behind. In packing for Stanbrook I was spared all this. I'd been sent a list – not unlike the boarding-school list of my childhood. So it was just a question of ticking off the various items: one black dress, two pairs of black shoes, long black stockings, and so on. For laundry purposes each person was allotted a number, and mine, which was number five, had to be stitched on all my belongings. This took some time.

Neither my sister Joan nor my brother Dermot knew then about my decision. I felt that they would not have understood. In Dublin, apart from my father, Sister Angela and Mother Ambrose at Sion Hill were the only ones I confided in. The last thing I wanted was publicity; and so the fewer who knew the better. Those who did know about my plans accepted my decision, though I suspected that some of them did so with reluctance. Up to this time my father was staying in lodgings in Dublin. Thinking it would be better for him to have a place of his own after I had gone away, the two of us moved into a flat out in Monkstown on the outskirts of Dublin. It was from there that I left for Stanbrook.

Some days before I travelled to England, I telephoned my good friend, Seán Óg Ó'Tuama (whose *claisceadal* music sessions I'd been attending on and off since my return from Australia), to see if he would give me a lift to the airport. I could have got a taxi, but I wanted to see Seán Óg and tell him what I was doing. When he arrived and saw the trunk full of black clothes, he was puzzled. 'Where on earth are you going?' he asked. When I told him, he was stunned. He and my father saw me off at Dublin airport and I left Ireland, as I thought then, forever. I wasn't to meet Seán Óg again or hear from him, until one day twelve years later he turned up unexpectedly at Stanbrook to see me.

As the plane took off over the Irish Sea towards England, I settled back in my seat and thought to myself that this was to be my last plane journey. It was the first step of a spiritual journey for which I had been consciously preparing for over four years. I felt a deep peace.

I stayed overnight in the Manchester area to attend to some family business and was joined the next day by my father on the final lap of my journey. They were expecting me at the monastery by late afternoon, but whatever happened en route I did not reach Stanbrook until about 9 pm, after Compline (i.e., Night Prayer which my father insisted on referring to as Complan) when the community was about to enter the 'Great Silence' and retire for the night. Not for nothing was I subsequently referred to as 'the late Sister Miriam'.

Father deposited my luggage in the front hall and, after a few words with the Abbess in the parlour, I gave him a quick hug and said good-bye. 'I'll see you in the morning,' he said and went off to stay overnight in the monastery guesthouse.

Then I did what countless people who aspired to live the Bene-dictine life have done down the centuries – I knocked on the enclos-ure door for formal admittance. Lady Abbess asked: 'What have you come for?'

And I replied: 'To give myself as completely as possible to God.'

I then stepped across the threshold into the monastic enclosure. From there, Lady Abbess led me to the church where the community was assembled and chanting psalms. After a few moments of silent prayer, kneeling at the altar steps, Lady Abbess put me into the charge of the Novice Mistress who, over the next few years, was to initiate me into the ways of Benedictine monasticism. Afterwards, each member of the community, in turn, gave me the welcoming kiss of peace and Lady Abbess bestowed on me the name Sister Miriam.

The Assistant Novice Mistress, or Zealatrix, as she is called, brought me to my cell in the novitiate, a building separate from the main part of the monastery. My cell was a small room about ten feet by twelve, with a high window from which trees were visible. It was adequately, if plainly furnished – a bed, a table, a chair, a priedieu, a small cupboard and a bookshelf on the wall. Above the priedieu hung a wooden crucifix. The curtains were dark green; the walls off-white and the bare floor of polished wood. My luggage was brought to the cell door by a couple of smiling novices. Neither of them spoke, nor did they enter my cell. Soon, all was beautifully quiet except for the sound of an odd bird in the trees outside, trying to settle down for the night. Before long I followed suit and did not hear another thing until I was called at six o'clock the next morning.

Having dressed in my black outfit, with a short black veil trimmed with white covering my long reddish-brown hair (pinned up), I was taken down to church by a fellow postulant, a tall, quiet Swedish girl. What a relief it was, from then on, never again to have to ask myself each morning: 'What shall I wear today?' After Mass next morning I was led to the refectory. There I was, struck by the beautiful adzed oak tables that ran down the length of the room. At the west end of the refectory sat the Abbess and, on either side of her, the Prioress and Sub-prioress. At the opposite end of the room stood the reader's pulpit.

After breakfast I went with Lady Abbess to the parlour to see my father. Clearly, it was a shock to him that I was already well and truly 'inside' with a double grille dividing us. I think he'd been expecting me to be able to stroll outside in the garden with him. For a while, the three of us chatted briefly and cheerfully together, which I think helped him. Soon it was time for him to go. We exchanged good-byes through the grille and he departed, making a valiant effort to hide his emotions. He had known from the time I told him of Richard's death that I'd wanted and intended to enter a monastery, but he didn't believe I ever would. He was very lonely at my going away, but wanted only my happiness. The rule obliged us to write once a week to our parents. For the next twelve years, my father was to visit me occasionally as the monastery allowed, looking forward eagerly to coming to Stanbrook. He used to refer to those trips as his journeys to the 'Happy Valley'.

My recollection of the rest of that first day in Stanbrook and, indeed, of the ensuing weeks is scant. It is much more difficult to get into a monastery such as Stanbrook than it is to get out of it. A person is admitted only after the authorities are satisfied about the person's suitability and, especially, motivation. On admission, the person became what was known as a 'postulant', one who seeks admission; after about six months she became a 'Novice', a year later a 'Junior' and, after three more years, she was solemnly professed as a Benedictine nun.

The monastic day began at 5 am, with personal prayer and spiritual reading until 6.25, when the community assembled in church to recite together the Morning Office, i.e. prayers to begin the day. Then after morning Mass and breakfast the work began (9.15-12.25). Everybody came together in Church for the recitation of the Midday Office (prayer). Dinner was in the refectory at 1 pm. This was the main meal of the day, and it was followed by a period of relaxation when the community met and chatted about matters of common interest. There was a rule of silence – not a vow – and this period after lunch, referred to as Recreation, was the only time during the day that we talked, except if one's work or if charity required one to speak. At the end of Recreation some of the younger ones took it in turn to wheel the older invalids around the enclosure in a Bath chair. Nuns don't run but when we were well out of sight, one particular old lady clearly loved it when I broke into a run with her in the Bath chair.

The afternoon was divided between work, prayer and study. On some days of the week, a half hour out of the work period was devoted to either choir practice or to a conference given by the Abbess. Vespers (evening prayers) was sung at 6 pm followed by spiritual reading or personal prayer and then supper at 7.30 pm. Compline (end of day prayer) was sung at 8.15.

The Stanbrook community at the time of my entry numbered about seventy people, including those in the novitiate – myself, another Postulant, one Novice and about three Juniors. New people were coming and going all the time. In the morning, the novitiate had various conferences which dealt with various topics: the Rule of St Benedict, Theology, the Scriptures, the Monastic Spiritual Writers, Church and Monastic History. Philosophy was added later. We were also trained in the Ways of Prayer, in the customs and traditions of the house, and in Gregorian Chant. Every moment was accounted for and, when the end of the day came, I was tired out but I felt it was a fruitful tiredness. This is what I had expected and indeed wanted.

How often one hears a vocation to the monastic life described, nay decried, in negative terms, such as 'turning one's back on' or 'running away from' something, anything, even life itself. A vocation is a call – derived from the Latin *vocare* – and one responds to, or answers a call, by turning and moving towards the caller. St Benedict even talks about running towards God and eternal life. To the eyes of non-faith this desire for eternal life may seem very like a death-wish, but to those who believe, it is in fact a life-wish. Let St Benedict have the last word. His injunction to his followers is clear. We must 'keep death daily before our eyes'.

Going into the monastery was also my way of saying 'thank you' to God for all the good things he had showered on me. He had given me a measure of rare happiness that I had no right to expect.

That first summer in the monastery came and went. I prayed and I studied and I worked in the fields, learning new things all the time. I grew accustomed to the monastic way of life, though I never got attached to it, nor did it ever become easy or routine. Soon the initial six months were up and it was time to take the next step. For my part, I was prepared to continue, but the decision of accepting me as a novice remained with the Abbess and the community. It was plain to me that I had made the right decision in coming to Stanbrook, but if my superiors had told me, as they had countless others, that I must leave, I would not have been upset. Richard's death had schooled me to bear any disappointment.

Eventually a day came when the Abbess and her Council met to decide whether I should be allowed to take the next step and become a Novice. As was the custom I waited in church while they deliberated and, after some time, I was summoned into their presence to be informed that I had been accepted. I did not expect to be emotional about it, but I was. I found myself weeping with gratitude. As I was hurrying back to the novitiate after I'd been given the news, I met one of the older nuns on the stairs. Misconstruing my tears she put her arms around me to console me, saying: 'Poor Sister Miriam, have you not been accepted?' Giving her a quick hug, I whispered that I was.

The Clothing was an important milestone on the journey towards becoming a fully-fledged Benedictine nun. Much was made of it in the community and it was a day of general rejoicing. The would-be Novice was allowed to invite her family and a few close friends to be present. The date chosen for the ceremony was 8th December, the Feast of the Immaculate Conception, a major feast in the Roman Catholic Church. It was a bitterly cold day. The land had been covered with snow for weeks and a great stillness had settled on everything outside. I did not invite many people. My father, Joan and Frank, Lesley Scott-Moncrieff, John and Mary Gray Hughes all watched the ceremony from the extern chapel. They were amused when, in the homily, the officiating retired Abbot reminded me that I had come to an 'approved' school. He was referring to a phrase of St Benedict's about a monastery being a school of the Lord's service, but to my uninitiated guests, the term was synonymous with a school for delinquents.

After the Clothing the guests had tea in the parlour, where I joined them for a while, the double grille dividing us. It was a rather awkward get-together, since few of my guests knew one another and when I joined them it was not possible to converse with everybody at once. The bell summoning the community to prayer put an end to the visit, which had lasted about an hour, and as the visitors went off into the night I got ready for my first Vespers as a Novice. The monastic habit now replaced the black dress that I'd worn daily for the previous eight months. It had been specially made for me in Dublin, (my 'little black number') and I'd never got such satisfaction and wear out of a garment before. It had become quite diaphanous in parts.

In a monastery, time seems to fly more quickly than it does elsewhere. My daily routine as a Novice was substantially the same as it had been when I was a postulant. I've always disliked having things on my head for any length of time and for that reason the headgear one had to wear as a Novice was something I distinctly disliked. It was a complicated pin-up job that I never seemed to get quite right, and the absence of mirrors in the monastery didn't help matters. After a while, I thought I'd got the hang of it, but obviously not, for one day the Novice Mistress was asked by the Abbess to 'see what you can do with Sister Miriam's veil to make her look less like a skinned rabbit'. So, I must have looked a lot less fetching than I thought. I was still not used to doing without mascara and lipstick. Of course, I didn't mind while among the community, but later, when on the occasions I had to see visitors in the parlour, I felt exposed. Vanity dies hard. Visits were restricted in number, something for which I was very grateful, and I believe that most members of the community felt the same way. Visits were also generally of short duration, as indeed they had to be, as they tended to disrupt monastic routine.

In one of her letters before I went to Stanbrook, Lady Abbess took me by surprise and asked me to bring my harp. It hadn't been my intention to do so, but since it seemed to be the Abbess's wish I looked on it as a sort of first step in obedience. A few months after I'd arrived was Lady Abbess's Feast Day, and I was asked if I would sing for the community. I was in a quandary. There was little or no time for the amount of practice I felt was necessary to give a proper perform- ance. Besides, the life was very tiring and one of Sister Angela's great maxims was: don't sing when you're tired. I'd been encouraged by the Novice Mistress to get out the harp and practise, but I'd never felt comfortable about it. There were other things I preferred to do. Besides, had I not made the studied decision to give up singing and playing completely? My present way of life took up all my time and energy. I did perform for the community on Lady Abbess's Feast Day, but after that I was not to sing for them for several years. In the novitiate I was prevailed upon by my fellow novices and Juniors to sing for them on a few occasions, but when they realized how reluc- tant I was, they soon stopped asking, and the harp was put away safely in the attic.

My presence at Stanbrook received no publicity whatsoever, a wish of mine that was also in keeping with the monastery's policy. Even regular visitors to the Abbey and people like John McEvoy, whose work on behalf of the monastery brought him daily into the enclosure, did not realize that I was there. I did not then know John McEvoy or his wife, Connie, but they had a record of mine from the early days. Later they became my good friends and only then did John tell me of an incident that occurred during my first year inside. One day in summer when he was passing the novitiate, he heard coming through an open upstairs window the sound of the harp, and recog- nized the voice of Mary O'Hara, familiar to him from his record. Somewhat surprised at hearing a record being played in the novitiate, he went home and told Connie: 'Some clot in the novitiate has a record of Mary O'Hara. Whoever it is, she is keeps starting and

stopping. That's certainly not going to do the record any good.' He
sent a note in to the Novice Mistress warning her that someone was
damaging the album. What he'd heard, of course, was not a 'stop and
start' record player but Sister Miriam Selig practising for her Lady
Abbess's feast day recital. It was long afterwards before he discovered
that the Mary O'Hara whose album he possessed was now a member
of the Stanbrook monastic community – though he must have seen
me around often enough.

After a year as a Novice I was asked whether I wished to take the
important step of Simple Profession, to become a Junior. The Junior
makes vows for three years: stability, conversion of manners and obedience – *stabilitas, conversio morum et obedientia.* Implicit in those are
vows of chastity and poverty. 'Stability' commits the person to living
the rest of her life in a particular monastery; 'conversion of manners'
means that the person turns away from worldly attitudes to embrace
the Benedictine Rule and to concentrate on the single-minded search
for God. 'Obedience' is self-explanatory. At the time of Simple
Profession the Junior receives a black veil in place of the white one.
After I'd made known my desire to take vows, the Abbess convened
the council to discuss my suitability and, having ascertained the
approval of the rest of the community, the verdict was communicated
to me. Lady Abbess chose 10th February to be my Profession Day.
What she did not know was that 10th February was the anniversary
of my engagement to Richard, seven years earlier. This happy coincidence I interpreted as a divine endorsement of what I was doing,
and I was deeply moved.

My three years as a Junior passed quickly and were outwardly as
uneventful as my novice year. In the life of a nun the adventure is
within. The ordinary everyday happenings in a monastery don't make
for exciting reading, but beneath the seemingly even tenor and, sometimes, even dullness of daily living spiritual revolutions and personal
discoveries can occur. As a cradle Catholic I had been brought up with
an emphasis on what are sometimes referred to as devotions, such as
the recitation of the Rosary, the Stations of the Cross and other time-
honoured extra-liturgical practices. There is nothing wrong with this
type of spirituality, but it is not the Benedictine one, which empha-
sizes worship, especially through the liturgy, which is the Church's cor-
porate prayer. One day I chanced upon a book in the novitiate library

which made me realise that I was practically ignorant of the deeper
meaning of the Mass, the Eucharistic celebration which is at the heart
of Catholic worship. This realization prompted me to explore the
mystery in greater depth, under the guidance of the Novice Mistress.
My studies soon led me to the 'discovery' of the Resurrection, the over-
whelming significance of which had escaped me until then, and with
this a spiritual joy I had never known before entered my life. Previously, my general approach to things religious had a somewhat som-
bre flavour about it. This could well be attributed to the Jansenism
which permeated Irish Catholicism, dating from the days when the
Irish clergy had perforce to receive their training in a Jansenistic
environment on the continent of Europe. When for political reasons
(to stem the flow of revolutionary ideas from continental seminaries),
the Irish Church was eventually permitted to establish a national seminary of its own at Maynooth, the Jansenistic tendency was confirmed.
Whatever the explanation, I certainly had a strong puritanical streak
in me, and I am grateful to Stanbrook for rinsing it out of my system.

I remember my mild irritation during the first conference Lady
Abbess gave in Easter Week on the day after my arrival. She talked a
lot about joy. I recall sitting there in the Chapter House with the rest
of the community thinking to myself: 'What is she going on and on
about joy for?' In those early days, mine was very much a cross-
orientated spirituality: I seemed to have got stuck at Good Friday. The
Easter Liturgy meant nothing to me. I'd never even attended the
Easter Vigil before I'd entered Stanbrook.

During my third year or so in Stanbrook, when my whole outlook
was becoming increasingly coloured by my new-found understanding
of the Resurrection, I started to re-read Richard's poems. A selection,
edited by Peter Levi, had just been published in Ireland. There were
some early poems which I didn't understand. One morning, as I was
sweeping the stairs, some lines from one such hitherto impenetrable
poem called 'Eros' kept going through my head. Suddenly I saw meaning in them. For me the whole poem, every line of it, was all about
the death and resurrection of the God-man Christ, though the author
may not have in any way intended it as such. Some years later I set it
to music, and have since recorded it on an album: *Recital*.

All through the novitiate years, the emphasis was on training. After five years, the candidate will have had ample opportunity to satisfy herself that she wants to spend the rest of her life in that one monastery. The authorities, too, and the community as a whole had to be satisfied about her suitability. Fitting in with the others was obviously important, and the community wasn't likely to vote for someone who was self-centred or incurably introverted.

From the start I threw myself into the life of the novitiate, shrinking from nothing, but having one of my biggest struggles with 'joining in' with the other postulants, novices and Juniors. During the hour or so of relaxation, conversation did not come at all easily. There were times when the Novice Mistress had occasion to point out to me that I should be making more of an effort to participate. One was expected to contribute to the general conversation even if one didn't feel like it or found the subject of no interest. Somebody once made the remark: 'Mention the subject of music and Sister Miriam will clam up.' I also never talked about Richard or my marriage, though he occupied my mind constantly. People seemed willing to talk about their families and books being read in the refectory and so on. There was neither radio nor television and I for one didn't miss them for a moment. Occasionally a newcomer to the novitiate brought odd scraps of information. For instance, one day it was mentioned that Marilyn Monroe had committed suicide. Conversation lingered briefly on the subject, but the Novice Mistress had never even heard of her. The first time I heard about the Beatles was when a postulant gave us a bar or two of 'Eleanor Rigby'. I thought the words were weird, but poignantly intriguing. I wasn't to hear mention of them again for over ten years, until after I left Stanbrook I was lent one of their records. Two of their songs are on albums of mine now.

The daily living out of the Rule of St Benedict was in itself penitential. At certain times of the year such as Lent and Advent we fasted. In those days I had (and still have) a very large, healthy appetite and wholeheartedly enjoyed my meals. However, I threw myself into the fasting with relish but, extremist that I am, tended at times to overdo things. Already I was setting myself a regime which in the end I could not sustain. From the beginning I tended to tax my strength too much. Not for me the Golden Mean. The hours for sleep were adequate for the normal adult, but being so highly strung I have always needed more than the average amount. Before I entered, I realized that in the monastery I might not be able to get enough sleep, but I gladly welcomed the opportunity for further self-denial. I declined the extra hours of rest that I could legitimately have availed myself of. The result was that, over the years, the lack of sufficient sleep was taking its toll. I was developing migraines, fibrositis and sinusitis, but I kept it all to myself. I presumed other members of the community suffered similar ailments, and I did not want to appear a softy by reporting mine.

A very important subject for study during the novitiate was Gregorian Chant. As I mentioned earlier, I was never enamoured of the Chant, nor did I grow any fonder of it with the passage of time. It seemed to me that it never quite got off the ground, perhaps because the mystique surrounding its interpretation prevented the voice taking wing. Singing the Chant in choir was, for me, a bit like dragging heavy chains. Surely it should be possible to *sing* the Chant in a detached and objective way without depriving it of life? It is a vehicle of prayer. I approached the Chant as I did all the other exercises: determined to do things the way I was told. I discovered there was an unspoken assumption that there were two kinds of vocal music: song and the Chant – and that they occupied different worlds and therefore the Chant should not be treated as a song would be. I willingly subordinated my singing instincts and used my voice as the collective body was directed to do. It was a strain. Whenever the choir mistress during choir practice rebuked the community for bad singing, I always took it personally, though I never betrayed my true feelings.

The difficulties did not decrease as time went by, but in those earlier days I had the resilience not to let choir practice and other irritations get me down. Having said all that, and acknowledging the unavoidable strain associated with choir, my time as a novice and a Junior was one of contentment and fulfilment, shot through with joy.

Members of Enclosed Orders often have wide-ranging interests, and appropriate hobbies were encouraged. People took up carpentry, botany, bird-watching, painting, flower-arranging and, above all, gardening. Each novice was given a flower garden to tend. I was not a successful gardener. One day another member of the community watched from a distance in horrified silence as I sedulously uprooted an entire bed of lily-of-the-valley believing they were weeds. To add insult to injury, it was she who had caringly planted those flowers there some time previously. Another time I was so anxious to be *seen* to have flowers blossoming in my patch of garden that, unable to wait, I went off and found some fully grown foxgloves which were flourishing by the roots of an acacia tree, and transplanted them. I did not realize that others consider them weeds. But then again what are weeds but flowers in the wrong place? And who would believe that many years later, I would find myself invited on to BBC 4's 'The Gardening Quiz'.

A number of us grew interested in the night sky. I suppose one could call it astronomy. We shared books on the subject, and it was all very fascinating. It was a study in accord with the spirit of silence and very conducive to prayer. On the one occasion we were lent a telescope, we went out with the Novice Mistress into the garden to observe the sky. It was a beautiful, unclouded night with a full moon. I had the first go with the telescope, but try as I might I was unable to locate the moon. By the time we'd got over our fit of laughing our limited time was up and we had to return the telescope, and we – rather I – still hadn't found the moon. I continued my star-gazing, but from then on using the naked eye.

My discovery of the Resurrection led to an all-consuming preoccupation with the mystery of the Parousia (Christ's Coming in Glory), of which the rising sun is a powerful analogy. My interest, therefore, was not confined merely to the heavens at night, but extended also to the sky at dawn. Words cannot describe the spiritual thrill and feeling of expectancy and longing which the beauty of a rose-coloured sky at dawn can provoke. Advent, my favourite liturgical season, produces some spectacular sunrises. While still in the Novitiate I was bowled over by Sebastian Moore's article 'Notes towards a Theology of the Redemption' and by F.X. Durrwell's book *The Resurrection*.

My father once asked me what I would do if I wasn't finally accepted in Stanbrook. 'I would look for a place where they accepted rejected nuns,' I replied. I meant it, too. Therefore as my novitiate ended and the time for my permanent commitment to the monastic life approached, there was no soul-searching on my part. I was content and had found joy in the life I had chosen.

News had got out, however, that I hadn't actually died, as some
had reported, but that I was a nun at Stanbrook. Sometime in the late
sixties the following typed letter arrived postmarked Australia and
signed Críostóir Ua Duinn:

MARY O'HARA

Beside your sweet voice,
A Mháire Ní Eadhra,*
The song of the nightingale
Is only the croaking
Of an old frog lamenting
A ditch without water,
And he deaf as a post,
On a dry night in summer;
Beside your light lilt
The little lark soaring
Is a hinge wanting oil,
And the rust from it scaling;

Oh why did you leave us,
A Mháire Ní Eadhra,
To chant Latin ditties
To God and his Mother,
They that have angels to sing,
A whole skyful,
And nuns by the million
Without you to join them:

I would rather to hear you
Sing '*Seóladh na nGamhna*'
Outside the door,
And myself on hell's hobstone,
Than me to be sitting
In glory and honour,
On the Throne of the Trinity,
Listening to nothing
But a choir of dull angels
That haven't the Gaelic
In word nor in whisper,
Unless that you teach it;

* The Gaelic version of Mary O'Hara.

And, now that I think it,
If only God grant it,
That, and that only,
Is justification
For this deprivation
On the ears of Clann Adam,
For the harp without strings
And the poets left lonely.

CHAPTER 12

Among Silence

I WAS ACCEPTED for Solemn Profession. The ceremony took place, as is customary, three years to the day after Simple Profession, on 10th February 1967, the eleventh anniversary of my engagement to Richard. Again, as with my Simple Profession, because I was a widow, the ceremony for Solemn Profession was somewhat shortened.

During the ceremony, three things were presented to the candidate: a breviary, a cowl and a gold ring. The breviary is the official prayer book of the Church, consisting mainly of the psalms and readings from the scriptures, which is used daily by the Solemnly Professed. The giving of the breviary by the celebrant symbolized that from then on the professed nun was delegated by the Church to pray in her name for all mankind. It so happened that the breviary being presented to me belonged to an elderly member of the community, Dame Anselma, who had once taught me Latin. She no longer used it as she had become too infirm to say the Divine Office, even in private. The cowl was a full-length, loose black garment worn over the habit for the liturgy. The ring stemmed from the bridal concept. I had my engagement and wedding rings melted down and made into one plain ring. This was to be the one I was presented with at my Solemn Profession ceremony.

On the morning of my Solemn Profession, as the community processed silently into church, the death knell gently informed them that Dame Anselma had gone to God. The measured tolling of the bell on the cold February air added an element of poignancy and drama to the event.

My Profession ceremony took place during Mass. My father, my twelve-year-old nephew Sebastian Barry and my great friend Scomo were there in the sanctuary, serving as acolytes. Sebastian seemed to have had a better grasp of what was required of him than the other two, who seemed a bit lost. Sebastian occasionally accompanied my father when visiting Stanbrook and worked in the monastery garden.

The whole ceremony took about two hours. 'Dame' is the title given to a Solemnly Professed Benedictine nun, so from then on I was known in the community as Dame Miriam. For the rest of that day and for the following two days, the newly professed kept total silence. This concluded a week of retreat that she had entered prior to the Profession day itself. There was always great rejoicing and a festive air in the monastery at the time of a Solemn Profession.

My three guests stayed in the village until my period of silence ended, when I could talk to them in the parlour. It was good to see them, but especially Scomo, whom I hadn't seen for five years. He was very happy for me, but he spoke yet again of his sincere regret that my singing was silenced. It was still a hope of his that I might some day make another recording. Reminding him that I had no desire ever to sing again, and besides it wasn't possible to make recordings in an enclosed monastery, he laughed and poked an imaginary microphone through the grille that separated us. I was to see this man of God, my most dear friend, only once more before his death, when he came for a brief visit a few years later with his second wife, Eileen, and their three tiny sons.

My father and Sebastian were still visiting the day Dame Anselma was buried. This time they were permitted to enter the enclosure to assist at the funeral and practise their new-found skills as acolytes. It was a hard, bright day. The community, following the coffin, processed from the church to the cemetery, carrying lighted candles in their hands. The singing of psalms was interspersed with the recurring promise of Christ's: 'I am the Resurrection and the Life. He who believes in me, though he die yet shall he live, and whoever lives and believes in me shall never die.' It was as much a celebration of life as a ceremony of burial. The ground was still hard from frost, and here and there small clusters of snowdrops had poked their way through the hostile earth. In a short while they, too, would be returning to their blind roots in the ground, seeming to die, but only to rise again the following spring. Nature conjoined with the Liturgy in a homily of hope: 'In the end is my beginning.'

The community strove to be as self-supporting as possible. There was a large vegetable garden, chicken houses, orchards, a bakery, a laundry, and various workrooms for making the nuns' clothing. The community derived income from the work of its artists, writers and printers. Each year the Abbess and her council met to reallocate the work for that year, in other words to have what Thomas Merton called 'the annual shake-up'. At the time of my Solemn Profession I was working in the garden, which involved a wide variety of jobs. I might be hoeing in the morning and afternoon could find me driving the little tractor, which was very enjoyable. It was largely used for cutting grass around the enclosure and for bringing the heavier supplies of vegetables in from the garden to the kitchen.

Once a year every able-bodied member of the community participated in harvesting the potatoes, something I hugely relished. A farmer came in with a special potato-digging machine and the nuns lined up along the drills putting the potatoes in sacks. During my early days as a Postulant, one of my jobs was to go round with a tin picking slugs off the winter lettuces. I gave myself the title 'Inspector of Slugs'. Another congenial chore was looking after the muscovy ducks that lived on the pond with the moorhens. In the spring and summer it was very pleasant working out of doors in the morning, sometimes as early as eight o'clock, picking vegetables for the kitchen or feeding the ducks. In summertime individuals often prayed outside between 5.30 and 6.25 am. Come spring and I was sent to sow seed. I was reminded of the parable of the sower in the Gospel. I punned in a letter to my father that I was still broadcasting...

With the passage of time my knowledge of gardening improved though I still made blunders. On at least one occasion I picked the wrong greens, which caused the long-suffering Sister Jane to remark resignedly: 'Between Sister Miriam and the pigeons we won't have many green vegetables this winter.' The same sorely tried Sister Jane put me in charge of the cucumber greenhouse where, in my ignorance, I painstakingly watered them to death. In those early days I liked working in the garden because I had plenty of energy. But during the final few years I found any physical work a strain. I had become perpetually tired.

Some time after I was Solemnly Professed, I was made Second Cook. It was interesting, if very hard work. My appetite was something of a byword and having to taste the food we prepared, far from reducing my appetite, only served to whet it. Someone affectionately nicknamed me Sr Yum-Yum. It was challenging work. One's wits were taxed to devise appetizing and varied dishes on a limited budget. The food was plain, plentiful, nourishing and quite varied. Preparing and cooking for about sixty or seventy people was strenuous. Added to that was the regular cleaning of the huge kitchen with its stoves and equipment. There was an added happiness in working in the kitchen because there the service to the community was obviously more visible and therefore personally satisfying. But the ascetic strand was still strongly present in my make-up, and even when I was exhausted, I kept pushing myself to the limit. It was the only way I could operate at that time of my life. To have done less I felt would have been ungenerous. But the true Benedictine life is one of balance and equilibrium: *virtus stat in media.* I was piling my own private discipline onto the monastic one.

It was during that fifteen months in the kitchen that I began to lose my appetite: unheard of for me. A general feeling of malaise became the norm, and the migraines were becoming more frequent. Lady Abbess, always careful to ensure that no one was overburdened with work, discussed my duties with me in case they were too much. But I was unwilling to admit to the strain. She advised me to make full use of the periods of rest the ordinary monastic timetable allowed and she was prepared to give me as much extra rest as I needed as well. But my policy was never to accept extras of any kind, or mitigations of the Rule, and so things continued as before.

After my Solemn Profession I was appointed Second Chantress. If anything went wrong with the singing in choir the First Chantress was responsible for putting matters right, and the First and Second Chantresses alternated every other week in leading the singing in choir. This was a trial for me from the start. I had been content to be in the ranks and would have preferred not to be Chantress. Among other things it is easier to pray the Liturgy when there are no distracting responsibilities. Being somewhat absent-minded at times, it was not unknown for me to intone Friday's hymn on a Thursday. In fact I became so conscious of the possibility of getting my days confused that at the slightest cough I would freeze in my vocal tracks, wondering what it was I had got wrong this time, or expecting the First

Chantress to wade in with the correct lines. My debut as Second Chantress for Benediction was a bit of a fiasco. It was during Advent so there was no accompanying music. For a long time, especially at the beginning, I'd found singing in choir uncomfortably low and, having a relatively high register, I had been solemnly warned, as Chantress, to avoid starting things too high for the choir.

I am not one of those people who can pick an isolated required note out of the air. Nervous and tense, I watched the celebrant's movements for the right moment to start the singing. Choosing what I felt was a reasonable note I started: 'Praise we our God with joy...' Dead silence. Heavens, I thought, I've started it too high. Another go, an interval of a good third down. 'Praise we our God with joy...' At this point I could feel my neighbour shaking with suppressed laughter. Still no sound from the community. I was in a sweat. In a last desperate bid to get a comfortable range for the choir, I did a Paul Robeson, singing virtually *basso profundo* dragging the notes up from my monastic sandals. 'Praise we our God with joy...' By now my neighbour, convulsed, had hidden her face in her sleeves. Terror-stricken at the fact that the choir still hadn't responded, I looked at the altar and realized I had taken not the wrong note but the wrong cue. Afterwards I put in a request for pitch-pipes which were duly purchased and from then on, I am glad to say, were in regular use – possibly my only lasting contribution to the choir.

After I became a Chantress I had, among other things, to become much more involved with the technical and non-prayer side of choir and this increased my general problem with tension. Although in line with the Church's thinking we moved to the vernacular, no radical change could be made about the Chant (as far as I know, Vespers still continues to be sung in Latin at Stanbrook). It was a period of readjustment and adaptation. The situation for me became acute when I was also asked along with others to contribute music for the new English Liturgy. The community, including the other members of the music commission, was steeped in a long tradition of plainsong, which was generally revered and loved. I myself was totally uninfluenced by it. Each member of the commission was given English words to set to music, and while everyone else, especially at the beginning, produced music unmistakably like the Chant, my contribution was a complete departure from it. I felt that Gregorian

Chant was meant for Latin and could not happily be wed to another language.

In singing the Chant in choir, the only time I felt free (or permitted myself any vocal liberty) was when I had solo bits, which I treated as my instincts prompted me they should be treated. Once Dom Bernard McElligott, an authority on Gregorian Chant, came to Stanbrook for a few days to help with the singing. I was working in the kitchen at the time and was excused from attending his sessions. As Chantress it happened to be my week for singing the Brief Responsory solo at Vespers. Next morning during his first talk Dom Bernard remarked: 'Whoever it was who sang the Brief Responsory solo at Vespers last night did it well. That's the way the Chant should be sung.' He did not know me, and when the remark was relayed to me later, I must admit I felt vindicated. He was surprised when Lady Abbess told him afterwards that the one he'd referred to did not actually like plainchant.

After my time in the kitchen, I was appointed First Portress for two consecutive years. This was a considerably less strenuous job. It involved fetching nuns when they were wanted on the phone or in the parlour, and letting the people who had to come inside the enclosure in and out. For those two years my afternoon work period was spent in the orchards. In winter it was generally relatively light work involving ladders and secateurs. Scything, during the summer months, and making compost heaps called for more muscle.

Once or twice since I'd entered, Lady Abbess had broached the subject of having copies of my records in the monastery, but since I objected to the idea she did not press the point further. After I'd been there about eight years, someone from the novitiate approached me for permission to play a record of mine that had been lent by a visitor. Eventually I reluctantly agreed, and then forgot about the matter. A few days later, while I was on duty as Portress, an unsealed package passed through my hands, being returned to the visitor. I realized that the package contained a record album and it suddenly struck me that it *might* be one of mine. Looking inside, I saw the cover of *Songs of Érin*, the first long-playing record I had made. It was recorded in the Decca studios in London three weeks after I was

married, and Richard had been present during the recording. I felt
weak at the knees and had a strong urge to listen to it. I spoke to
Lady Abbess and told her that I'd opened a package which I
shouldn't have opened and that, with her permission, I'd like to
listen to the record before I sent it out. So together the two of us listened to the record in her room and I was totally unprepared for my
strong emotional reaction. I was strangely affected by what I heard.
I'd never listened to my records without feelings of discomfort, being
keenly aware of my flaws and imperfections. But this time it was as
though I was listening objectively to someone else. I was struck by
the sincerity of the performance. The words of 'My Lagan Love' and
'Danny Boy', for instance, together with the recollection of the circumstances under which they were recorded, combined to move me
to tears.

Deeply understanding as she was, Lady Abbess let me have 'a good
cry' as she put it. We discussed the record, and I told her that this was
the first time I had come to recognize that my singing probably did
give pleasure to many people. Gently she said: 'My dear Sister, I've
been trying to tell you that for the past eight years.' There and then
I told her that yes, she could indeed go ahead and buy my albums for
the community.

When I first entered Stanbrook, Lady Abbess encouraged me to
keep up singing and playing the harp, but my heart was not in it.
Apart from giving in to repeated pleas from other members of the
novitiate very early on, only on two major occasions, and under great
duress, did I unpack my harp and play it during my first years in the
monastery. One was on Lady Abbess's Feast Day, already referred to
and, much later, for an ecumenical carol service held in the monastery
Church. In preparation for this latter event, I squeezed in whatever
practice I could get in my free time, but I was still acutely nervous.
I was to sing and play the harp beside the grille on a narrow step on
the sanctuary. Everything went fine during rehearsals, but all of us
forgot that during the actual ceremony the grille was opened, and
when I came to reach the top notes of the harp I couldn't, because
the opened grille had gobbled up all available elbow room. There was
a moment of embarrassment for everyone, and something akin to
terror for me, while proceedings were halted and stool, chair, harp and
nervous nun were all re-positioned. But in spite of that the evening

was a success and the singing of various local non-Catholic choirs enjoyable.

As a result of listening to my album with Lady Abbess and our subsequent conversation, my interest in singing with the harp started to revive. Now I felt willing to start again, and took my harp out of its cover in the attic, where it had safely waited, observing the rule of silence for almost eight years. I started re-stringing it in my free time.

Just about then the French Benedictine monk Dom Jean le Clerc came to visit us to give talks. Here was a singularly joyful man, at times patently drunk with the Spirit of the Lord and radiating godliness. During one of his talks he recited:

> I danced in the morning when the world was begun*
> And I danced in the moon and the stars and the sun
> And I came down from Heaven and I danced on the earth
> At Bethlehem I had my birth.
>
> *Chorus:*
> Dance, then, wherever you may be
> I am the Lord of the Dance, said he
> And I'll lead you all wherever you may be
> And I'll lead you all in the dance, said he.
>
> I danced for the scribe and the Pharisee,
> But they would not dance and they would not follow me.
> I danced for the fishermen, for James and John
> They came with me and the dance went on.
>
> *Chorus*
>
> I danced on the Sabbath and I cured the lame
> The holy people said it was a shame.
> They whipped and they stripped and they hung me high
> And they left me there on a cross to die.
>
> *Chorus*
>
> They cut me down and I leap up high
> I am the Life that will never, never die.
> I'll live in you if you'll live in me
> I am the Lord of the Dance, said he.
>
> *Chorus*

* 'Lord of the Dance', © Sydney Carter, 1963, reproduced by kind permission of Stainer & Bell Ltd.

Dance, then, wherever you may be
I am the Lord of the Dance, said he
And I'll lead you all wherever you may be
And I'll lead you all in the dance, said he.

The words bowled me over, for they succinctly articulated the things that mattered most to me. A million bells were set ringing inside me. Those words emphasized so beautifully what I think Christianity is all about: the unavoidable presence of the Cross transformed by the certainty and joy of the Resurrection. When I discovered later on that the words were set to music, I could hardly wait to get at the song and adapt the piano accompaniment for the harp.

For several years the 'Mount Street Master Tapes' had sat in the basement of the Dublin studio gathering dust. I was too preoccupied with other far more important things to give them any thought. I had arranged for my father to look after all my business affairs, including my income from royalties, until such time as I could officially sign everything over to him at the time of my Solemn Profession. In the meantime, all my income went to my father to do with as he wished. I considered it to be no longer mine. A number of record companies, one of which was Vanguard, the Joan Baez and Odetta label, were keen to release the material on the 'Mount Street Master Tapes' but they wanted to be selective about what they'd use and I felt strongly that the material shouldn't be chopped and changed at the discretion of someone I did not know. They also wanted to control the art-work on the cover. My fear was that they might wish to exploit my monastic situation. Over the next few years, beyond the walls of my sequestered world, this hassle over the 'Mount Street Master Tapes' dragged quietly on.

By around 1970 the business of the tapes was becoming tiresome and distracting and an unavoidable correspondence was eating into my precious time, so much so that Lady Abbess decided I had better listen to them myself and find out what the fuss was all about. She also felt that they should be available as records for people to hear and enjoy. I contacted John Nice, a professional friend and music publisher in London, to see if he could help by bringing equipment to Stanbrook so that we could listen to them. He explained that this was not possible as they could only be played on special machines available in recording studios. So Lady Abbess decided that I had better go to London to hear them. I very much wanted to bring Sister Raphael with me for the sake of getting a second, less subjective opinion. I felt strongly that Sister Raphael would be indispensable for several reasons, as indeed she proved to be. She was musical, a singer herself, sympathetic towards my work and had shown from her pertinent observations about my records after she'd listened to them that she also possessed a knowledge and understanding of the technical side of the production of records, something which I lacked. Not only was she one of my closest friends, but she was also a good organizer. When I asked Lady Abbess if she would allow Sister Raphael to accompany me she was very reluctant at first, but later agreed and sought the necessary permission for both of us. When the leave came through, I approached Sister Raphael. She was very willing to accompany me but asked, 'Why me?'

'Because if needs be, you can be bossy,' I said. 'And you may be called upon to exercise that trait.'

In London, we were graciously received at Decca House by John Nice, taken to lunch and then into the studio. The deference with which we were treated was, I suspect, mixed with curiosity. It must be rare to have two nuns in black maxis quietly invading the Decca recording studios. Sister Raphael gathered from the chance remark of one of the technicians that the studio we were assigned was not a very good one. Adopting an authoritative, nay, a bossy tone, Sister Raphael made it known that we wanted the very best facilities and in no time had them book a top quality studio for the following morning.

After hearing all the tapes Sister Raphael compiled pages of detailed notes, which were enormously helpful. Her assistance was invaluable, as I had known it would be. Someone in Decca had done a very bad job of reprocessing the original mono tapes for stereo. This had been the root of much of the trouble. Now Philip Wade, another of the Decca engineers, very kindly offered to re-do the job properly. John Nice put me in contact with Mervyn Solomon in Belfast, whose company, Emerald Records, had a tie-up with Decca, and the records were eventually released as *Mary O'Hara's Ireland* in 1973, *Mary O'Hara's*

Scotland in 1974 and *Mary O'Hara's Monday, Tuesday – Songs for Children* in 1977.

There was one more piece of business to be attended to before returning to Stanbrook. Photographs would be needed for the sleeves, and we hoped that the studio in Wigmore Street, where I'd had photographs taken around 1960, would still have the negatives. When we got there we found it had changed hands. We didn't exactly receive a warm welcome from the new owner, whose first words were: 'What have you come to beg for?' The hostility was humiliating.

I remained silent and Sister Raphael, with a cool, businesslike air, took over. Ignoring his remark, she explained our reason for coming, finishing with: 'These photographs were taken some years ago. Of course, she was not in her present disguise then.'

It had been an eventful two days and we'd achieved a lot, but we were both very relieved to find ourselves on the train heading back to Stanbrook. We had been out of our element. Stanbrook was where we belonged.

As soon as I was Solemnly Professed, my father went off to work in the US. Every now and then, a particularly lovely autumn leaf, indigenous to whatever part of North America he was in, would arrive from him in a letter. He would pick them up on his rambles, press them and send them on to me. They were so attractive that I began sticking them onto cards and using them as markers in my choir books. One day Dame Hildelith, the Printer who had seen my leaves, asked me if I'd join forces with her and produce some leaf cards for the annual display of the handmade gifts from members of the community for Lady Abbess on her Feast Day, and I agreed. However, shortly after that, Dame Hildelith had to drop out of the project because of other commitments, so reluctantly I continued on my own. Eventually the finished leaf cards went on display among all the other community gifts. It was a lovely surprise to discover that not only did Lady Abbess like them, but so did other people including the Cellarer, who asked if I'd produce more for sale in the monastery shop. So I went on happily making leaf-cards in my free time, little thinking that it was to develop into a fascinating hobby.

To me each leaf I worked with was a new source of wonder because each was a unique creation and something living. The combinations of leaf and paper were myriad. I was in the enviable position of having access to off-cuts, and sometimes whole sheets of what must have been some of the most beautiful hand-made papers in the world, from Japan to England. My sources of supply were all within the monastery walls, and contributions came from the printing room, where they also did Fine Printing, the scriptorium, the bindery and the artists' studio. Besides hand-made paper in white and in various colours, shades and textures, and Japanese veneer, I was also given good quality machine-made papers, sometimes hand-dyed. Soon it became the most fascinating work I've ever done.

Eventually, as the work expanded, I was given a special cell to work in, which I called my 'Leafy Bower', and was also provided with a table, shelves and a guillotine for cutting paper. It was absorbing and enjoyable work. Sometimes I referred to them as my Zen cards.

'And the leaves shall be for the healing of the nations,' says the Book of Revelations. There was a healing property in the stillness that working with leaves generated. One prayed that the leaves, through their beauty, would bring moments of inner peace to those who received them. As I worked, I was reminded of the words of the leader of the Elves in Tolkien's *The Lord of the Rings:* '... for we put the thought of all that we love into all that we make.'

One day we had as a visitor an American psychiatrist named Harold Kaye, who had a practice in London. A patron of the arts, he had a standing order for the Fine Printing productions from the Abbey Press. As he was about to leave at the end of his visit, he expressed the wish to buy some Christmas cards. He was directed to the display in the shop and looked at the various printed cards. Seeing my small box of leaves he seized upon them and said excitedly: 'This is what I'm looking for.' Then he asked to see the person who made the leaf cards, saying he wanted to buy all that were available. Puzzled by all this, I went to the parlour as instructed and was introduced to a quiet, dignified, middle-aged man with the sort of inscrutable face that gives nothing away. But his words were enthusiastic and he began by asking me why I didn't sign the cards. Mystified, I asked why. He replied:

'Because each one is a work of art.' I felt flattered and very pleased. It didn't end there.

He ordered 150 cards for Christmas. Eagerly I set to and used all my free time to try and meet the order. By then I was making envelopes to match. He didn't seem to mind when I was short of the 150 by the time Christmas came, and was content to have the remainder later. He ordered more for Easter. He wrote to the printer that he liked his leaves so much that he couldn't part with most of them. He had a special cabinet built by another member of the community to house his beautiful Stanbrook books and also my leaf cards. All the cards I made for him were different, as I made a point of never repeating any one.

All this time the physical troubles were still present and I seemed unable to pull out of them. My appetite was still on the wane and I was sleeping badly. Duties that I had previously taken in my stride were becoming increasingly difficult. During Vespers one evening I had a particularly bad migraine attack and I had to leave church and go to my cell, where I became violently ill. Lady Abbess came to see me and for the first time I told her about my recurring headaches. She sent me to a homeopathic doctor, who diagnosed the headaches as migraine and gave me a course of treatment. He also diagnosed fibrositis and sent me to an osteopath by the name of Eric Twinberrow. Eric and his wife Jacqueline were to become my good friends. It was Jacqueline, a charming and vivacious Frenchwoman, who translated 'Scarlet Ribbons' into French for me and it's now on the album *Mary O'Hara Live at the Royal Festival Hall*.

During the course of conversation during my first treatment, details of my past emerged and Eric casually asked if any of my husband's poems had been set to music. This resulted eventually in my setting 'Among Silence', a prose poem of Richard's, to music. That, too, is on the Royal Festival Hall album.

But my health deteriorated even further. Very concerned, Lady Abbess arranged for a thorough medical examination. The result of this was that I was sent to a Benedictine monastery on the Isle of Wight for a complete rest. To my utter surprise, Lady Abbess told me to take the harp, encouraging me to sing and play again. The community there was loving and welcoming and had already been acquainted with my work prior to my entering Stanbrook. I gave a few recitals for them, brushed up on some of my repertoire and tried my hand at composing. These were pleasant days, but recovery was slow and it was a good two months before the authorities considered me sufficiently improved to return to Stanbrook. The sea air and the wholesome Jersey milk had partly restored my appetite, but sleeping still remained a problem. I had not yet fully unwound.

Back in Stanbrook I was very gradually eased into the monastic routine again. Lady Abbess, a woman of great compassion, had acquired a good deal of medical knowledge during the time before she was elected Abbess, when she worked in the Stanbrook infirmary. The Benedictine Rule is strict but never harsh, and, as I've already pointed out, Lady Abbess made every effort to see to it that the work-load was evenly distributed and that everyone had a reasonably balanced day with enough time for spiritual reading and prayer and sufficient physical rest for the body. The abbess now informed me that from now on, I must devote the afternoon manual labour period to practising singing and the harp.

Benedictines encourage the arts if they are in accord with *community* life. Obviously, in my case, as my husband Pat has pensively observed, the Abbess would have had to think long and hard if my expertise had been on the bagpipes.

In the morning I worked at making and mending the monastic habits with Sister Rosemary, whose friendship and keen critical mind were to be of such value to me in coming years. Soon I was back into the mainstream of monastic living. Once or twice on very special occasions I gave (but only when asked) a recital to the community, and I continued to build up my repertoire of God-songs, for these were the songs that interested me most. Among my papers I recently discovered the programme for one of those monastic recitals. I know the date exactly because it was written on the blank side of a local government voting paper. We nuns wasted nothing.

After about a year I had a sufficient number to constitute an album, and I started to think about the possibility of recording them some day. I discussed this with Lady Abbess, and she thought it would be a good idea, so I approached John Nice once again. He pondered the matter for a time. After some correspondence he decided that I should go ahead with the recording and that he would make all the necessary arrangements. Lady Abbess obtained permission for me to leave the enclosure for three days, and in August 1974, when I had all the material ready, I travelled to London.

It was very warm weather and midday London was full of noise, swarming crowds and traffic fumes – an uncomfortable contrast with my sequestered life in rural Stanbrook. I was being driven by John and Connie McEvoy, and in the midst of London traffic, as we started on our way out to Wimbledon where I was to stay for two nights, I was very sick and vomited almost non-stop for an hour into a plastic bag with which Connie had the foresight to arm herself. On top of this a monstrous migraine made the journey well-nigh unbearable. I was staying at the Ursuline convent and as soon as I arrived I went to bed, but despite the kind ministrations of Sister Infirmarian, I had a sleepless afternoon and night. I was feeling somewhat better next morning and after breakfast went off to the studio. The recording took two whole days. Side one consists of secular love songs, a mixture of traditional and art songs ending with Richard's poem 'Eros', and side two has God-songs on it. It was released under the title *Mary O'Hara: Recital*.

Despite the debilitating effects of all the sickness on the previous day, my stamina was such that I managed to do the recording successfully without a hitch.

After two nights in London I was glad to be back in Stanbrook and in the silence of my own cell. For some time I had again been physically at a very low ebb, and, although I was availing myself of every opportunity for rest, my health did not seem to be improving. I was losing weight and I had little appetite for food

It was now almost two years since I'd been away for a rest. I looked poorly, or so I was told. As one elderly nun put it: 'Darling Sister Miriam, I look at you across the choir and there you are like a lily among the roses.' At times Lady Abbess sent for me or came to my cell saying: 'I'm very worried about you, Sister Miriam. How are you feeling?' Answering her questions I was able to tell her that now every day was a constant strain and struggle. Things that went against the grain, but which, hitherto, I was able to ride, so to speak, were getting – and staying – on top of me. I was exceptionally jumpy, reacting acutely to the slightest sudden sound or movement, and there were nights when I didn't sleep at all.

Deeply concerned, Lady Abbess once again arranged for a thorough medical examination. Two doctors examined me and gave me various tests. The verdict was that I was suffering from severe physical and nervous exhaustion and once again needed complete rest away from my normal monastic routine. I dreaded the prospect, as my previous two-month break had not really solved anything. Out of the blue one of the doctors said: 'How do you feel about continuing with the monastic life?' I was stunned, and for about a minute couldn't say anything. Throughout all the times I had been sick, the idea of leaving the monastery had never for a moment entered my head. When I recovered the power of speech, I replied: 'I've always found it difficult, but I've no intention of giving it up.'

My first reaction was to go immediately to Lady Abbess and report what had happened, but she was away at a monastic conference and would not be back for some time. During the following days I prayed and thought about everything the doctor had said. Very gradually I was beginning to see that the doctor's suggestion about leaving merited serious consideration. I discussed the whole matter separately with two of my closest friends in the community, who knew me better than anyone else there, apart from the Abbess.

When Lady Abbess returned, I told her all that had happened and of my realization that I should leave. Lady Abbess, ever solicitous about my well-being, patiently listened to my story. After I'd finished, she gently asked: 'Does this mean that you are asking to be dispensed from your vows?' This was probably her way of reminding me of the gravity of what I was contemplating doing.

I answered: 'Yes.'

She said that if I felt sure I was doing the right thing, might it not be wiser to ask for a year's exclaustration (living outside the monastery, but still a member of the Order) before making the final break? I agreed. She then asked me if there was any particular person I would like to talk to before she finally wrote away for permission for exclaustration. When I mentioned Father Jock Dalrymple, who was known to both of us, she readily agreed.

Jock came to see me. Ironically, it was Scomo's funeral that made it possible for Jock to be in the country and available at that time.

I suspect dear Scomo had a hand in this for I felt the loving concern of our mutual friend had not ended with his death. After a lengthy discussion with Jock I felt relieved and happy, for he firmly endorsed my decision to leave. When I said to him: 'But what about my Solemn Vows?'

Without any hesitation, Jock said simply: 'You became a Consecrated Widow; you never became a Benedictine Nun.'

Added to all that, the loving support of Sister Rosemary and Sister Raphael and the fact that they, too, concurred with my conclusion that I should leave, meant much to me and strengthened me. It is no easy matter after twelve years to leave a monastery that one expected to live in for the rest of one's life. Having reached my final decision, all the anguish had melted away and was replaced by an extraordinary sense of peace and, above all, a torrent of inner gratitude that words simply fail to describe.

The Cellarer always kept in the attic some secular clothes, cast-offs of those who entered and stayed. And from these, on the day before I left, we got together an acceptable outfit that would do for the time being. Lady Abbess could not do enough for me. With her characteristically maternal foresight she had even made an appointment for me at the hairdresser. It was not until after Lady Abbess had announced to the community that I was leaving and people came individually to say good-bye, that I realized how strong the bonds of affection were between us. A letter from the Cellarer to my father confirms this.

> Stanbrook Abbey
> Callow End, Worcester
> 7th November, 1974

Dear Mr. O'Hara,

... I am glad of having this opportunity of writing to you. It must have been a shock to you to hear that Mary had gone to Cambridge, but I would like you to know that she is very dearly loved by every single member of the community — and I think loves us all in return. Like you, we only desire her peace and happiness and we can trust the Lord to hear our prayers. And you, of course, are still part of our family even while she is away.

> Yours affectionately
> Sr. Gertrude
> Cellarer

On Saturday afternoon, 12th October 1974, I said good-bye to Stanbrook. I left with Lady Abbess's blessing. I have no regrets. I treasure every hour of those twelve years and would not have exchanged them for anything in the world. Though I emerged from Stanbrook physically depleted, I felt spiritually invigorated and incalculably enriched. I knew that the road back to full vitality and health would not be easy, but with God's help I was prepared for whatever the future might hold.

A friend of mine, the calligrapher John Smith, with whom I had become acquainted during my years in Stanbrook, sent me the following quotation. His beautiful calligraphy is written over the shadow of a harp and, in the circumstances, it proved to be very apposite. Song was once more about to take over my life, though I had no intimation of this at the time.

> Close by the hilltop stood a cairn,
> and each traveller as he passed
> laid some token by.
> Some a stone, some a flower
> and some a song.
> And the stones fell to dust
> and the flowers withered,
> but the songs,
> the songs laughed and cried
> and swept into the sky
> for evermore.
>   ANON.

CHAPTER 13

Back Into the World

O N MONDAY MORNING, John Ginger, a writer friend of mine, drove me to the hairdresser, and from there on to Cambridge. John was the first of a string of kind friends whose generosity and understanding was to help me get back on my secular feet again. He delivered me safely to the Bennetts' home in Adams Road. Jack Bennett had moved from Magdalen College, Oxford, to Magdalene College, Cambridge, to succeed his friend C.S. Lewis as professor of Medieval and Renaissance Literature.

It wasn't an easy time for Gwyneth to have me. There had been illness in the family which was the cause of strain and anxiety but she coped nobly and did her best to make me comfortable. I think my inevitable bewilderment and consequent inability to make small decisions was something of a trial to her at times, but she was genuinely concerned that I should be my old self again, as soon as possible. Pragmatist that she was, Gwyneth told me to go shopping and open a bank account the morning after I arrived. My shopping list read: tights, bra, slip, open bank account, cleansing cream, seek out hairdresser, Eden Lilly for skirts (tweed), suede coat, stamps, notepaper and envelopes, tweezers, paper hankies, umbrella. These, I must have deemed, were my immediate needs.

I was accompanied by a French girl, who was staying with the Bennetts at the time. With my friend, John Ginger, I'd felt protected and secure because I knew that he understood what I was going through and the difficulties I was facing readjusting to the outside world. But it was different with Veronique. There was no communication between myself and this sixteen-year-old schoolgirl, for she had little English and could not be expected to be sensitive to my particular situation. I felt disorientated. To open an account in the bank I had to give my signature. Trying to control the pen was well nigh impossible. Some time ago I had occasion to see that sample signature and I was awed by the great tension evidenced. It was barely legible. From the bank I went to one of the big stores to buy clothes. As soon as we arrived at the skirt department Veronique breezed off downstairs saying she'd meet me there in a little (unspecified) while. After some time I decided on a skirt and moved across to the underwear section. While I was deliberating over some items, I felt a frightening sense of panic take hold of me. I was breaking out in a cold sweat and felt utterly exhausted, longing to sit down. But there were no chairs in sight and I feared that, if I sat on the floor, people might think I was a nutcase. If I went off to look for a chair, Veronique might return, find me gone, and leave. And I didn't know how to make my way back to the Bennetts' house. Desperately I prayed that Veronique would come back. Just as I'd reached the stage where I thought I couldn't hold out any longer, she turned up. I said nothing, for neither her English nor her understanding could have coped, and I followed her out of the shop. Walking back through the town and out to Adams Road, I had the uncanny sensation of not being in command of my feet.

In the security and shelter of her house I told Gwyneth about my weird and frightening experience. I voiced the thought that the antidepressants which had been prescribed for me while I was in Stanbrook might in some way, if not directly, be responsible. Wasting no time, Gwyneth whisked me off to her own GP. Briefly I relayed my case history to her, ending with the words: 'If you think these tablets are the cause, I'm ready to stop taking them.'

The doctor put out her hand and took the bottle. The doctor who had prescribed these tablets had warned me not to attempt to stop taking three per day for at least six weeks, no matter how well I felt. But I gave them up that very day in Cambridge and have never touched them or their like since. There was no repeat of the stark panic.

My friend, Adrian Hastings, was at that time living at and working from St Edmund's House, a few roads away. During a concert one evening Adrian dropped a veritable bombshell by offering to arrange a recital for me at St Edmund's House. Alarmed at the prospect,

I made every sort of excuse. It was too soon; I wasn't well enough yet; I needed more practice; wouldn't it be better to wait and do some work in RTE in Dublin first, perhaps in the spring? But Adrian overrode all these specious arguments and eventually, with many misgivings, I allowed him to go ahead. He arranged the recital for some time in December, before term ended.

Early in November my father telephoned to say he was to undergo a serious exploratory operation for suspected cancer. I flew at once to Dublin, initially staying with my sister Joan whose house was adjacent to the hospital. It was a time of great anxiety and, for a while, the outcome of the operation had by no means been certain. The growth was discovered to be malignant, but the operation was a success.

During that visit I moved around a bit, staying a day or two at a time with different people and renewing old friendships. While I was staying with Michael Garvey and his wife, Mercedes Bolger, Gay Byrne, presenter of the 'Late Late Show' phoned to ask if I'd appear on his programme the following Saturday. I'd never seen the show and was very reluctant to take part. Michael – who was RTE Controller of Programmes at that time – and I debated the matter for a long time. Gay said I must let him know my decision by eight o'clock on Saturday morning. The 'Late Late Show' goes out live and is the most popular programme on Irish Television. Eventually, after considerable inner struggle, I agreed to appear. In conversation with my husband Pat thirty years later, Michael said to him: 'You don't lead Mary down to the water's edge. You throw her in off the deep end.'

Michael drove me to the studio in virtual silence as I steeled myself for the ordeal ahead. Gay did a probing, fairly lengthy interview touching on my life in the monastery; why I went in and why I came out and what my plans were for the future.

I sang 'The Quiet Land of Érin', which had become my theme song before I went into the monastery. The viewers' response throughout Ireland was so favourable that I was invited to return the following week, which I did, and sang two more songs. Strangers stopped me in the street to tell me how glad they were that I was back. It was exceedingly encouraging and heart-warming to receive such a welcome. Indeed I was invited on for a third time before returning to England.

This unplanned return to singing took place amidst daily visits to my father in hospital. He recovered quickly in the capable hands of David Lane, the gifted surgeon. He's also an accomplished oboist, who at one time played with the Radio Éireann Symphony Orchestra. The twin gifts of healing and music go well together.

During this period I spent a few days with Gay Byrne and his wife Kathleen Watkins in their house in Howth overlooking Dublin Bay. They could not have been more welcoming and helpful about all sorts of things, eager to get me back on my feet again.

Despite the success of the TV appearances, I still was not at all sure that I wanted to take up singing again; certainly not so soon. My intention was to rest and get well again over a period of some months. That I had to earn my living was obvious; it was only common sense to try to do so by singing, as I had already successfully done before I went into the monastery.

As soon as my old producer friend, Ciarán MacMathúna, a soft-spoken, self-effacing man, heard that I was back in circulation, he offered me radio work. Several times during the next two or three years I recorded songs for inclusion in his tremendously popular Sunday morning programme, 'Mo Cheól Thú'. Ciarán's soporific voice introduced the various items of music, poetry and song. 'Mo Cheól Thú' was generally confined to Irish material, but I often included English songs, Elizabethan songs and 'god-songs' and some of my own compositions among my contributions. Ciarán must have had some complaints because I was told that he once announced: 'Any song Mary O'Hara sings is an Irish song.' I also recorded numerous fifteen-minute special programmes for Ciarán and RTÉ.

A couple of days after the 'Late Late Show' I flew to England to see friends. First I visited Peter Levi at Oxford. After twelve years Peter had lost his attenuated El Greco look and was heavier in build, but he still had his dark good looks and his fine head of thick black hair. While I was in Stanbrook, at my request, he'd written verses for me called 'The Clown', which I'd set to music. It eventually went on my Chrysalis album, In Harmony. The clown concept was one which had long fascinated me. In the Edinburgh days, that 'grave-merry man' Scomo and I had talked about it.

Over dinner Peter and I talked about doing some more songs together. We decided that any subject could be considered for a song, when along came the waiter bearing our first course, which was snails. We looked at each other.

'Snails?' said Peter.

'Why not?' said I.

Not long afterwards he sent me 'The Snail' which eventually I set to music, and it's now on my Chrysalis album, *Music Speaks Louder than Words* and on *Live at Carnegie Hall,* as well as in my *Travels With My Harp* voice and harp collection.

A friend drove me to visit Joyce Grenfell in London. During my time in Stanbrook, Joyce and I had kept in touch, and that summer of 1974 she had written sleeve-notes for the *Mary O'Hara: Recital* album. She received me warmly and we talked for a long time. She'd only just retired from the stage and while I was with her she phoned her ex-agent, who had started out on her own, and arranged a meeting between us. Joyce was enthusiastic about my re-starting a career and predicted that I had another good twenty-five years of song left in me. This was especially encouraging since Sydney MacEwan had advised me against it, saying I should train to be a music teacher because there was no audience for my sort of singing any more. It is amazing how often over the years I've heard this same opinion expressed but, just as often, the same songs push through again just as daffodils do in the spring. I believe it is due to their uniqueness. Before I left, Joyce took me to her wardrobe and presented me with two beautiful full-length Thai silk designer stage dresses and some beads, which she didn't intend ever to wear again.

Joyce Grenfell's encouragement and touching concern continued even during the last few months of her life, when unknown to most of us, she was dying of cancer. After she attended one of my concerts at the London Palladium, she came back-stage. I had not mentioned I was having problems with Jo Lustig's management but she had somehow sensed my distress and wrote to me at great length about it all. She was a pillar of strength, a true friend.

While I was in Stanbrook I'd had a brief correspondence with Lord Moyne, who, learning from a mutual friend that I was there, had written to invite me to sing at the Salisbury Arts Festival in 1975. At the time, of course, this was out of the question. Now that I was outside of the monastery, I contacted him and received a very enthusiastic and warm reply, assuring me that the engagement at the Salisbury Festival still stood and inviting me to Knockmaroon, his Irish country estate.

It so happened that I had agreed to take part in a concert, which included other musicians, to mark the publication of a harp book by Nancy Calthorpe (Nancy had taught me the piano when I was about nine years old). It was a private concert before an invited audience and I was asked if I wished to invite anyone special. Knowing Lord Moyne liked my work, I gave his name to the organizers and they invited him and his family. Lord Moyne was the poet Bryan Guinness, a man of exquisite manners and great gentleness in whom there was not a vestige of guile or arrogance. If asked, he'd have said he was not a believer, but in my opinion he was a Christian to the core.

A few days before the concert, my very good friend, Caroline Mahon (we had done Beauty Culture together when I was seventeen), brought me along to meet Mary O'Donnell, well-known as a dress designer on both sides of the Atlantic. By the time I'd left her boutique, I was the happy recipient of a blouse of white, hand-made lace and a skirt of peacock blue Thai silk. On the morning of the concert I purchased a pair of silver, sling-back evening sandals with high heels. That evening, as I walked towards the stage, I found to my consternation that the sling-back part kept slipping off my heel. Keeping my shoes on more or less by means of sheer willpower compounded the tension that is normally part of a public appearance and slowed down my progress. As I settled myself on stage, I caught a glimpse of Cearbhall Ó'Dálaigh, then President of Ireland, seated directly opposite me in the front row. We were old acquaintances since my pre-Stanbrook days, and his warm smile and welcoming nod encouraged me on this, my first re-appearance in thirteen years on a concert platform.

When I first knew Cearbhall Ó'Dálaigh, he was a judge, a noted linguist and a Gaelic scholar. He was a descendant of the poet and musician who composed 'Eibhlín a Rún' and was deeply interested in all aspects of Irish culture. After the concert we had a pleasant reunion. Several years later I was very honoured when he invited me to accompany him on an official State Visit to Japan. Unfortunately, my touring commitments did not permit me to take up the offer.

On New Year's Eve, Lord Moyne collected me from my sister's house to dine at Knockmaroon.

Lady Moyne had been at the concert, but it was only now at Knockmaroon that I met her for the first time. She was a strikingly handsome woman with the loveliest laugh I have ever heard. I think one might hear its like in Lothlorien. She was an ardent lover of children and horses. Of her nine children, Tamsy, Kieran, Erskine, Catriona, Fiona and Mirabel were there that night. After dinner I sang in the drawing room and Tamsy drove me back. It was a memorable evening, and I was to meet the rest of the family and to get to know them all better during the next few years.

My father was making very good progress and early in January he was discharged from the private convalescent home. It was time for me to return to England.

I had consulted various people in the music and entertainment worlds, both in Ireland and in England and the consensus of opinion was that, if I wanted to re-establish my singing career again, my best bet was to base myself near London and near Heathrow. For a year after I left Stanbrook I received a monthly allowance from the monastery, and there was a small income from my record royalties. Money was slowly starting to come in again from the odd concert, TV and radio work in Ireland and elsewhere. Once it became known that I was available for engagements, old radio and TV producer friends in the UK were getting in touch.

The recital at St Edmund's in Cambridge was a success, and gave me the added confidence I needed to go on singing. Lord Moyne invited me to join the family and their friends for the local hunt ball in Wiltshire and to bring my harp. I travelled with it as far as London, but found it too heavy in my weakened condition and had to leave it with a friend.

Dinner at Biddesden was splendid, but the hunt ball itself was unexciting – though I love dancing. Nobody asked me to dance apart from Lord Moyne. He knew that I was looking for a place to live and generously offered the use of the Gardener's Cottage on his estate. I considered the matter for a couple of weeks and then decided to accept the offer and moved from Cambridge to Biddesden on the Wiltshire border towards the end of January 1975. I stayed with the family at Biddesden House for over three months while waiting to move into the Gardener's Cottage in the farmyard. During this time I spent a couple of hours each day in the cottage doing a bit of house painting and decorating. I went up and down to London fairly frequently.

My old friend Fred Macaulay, senior Gaelic producer in the BBC in Scotland, asked me to do some radio broadcasts from Glasgow. I was also preparing more programmes for RTE radio.

There hadn't been an opportunity to relax thoroughly since leaving Stanbrook and I felt a great need to get away where there was quiet, sun and sea, preferably a Greek island. Peter Levi suggested the tiny island of Antiparos, so I arranged a three-week holiday there late in March 1975. It would have been preferable to have had a companion, but all my friends were working, so I went ahead and booked a holiday for myself. The sum total of my knowledge of Greek was *kyrie eleison,* so travelling in Greece wasn't all that simple.

Armed with a Greek phrase book and, hoping for the best, I flew to Athens where I stayed the night. Next morning I set out for the ferry to the Cyclades. No one spoke a word of English and I couldn't read their language, so I had no way of knowing which island to get off at. My phrase book didn't help. Having a cabin, I slept for a little while because I knew I would be a good twelve hours at sea. When we started calling at the islands I tried to find out which one was mine. Nobody understood what I was trying to ask. My attempts at communication must at times have resembled charades, but I eventually found a lawyer with enough English to understand me. When we reached Paros he called me, and together we made a dash down the crowded pier to catch the small motor-launch, in which he deposited me and my luggage. The boat took off immediately for Antiparos. Within half an hour I was lodged in the only hotel on the island.

I was the only visitor on Antiparos. When I wasn't swimming, reading, or skimming stones by the water's edge, I walked for hours across the rocky hills which were brightly covered with exquisite tiny spring flowers. I became friends with the Athenian wife of the local doctor and we went swimming together. Breakfast was in the fishermen's cafe beside the wharf, and the rest of my meals I took in the kitchen of the hotel owner's family house. My appetite revived and I came back to England in much better shape than when I'd left.

Shortly after I returned from Greece, I moved into the Gardener's Cottage. At first I lived, practised music, entertained, ate and slept in the larger of the two rooms upstairs. It didn't matter how loudly I sang or played, or at what hour, for there was nobody to be disturbed.

I was content to do work as it came along, unplanned and unsought, and it seemed to me I was getting quite enough to keep me as busy as I wanted to be. A large part of each day was spent polishing up old material and learning new stuff. I was anything but idle.

It was at this time that I met Pat O'Toole (now my husband). 'An untetherable bird' was the very succinct appraisal of him once given to me by his friend the Irish poet John Montague. A free spirit he most certainly is and a very colourful character. Already acquainted with my work before we ever met, Pat now took a keen interest in helping to get me re-established again. Shortly before we met, Pat had been brought home seriously ill from Africa where he had been a missionary for eight years. While there he set up and was for some years Headmaster of a Co-Educational Moslem High School and lived, incidentally, in the so-called 'palace' of the Moslem Emir of Lafiagi, who had ten wives. Back in Ireland Pat had edited a religious magazine, trained as a radio and TV producer in Dublin, and had done some freelance journalism on the side. When I first met him he was, as he explained it, 'killing time' working in a parish near Stonehenge, Wiltshire – a suitable location, he opined, for the likes of him, a disengaged missionary aged thirty-six, vaguely searching for a new meaningful role in society.

Our first meeting was quite prosaic. Every Sunday I borrowed Lady Moyne's 'sit up and beg' bike – a war-time relic no longer in use – and cycled the three miles to Mass in the nearby village of Ludgershall. Pat, as the parishioners called him – though he always signed himself Pádraig – was chatting to a group of teenagers in front of the hut acting as a church. I was briefly introduced as Mrs Selig and went on my way. After a few weeks I got to know him and the other parishioners better and one day, mentioning that I was 'moving house', so to speak, wondered if anyone would like to give me a hand to shift some furniture. Pat immediately offered to help and asked when?

'Any day now,' I replied.

Pat said that on the following Tuesday after he played squash with his army friend Seán Trodden they'd come over and help.

Tuesday I was upstairs practising for a BBC radio broadcast. Engrossed in my work, I did not hear the car driving into the yard or the knocking on the door but I heard the car horn. I put my head out the upstairs window and called to them as they were just leaving. They had driven seven miles from Amesbury. Pat rather testily wondered what it was that I was doing that I did not hear the knocking on the door. Shamefacedly I replied: 'I was practising.'

'Practising what?'

'A new song with the harp,' said I. A pregnant pause was followed by Pat's next question: 'Do you have any other name besides Mrs Selig?'

'Yes, Mary O'Hara,' said I. Another pause.

'Ah ... I saw your interview on Irish television some weeks ago and I can tell you that you did more good for the Church through that one interview than if you'd spent a lifetime as a nun.'

Obviously all was now forgiven.

That was how our friendship started. I made some tea. The furniture was moved, we touched on how my work was going and my visitors departed. I continued practising.

I hadn't occasion to talk to Pat again for some time. He enquired how my broadcasts with the BBC went. He asked me how my work was doing, did I have a manager and how I was going about finding work. Pat, as I was soon to find out, is a consummate organiser and I began to suspect that I was not impressing him with any organisational skills on my part.

'How many albums have you recorded?'

'Seven.'

'We had one of them in the seminary,' he said. 'We played it most Sundays. Do you have copies of all of them with you?'

'I don't have any.'

'Can they be purchased in the shops?'

'I don't know.'

'Do you have any flyers or brochures about your work?'

'No.'

'Do you have anything at all that tells about your music and work?'

There was a long pause when Pat, as he told me later, was wondering if he was talking to someone living in the real world.

'I have reviews of my concerts and of my recordings and TV programmes,' I explained, attempting to rescue my reputation. In fact the bundle of reviews was one of the few things that weren't discarded when I entered Stanbrook. Pat seemed more pleased and I agreed to lend them to him. At his suggestion, I agreed to go to the local record shop and order one copy each of my recordings. To my surprise they were still available after more than twelve years of publicity-less monastic seclusion. Before we parted, Pat thought it necessary to explain that, in his view, there were two things I urgently needed: 'One, you need a good manager, but finding the right one will take time and patience, and, two, you also immediately need a flyer or brochure explaining what you do and did. The reviews should supply the material for that.'

Within a week or so, I ran into Pat again as he talked to the young-sters outside the makeshift church. He handed me an A4 flyer. It was the first promo hand-out I ever studied, never mind having one myself.

'Have a read,' he said. 'If you like it, we can have a few hundred printed.'

As I read through he obviously saw the expression on my face change.

'What's the matter? Don't you like it?'

The brochure said very lovely things about my work but 'blowing one's own horn' is something anathema to me. I'd feel uncomfortable about circulating such a document. It sounded like boasting and I told Pat as much.

'For heaven's sake!' he said, 'This is what's called publicity. It is just quotes taken from the reviews you gave me. It is not you that is claiming this but the reviewers. This is how agents always promote their clients.'

I was not convinced and I was aware Pat was disappointed.

'Ah well,' he sighed, 'let's leave it then. I only tried to help.'

I gave him back the flyer but as we were parting he handed it back to me.

'Here, take it and try it out on Lord Moyne. If he says it is useless, then bin it.'

I showed the flyer to Bryan Guinness and he thought it was very good. He persuaded me that I should get more copies printed, so I telephoned Pat with the good news.

'I'm glad,' he said. 'I'll drop off three hundred copies at the cottage. I had them in the boot of the car all the time.'

'And what would you have done if I didn't get back to you?'

'Thrown them away, of course.'

Pat had used his own money to print these flyers and I knew he would have had little to spare.

His next step was to organise some charity concerts 'to get some useable quotes from current reviews', as he explained. Together with his friend, Sean Trodden, he organized a concert at St Edmund's Art Centre in Salisbury, and another in Bath. All the reviews were more than generous. The proceeds from one concert went to the homeless and from the other to a favourite charity of Pat's back in Africa. Pat's efforts on my behalf made my comeback to singing much easier than it might otherwise have been.

In my youth in Dublin, I knew of nobody who had an agent. Engagements just dropped through the letter-box. I wanted to keep my independence but friends kept suggesting I should have an agent or manager. Times had changed, they said. Understandably, the interest of people like agents is centred on their own financial gain and there is a tendency for them to *push*. What pleases them most, and quite understandably so, is to work with someone who has talent but who is also hungry for success, if not exactly possessed by greed, either for money or stardom.

Pat was on the look out for potential managers. One name that kept cropping up in the media was that of Jo Lustig. Pat researched him thoroughly and found he had a mixed press. Friends in the media that I consulted counselled me against Lustig. One of those was Robert Ponsonby, comptroller of BBC Radio 3, for whom I had done some recent radio work in the Heritage series. He had been director of the Edinburgh International Festival in 1956 when I was the guest in 'Pleasure of Scotland'. Over lunch, he pointed out that with Lustig I might be led along an unsuitable avenue. Pat was still very much in favour of Lustig. Eventually I wrote to Jo Lustig, sending him copies of reviews and Pat's recent flyer and asking if he could point me in the direction of a suitable agent or manager.

In the meantime, Pat had left for Canada. While there he found time to arrange a number of concerts, radio engagements and TV appearances for me. He also organised a few in the US. Pat has an astounding appetite for work, and his steady, unstinting support instilled in me a resolve to forge ahead. Apart from Lord Moyne, no one has done more to re-establish my career than he. To both of them I owe a debt of gratitude that I can never hope to repay. Whatever project Pat decides to undertake, he brings to it an enthusiasm, perseverance and energy that carries him along to its successful conclusion. I do believe it is in Pat's DNA to help people with no expectation of reward or favour returned. He never turns anyone away. I've seen this time and time again. When we were first introduced I found him very cheerful and charming and soon discovered he was the same with everyone he met or with whom he had dealings. Endowed with remarkable patience and self-restraint, he had ample opportunity to exercise these last two traits in particular in his dealings with me and my work.

Lord Moyne arranged for my appearances at a number of important venues, among which were the Salisbury Arts Festival and the Wexford Music Festival. John Paddy Browne, an authority on folk music, had been writing favourable reviews about my records from the beginning. Hearing that I was to take part in the Salisbury Festival in summer 1975 (he could hardly believe his ears), he arranged to interview me for the magazine *Folk Review*. That first meeting was the start of a warm friendship. John is another person who had strongly supported my return to music, doing everything in his power to get my name circulating again and letting me borrow at will from his prodigious record collection. He took great pains to produce an extremely tasteful, glossy brochure, and presented it to me before one of my visits to the US.

My first reappearance on BBC Television was from Scotland that summer of 1975 on 'McCalman's Folk'. The following summer I appeared on their programme again. That autumn I sang at the Newcastle-on-Tyne Arts Festival. My friend, Lucy Broughton, drove me there and back – this was Lucy's introduction to the rigours, the fun and the frustration of touring, for she was subsequently to become my personal assistant during my earlier tours of the UK and Ireland. Lucy, a mother of five, one of the most colourful characters I ever knew, took delight in flouting convention, and her good humour was infectious. Thoroughly English, she once told me that her father was one of the last British Army sergeant majors in Ireland before that country's independence. Part of her early childhood was spent on Bere Island, off the south coast of Ireland. Lucy adored touring with me in

Ireland. She was unflappable in a crisis – of which there were plenty – like the time when she forgot to pack my stage shoes and I had to give a concert in my bare feet.

At Carnegie Hall early in 1976 I took part in 'The Best of Ireland', an event organized by Irish-Americans to commemorate the bicentennial of American Independence and celebrate the Irish contribution to American culture. Cyril Cusack, Peter O'Toole, Siobhan McKenna, Frank Patterson and others participated. The programme was televised.

In New York I met the instrumental folk group The Chieftains for the first time. We were all staying together at the Statler Hotel, Madison Square Garden: Peadar Mercier and Derek Bell shared the same room, and one day after rehearsals I went with them to look at Derek's harp box. I left my harp on Peadar's bed and the three of us went out. Next morning when I went to fetch my harp the following lines penned by Peadar were attached:

> Mary O'Hara
> Upon my made-up bed
> I laid your harp, Mary
> Upon my word!
> I was disturbed, a *chroí*,
> To see it resting there.
> For where this coming night
> Might I seek sweet repose,
> For those as susceptible as I
> Even an eiderdown, from *no éadtrom*,*
> Can frown at displaced imagery.
> As surely as my bed has springs
> As surely as your harp has strings
> As surely will I sit all night
> Voluntarily, Mary
> My pillow be your willowy form
> I'll be of this sweet madness shorn
> By early morn.
>
>   PEADAR

* The *'éadtrom'* refers to an RTÉ bilingual TV programme called 'Trom agus Éadtrom' (Heavy and Light), on which I appeared several times.

It was on the flight back from New York that I had a chat with Jo Lustig for the first time. He showed an interest in managing me but, beyond that, seemed in no hurry to commit himself.

Back in England after 'The Best of Ireland', I found work was piling up. I felt honoured when BBC Radio 3 approached me to do three programmes for their 'Heritage' series. Leaving the choice of material to me, I decided to do programmes on (1) Irish Traditional Songs, (2) Irish Art Songs, and (3) Elizabethan Songs. Three more times during the remainder of 1976, I went to the US and Canada for engagements in places as far-flung as Montreal and California. Of one concert in Toronto I have a lovely memento: an Inuit soap-stone carving, specially commissioned by Russ Kempton which he presented to me himself, on stage, at the end of that concert. A friend of Pat's, he had travelled all the way from Moose Factory in the frozen north, where he worked as a medical doctor among the native peoples.

I found myself going back and forth to Dublin appearing on television, recording radio broadcasts and giving concerts, sometimes in beautiful settings such as Slane Castle, where I shared the programme with Lord Moyne and Richard Murphy reading their poetry.

Through the autumn and winter of 1976 and into 1977, I travelled around Ireland, north and south, east and west, giving recitals in schools and public concerts in the evening for the Music Association of Ireland (MAI).

During these protracted visits to Ireland I usually stayed with Eibhlín Ní Chathailriabhaigh. Eibhlín, a retired civil servant, had a zest for living that would wear out many half her age. She was a Gaelic scholar and gave adult classes in the language. She was also secretary of *Cáirdre na Cruite*, the Harp Association of Ireland, and a dominant figure at every Celtic Congress.

Driving a battered Renault, Eibhlín accompanied me on the MAI tours round the country. We had a hilarious time and hugely enjoyed each other's company. We seldom arrived on time anywhere because Eibhlín was not exactly a speed merchant. She would say lovely fairy-tale things such as, 'Mary, I have a very definite feeling that this road is going somewhere,' when in actual fact we were sometimes cruising in the opposite direction to that intended, because some practical joker with a misguided sense of humour had decided to turn the signpost round. At that time I hadn't got my own driving licence, but the first time I had the pleasure of chauffeuring Eibhlín anywhere, a tree fell on the car, almost killing us both. It was in England. I was driving her and my father to Stanbrook. Considerable damage was caused to the vehicle, and it was a miracle that we were unhurt, but we managed to get some laughter even out of this.

Concerts and television work took me to France, Luxembourg, (staying at the Irish Embassy as guest of poet Val Ironmonger and his wife) Germany, and yet again across the Atlantic. The BBC television people came and did a documentary on me, and on Southern Independent Television I had a series of seven late-night programmes with Alec Taylor.

There was no shortage of work, and it was getting ever more difficult to keep up with the correspondence and organization that the business side of singing unavoidably entails.

CHAPTER 14

Reluctant Diva

I N 1977, after a year observing me in action – attending my performances, watching me on TV, etc – Jo Lustig offered to manage
my career. I signed a three-year contract. Jo had come to the UK
in the 1950s as publicity manager for Nat King Cole and decided to
stay. At one time or other he had managed performers like Jethro Tull,
Steeleye Span, The Chieftains, Ralf McTell, Julie Felix, Dana and
others. He was known to be a tremendously effective drum-beater but
there appeared to be an established pattern of his alienating people.
I was aware of all this. When I mentioned to Paddy Maloney of The
Chieftains that I was thinking of signing with Lustig his only comment was: 'He'll take you to the cleaners.' At the time I wasn't sure
what he meant.

Jo's first move was to secure a recording contract for me with
Chrysalis Records, in which as I found out later, he had a financial
interest. Living in the country can be idyllic, but for someone whose
work necessitates constant travel, rural life has its drawbacks. Having
struggled with taxis, trains and buses for a couple of years, Jo encouraged me to learn to drive and get my own car. Despite the predictions
of my friends I passed my test first time. I was jubilant. To commemorate the success, my instructor presented me with a Jubilee coin, and
we celebrated with mugs of coffee in a Salisbury cafe. Passing that
driving test first go did more for my ego than being told that my
album *Tranquility*, within about two weeks of its release, had gone
platinum (sold over a quarter of a million copies). I christened my new
car 'Marco the Red Dragon'. My new-found mobility enabled me,
among other things, to visit Stanbrook occasionally – not because of
any desire to return to monastic life, but because the friendships
I forged at Stanbrook are very precious to me.

The one event that gave the greatest single impetus to my work at this time was my appearance on the Russell Harty Show on London Weekend Television. What took place that night is best described by Russell Harty himself in an *Observer* article, which was subsequently reproduced on the sleeve of my Royal Festival Hall album and from which I take the liberty to reproduce an excerpt here:

> She agreed to talk to me on my programme. She also agreed to sing. I crept into the back of an empty studio to take her measure during rehearsal. It is always a profitable course of action to watch hardened technicians in their reactions to artists in rehearsals. These, on this day, were buzzing about their normal activities until Mary started her first song. The floor manager, who normally has to shout above the din for order and silence, was relieved of this task. There was a natural, or more precisely, unnatural attention to this woman. When I emerged from the back gloom to say hello, I felt enough confidence from her warmth to ask if she would sing two songs, since one would be short changing me and the rest of the world. She chose a little Gaelic song about two cuckoos, two lovers, who echo their plans and their joy. She sang it so beautifully that, when she had finished, the entire studio put down their cables and lights and microphones and cheered. It was an astonishing moment. I was glad that it was rehearsal because it took me half a minute to find any sensible word to say to her.
>
> In the evening of that day, she came quietly to her chair and stormed her way into the heads and hearts of everyone. The next day my colleagues and I had seriously to think about opening a sub branch of the Post Office and hiring fresh staff to man switch-boards. The response was staggering.

The appearance on the Russell Harty Show provided invaluable publicity for my forthcoming concert at the Royal Festival Hall, London on 5th November 1977. As was the case with the 'Late Late Show' on RTE/Irish Television, I was invited back the following week and again a third time before the season ended. My new manager, Jo Lustig, was, of course, very pleased.

In the same week as Russell Harty, I was filmed and interviewed for the BBC 'Tonight' programme by David Lomax, who came to the cottage with a film crew and a jar of delicious honey from the bees he kept. To my astonishment the BBC had unearthed a snapshot of

Richard and me in deckchairs on the *Queen Elizabeth,* as we sailed to New York in 1956.

The Royal Festival Hall was my first major concert since leaving the monastery, and it was recorded live for a Chrysalis album. It sold very well and quickly 'went silver'.

The concert was sold out two weeks beforehand, and on the night itself the tension was heightened by the possibility of a power cut, which threatened to plunge the whole place into darkness at any moment. For this reason it was announced, before the concert began, that there would not be an interval, thus leaving me with just a few minutes in which to change dresses and proceed with the second half. Jo was justifiably over the moon about the way things were going and shortly before the concert began he put his head around the dressing room door to wish me well, he whispered: 'Mary, I'm off now, otherwise I'm going to cry.'

And I'm sure he meant it.

The period following the Royal Festival Hall concert was hectic, what with publicity for the new record, the London Weekend Television Special, my own half hour on BBC TV (shown on the same night as ITV), guest appearances on various TV and radio programmes and, in February, a concert tour of the UK that took in Dublin and Belfast. I lost track of the number of press, TV and radio interviews.

Lustig talked enthusiastically about his plans for the future. For him success in the UK was small fry. His planning was always meticulous and long-term and he had already started on America, where he wanted me to be. He asked me if I'd consider living in America for at least six months. He needed that much time to 'break me' there and I have no doubt but that he would have succeeded. But then again, he might not. I read in the newspapers that Hollywood was interested in the story, which at the time meant the autobiography, about which (as mentioned in the prologue to this book), I was becoming increasingly unhappy. Unfortunately and, probably most annoying for Lustig, I did not show any great joy or share his enthusiasm or plans for the future. I found it difficult to become enthusiastic about becoming rich or famous. In the eyes of Jo Lustig I was lacking in ambition. I now recognise how frustrating this would have been for any manager. But that is how I am made.

From the very outset I made it clear to the management that when I was on tour I would never sing two nights in a row unless it was in the same city, as was the case with my week at the London Palladium which started with my appearance on the Royal Variety Show. My main instrument was my voice and a delicate one at that. And travelling is tiring. I for one knew that I couldn't give of my very best if I was tired – and audiences deserve only the best a performer can give. Surely this is a form of ambition. So, on tour: concert only every second night. For the same reason I avoided doing publicity or interviews on the day of a concert. In fact I avoided all unnecessary speaking on the day of a concert, saving the voice for the evening performance. I also insisted that no tour be longer than six weeks. All this was agreed to by the management before I signed on. Extenuating circumstances always seemed to crop up but I refused to budge. It seemed to me that, like many successful entrepreneurs, Jo lived and breathed 'the music business'. All very commendable but I was getting the impression that he expected the people he managed, in this case me, to be similarly committed, like being at the other end of a phone 24/7 as they say, even during my holidays. It was after one such holiday when I briefly disappeared from Jo's radar screen that he accused me of not being serious about my work. On the contrary, I felt that I was being ultra serious about my work, conserving my voice and not jumping at every opportunity to increase my income.

Catching a cold is an occupational hazard facing every singer and can be particularly disastrous during a tour. As I've said, the singer's voice is her instrument. Using a damaged instrument, such as the vocal chords when one has a cold, not only detracts from the listener's enjoyment, but also risks causing long-term, and perhaps irreparable damage to the singer's voice. It was around this time, while appearing on one of James Galway's BBC TV programmes and battling with a cold, that a throat specialist was summoned by my management. Later, I was horrified to discover that the injection he gave me was in fact a steroid. I hadn't been consulted and, had I been, I'd have refused it. It was my manager who had given the OK.

It took nine weeks of rest, visits to the Harley Street specialist and a special trip to Dublin to consult with Sister Angela, my old singing teacher, before my voice got back to normal.

All my professional life, the core of my work had been my traditional material, especially the Gaelic songs. The amount of this material available is understandably limited and the audience for it is also some-what restricted. The big difference between my first Royal Festival Hall concert and all my previous work was the inclusion of songs known as Middle of the Road (MOR). I've forgotten what sparked off Jo Lustig's idea of including MOR material in my repertoire. It might have been my performance of Gordon Lightfoot's 'Song For a Winter's Night', with my own harp accompaniment, on a TV programme in the UK in 1976. I had come across Gordon Lightfoot's work during one of the many trips to Canada where Pat O'Toole, despite his own very busy life, had organised several TV appearances and recitals. The Chieftains were also performing on that same TV programme and Jo Lustig, their then manager, was in the audience. He evinced genuine surprise at my inclusion of that kind of song and told me so. Jo, not yet my own manager, was following my work closely and for all I can remember now, it may well have been that performance that triggered his notion that I should consider learning more contemporary songs of that genre. I was delighted with the suggestion and very willing indeed to have a go. For my Royal Festival Hall concert, Jo had assem-bled a group of five musicians – piano, guitar, base, woodwind, per-cussion – to accompany me. This was a big departure for me, who until then only sang sitting down accompanying myself on the Irish harp, or *a capella*. We decided to experiment with different combin-ations: voice, harp and the other instruments for some songs, whether traditional or MOR, and some without the harp. I concurred whole-heartedly and was very comfortable with the songs we eventually chose for that first venture. In fact I never objected to the inclusion of MOR as long as I was happy with the choice. I never sang a song I did not like or that expressed a sentiment with which I could not identify but on my second Chrysalis album, which came fast on the heels of *Live at The Royal Festival Hall*, due to the pressure of time, I felt a bit rushed about the choice of songs.

Quite out of the blue one day, apropos of nothing, Jo said to me: 'I'll never interfere with your repertoire.'

This took me by surprise, having assumed he'd never do so anyway. I thought no more about it. This was very early on in our association when relations were warm and easy. But 'interfering with my repertoire' turned out in fact to be the fly in the ointment, the fatal flaw that soured our hitherto amicable relationship. I went on tour almost immediately after my first Festival Hall concert and perhaps here is the place to attempt to explain my 'reluctance' to perform, which not everyone sympathised with or understood.

For me a forthcoming concert was always 'the dark cloud on the horizon'. I could never get eagerly excited about performing in public and this can be sometimes 'disappointing' to those behind the scenes who so enthusiastically spent time and energy setting up the event.

In fact they knew in Jo's office that the bigger the venue, the more depressing was the prospect before me. I can only describe it as fear – stage fright. In his office one day, Jo said to me with a smile: 'Now that the RFH is behind you, here is something new to be 'depressed' about: you are giving a concert at the Albert Hall on the 11th February.'

Actors have an expression: 'first-night nerves'. Not everyone can understand this 'shying away' from performing. But my older sister, the actress Joan, did. After seeing me in concert a few times, she said to me: 'Mel, I can see that for you every night is a 'first night'. If the nervous energy coming from you on stage could be measured, it would be weighed in tons.'

Whether on tour or not, the routine on a concert day was more or less this: in the morning, after my usual bout of callisthenics, I had breakfast, followed by vocal exercises, then harp exercises and finally a run through of that night's concert programme. Next, if at all possible I liked to play tennis or else have a brisk walk. From lunchtime on, I was incommunicado – relaxed, took a nap, washed my hair and got ready to go to the concert hall or theatre for the sound check. Two hours before the concert was due to start, I had a light meal consisting of a lightly boiled egg, a couple of slices of brown bread, toasted, and light tea or lemon and honey. I had been doing this since I first took part in concerts in my teens. However much I enjoyed dairy products, on tour they were out. They create phlegm, the bane of a singer's life. Lucy became expert at spiriting away the toast from the dining room after breakfast, and we generally travelled with a supply of free-range eggs, fresh lemons, or a bottle of lemon juice, a jar of honey and tea bags. This meal nourishes and sustains, but doesn't tax the

digestive system. I needed to have complete control over my dia-
phragm and abdominal muscles in order to deal with nervousness and
control my breathing. All my energies are concentrated on the
performance. In a full, two-hour concert (which included a twenty-
minute interval), I usually did twenty-five songs, half of which I sang
accompanying myself on the harp, whilst for the rest of the songs
I was joined by my accompanying musicians.

It was essential for me to have time to be totally alone just before
the concert begins, so that I could get myself inwardly together,
concentrated and attentive, my mind focused on what I was about to
do. Once the concert was over I was elated, relieved, and a sociable
person again.

I preferred not to know how many were in the audience or if someone I knew was there or if it was sold out. All hands were instructed
not to tell me. I can identify with two stories told by the accompanist
Gerald Moore in his autobiography *Am I Too Loud?* When Pablo
Casals, the renowned cellist, injured his hand severely in an accident,
his immediate reaction was: 'Thank God, I don't have to play [the
cello] any more.'

And the other story: Gerald Moore asked Dietrich Fischer-
Dieskau's little son if he too would like to be a world-famous singer
like his daddy.

'Oh no,' came the reply.

'Why?'

'It makes Daddy so unhappy.'

When an important sold-out concert at the Barbican, London, had
to be cancelled at the last minute because of my laryngitis, I sat at
home by the fire reading a book, secretly relieved.

Doing radio work or recording in the studio, one is invisible, as it
were, nonetheless nervous, but on stage one is totally exposed. I was
uncomfortably aware of this when I first started performing. There
was a subconscious sense of security sitting on a chair playing the harp.
It is difficult to imagine that in the very early days I could not bring
myself to sing the *a capella* songs standing up; I did so while sitting
on the chair. I eventually conquered that one.

In 1978 I took part in both the Royal Variety Show at the Palladium
and The Golden Gala – a Tribute to Queen Elizabeth The Queen
Mother. It was not to be my last performance for the Queen Mother.

Shortly afterwards, I was invited to give a private (voice and harp) performance for her after a dinner party in the town-house of a mutual friend. It was kept quiet even from my management to avoid any media attention or publicity. The Queen Mother spoke to me very graciously and thanked me, especially for the lovely songs in Gaelic. On the Royal Variety Show, my first song had been the Gaelic song *'Cucúin'* with the harp and afterwards Princess Margaret remarked how much she enjoyed the *'Cucúin'* with the echo effect at the end of each line. For the second song, 'Music Speaks Louder Than Words', I was accompanied by my five musicians. I always performed this standing at the mike. Can you imagine my utter horror then, when the producer at one stroke removed all my 'props' during the rehearsal: 'No you cannot sing at a standing mike.'

'No, you can't sing sitting on the stool.'

'You'll just have the mike in your hand and move about.'

And there she left me with my terror. I'd never done this before and were it possible, I'd have opted out of the programme altogether. I felt trapped. My back-up band whispered encouragement, saying: 'Mary, of course, *of course*, you can do it.'

When it was broadcast a few nights later I made a point of carefully studying my face and demeanour. Nobody, not even I, could have guessed what I was going through. Even *I* was fooled: what I was watching on the screen was serenity and confidence personified. It sounds very trivial now but it was an important break-through for me.

Gradually, with the pressure of work, my amicable relationship with Jo Lustig started to fray at the edges. Doubts began to creep in that he, as he so often emphasised, was doing things solely in my interest. My first doubts started when he explained that putting me into the Royal Albert Hall was going to cost a mint and that if I was willing to accept a modest fee, he was willing to absorb any loss. After the success of the Festival Hall I thought this a bit odd, so I called Pat O'Toole in Canada for advice. His response was typical: 'Mary,' he said, 'this is a no-brainer. If you believe in yourself, take the loss. Jo knows it will be a 'sell-out'. He cannot afford a flop after all the recent hype.'

I followed Pat's advice and was well rewarded. The concert sold out. However, the episode left a sour note. After that I began to be less trusting about what Jo was up to and more questioning about the logistics of touring. On my tour and concert brochures there seemed to be many names of people who, it seemed to me, did nothing but collect salaries. Managers always signed contracts on my behalf. This worked well when there was trust. In one case I found, much later, Jo had signed the rights to a televised concert over to himself. His contract with the TV station forbade them letting me know where the programme was subsequently broadcast. After receiving letters from people who watched the programme in Norway and elsewhere, I wrote to the TV station concerned seeking information, only to be told by the head of contracts that their contract forbade them letting me know anything about this programme. Correspondence with my new management showed that Jo had frustrated the showing of the programme in areas where I was scheduled to tour.

Towards the end of the second year of my contract with Jo, our relationship became even more fraught. Possibly frustrated by my lack of cooperation with all his wishes, Jo's manner became hostile.

My way of dealing with agro is to go quiet; the reaction of Jo, an impatient man by nature, was the opposite: I bought an answering machine so as to minimise the opportunity for further confrontation but this infuriated him all the more. The tapes are still somewhere in my attic. In one he threatens to destroy me and finish my career in music.

As mentioned elsewhere, I was not a hundred per cent happy with the selection of songs on my second album with Chrysalis but management tried to steam-roll me into using more than I would wish of the MOR songs from the album in my coming UK tour. This probably made good commercial sense. With hindsight I now suspect that Jo would have been pleased had I dropped all the Gaelic songs from my repertoire. One day in frustration he came out with it: 'Mary, you're too ethnic!' – the same unspoken attitude displayed by Decca twenty-two years earlier. But this was my 'roots' and I stuck to my guns. It irritated Jo that I was not more commercially minded, more hungry for work. This conflict elicited the following 'cautionary letter' to Jo.

Dear Jo

I've studied the suggested list you sent me for the tour programme. I've decided to return to the majority of songs used at the Royal Festival Hall concert. Only at the Albert Hall will I substitute a few new songs. For the provincial concerts the songs with the group will remain as for the RFH. Adding the songs 'Follow Me' & 'Oceans Away' & 'Scorn Not His Simplicity' to the original selection of songs with the group.* is out of the question as this brings the timing way beyond 2 hours. I do not intend to cut down on the number of my songs with harp accompaniment alone (as was clearly established when I signed with you). The choice and order of the songs will remain my province: As soon as I can on my return on Thursday I will discuss with David Gold the selection of new songs with the group at the Albert Hall. A few changes I think, so that some of the material on the latest album material can get well aired there.

Kindest Regards
Mary

P.S. I trust that you will endorse my decisions as outlined above. It can be a cause of real unhappiness and distress to feel that the management is standing in the wings, so to speak, disapproving, even tacitly of my programme. And I'm sure you would want to create an atmosphere conducive to my giving a joyful, confident, free-from-distress performance.

* Already the selection with the group is crowding out the other so-called 50% of my concert.

Sadly this letter only gained me a temporary breathing space before disputes over repertoire resumed.

Later, after my contract with Jo finished, I went on to record the occasional album of traditional songs, including one entire album of Gaelic songs (a live concert at the National Gallery in Dublin), but the Royal Festival Hall format broke new ground for me. The old 'pre-Lustig' format worked well for the occasional recital and broadcast; it worked less well for an expanded multi-cultural audience and with the multiplicity of performances. Also, in order for my recording contract to work it required a broader repertoire, which I welcomed as long as I chose the material. For a song to be effective it must retain its freshness and I found that this proved well-nigh impossible after singing the same song hundreds of times. This happened in the early days with

that beautiful song, 'The Quiet Land of Érin', for example, a song I
love. Luckily as time went on I discovered several other beautiful
songs, some contemporary, some ancient, that I also loved to sing.
There were some people, I well realised, who would have me sing
nothing but the old Irish songs and they made no bones about telling
me – I was betraying them and my own culture etc, etc. I never
allowed myself to become bored by singing the same song too much
– no matter who requested it – and that is what would have happened
if I wasn't fortunate enough to have found other material that I liked
to sing. I made a point of including one or two Gaelic songs in all my
recordings.

Two days before the concert in the Royal Albert Hall I developed a
severe sore throat. I was staying at the Aer Lingus Tara Hotel in
London, and Mr Dillon, the manager, sent for a doctor. After examining me, the doctor gave me antibiotics and next morning put me in
touch with Mr Holden, a Harley Street throat specialist who diagnosed the 'red flu' and prescribed appropriate treatment (there was an
epidemic of the red flu in England at the time). That night I slept
fitfully. My throat and sinuses were badly inflamed and very painful.
The Albert Hall was sold out, and the next day I had to decide whether
to go ahead with the concert or not. It was a difficult and momen-
tous decision. By mid-day I still hadn't improved, so I telephoned Lady
Abbess at Stanbrook. She was most sympathetic and promised that
the community would pray specially for me for the rest of that day.
Buoyed up by this and armed with throat sprays (which I loathe
using), I decided to go ahead with the concert. Mr Holden was in the
audience ready to leap to my assistance if need be, and came backstage during the interval to administer more sprays. I had with me on
stage a hot lemon and honey drink, and on Mr Holden's advice (as a
precautionary measure), I warned the audience.
    After a few songs I said: 'I bet some of you are wondering what's
in the mug.' They laughed. 'Lemon and honey,' I told them. 'I'd like
to tell you that I've been informed by my doctor that I'm suffering
from the red flu.' And I continued with the concert. I'll never know
how I got through that night: But the audience was happy and the
reviews next day in the London papers were all good. The critic in

the *Telegraph* commented: '... if she hadn't mentioned the fact that she had the flu, we would never have known;' the *Times* critic wrote in a similar vein: '... neither the problems created by a heavy cold nor the acoustic vagaries of the Albert Hall could dim the almost ethereal purity of Mary O'Hara's voice, throughout even the most taxing song of her concert last night.'

Another time I got through a UK winter tour battling with a bad throat. Each city I came to I consulted with the local GP hoping he would take the responsibility about whether or not I should sing with my throat is such a condition but each time he passed the buck. I made it as far as the last concert, sold-out at the Barbican, but when I rose in the morning to head for London there was no voice. That solved the problem and my GP confirmed that I simply could not give a concert. Full-blown laryngitis.

Audiences were appreciative. In some places they started off rather shy, perhaps not knowing what to expect, but by the time I'd reached the second half they had warmed to me. 'Don't risk going to Belfast,' family and friends kept saying but in the end, I ignored the warnings and started to sing there. There was something special about the enthusiastic response of a Belfast audience that I can't quite put my finger on. Despite the potentially dangerous situation in that city in those days, the kindness and cheerfulness of the inhabitants made one forget all that and I loved singing to them. Belfast was always included in my Irish tours. On one occasion the concert which was to start at 7.30 pm was inexplicably delayed until 8 pm. It was not until after-wards that I heard that the hall was practically empty at 7.30 because a bomb had exploded two streets away and the army had cordoned off the area, restricting all traffic. The ban was lifted at about 7.40 and the hall was full by 8 o'clock.

I was especially pleased when Sammy Crooke, Dean of St Anne's, the Protestant Cathedral, invited me to take part in a concert in the Cathedral. The audience consisted of enthusiasts from both sides of the religious divide – which is continually narrowing, I'm glad to say. And the two or three days staying with Sammy and his wife in their lovely home was the icing on the cake.

People from my distant past often turned up when I was on tour. My first evening at the Great Southern Hotel in Galway, the phone rang. I picked it up to hear: 'Miss O'Hara, I think you're absolutely marvellous. I'm the mayor of Galway, and I'd like to say what a fantastic privilege it is to welcome you to our city.' Something told me that I'd heard that voice before, and suddenly I knew: 'Would that by any chance be a rogue called Pascal Spellman?' Mayor of Galway, my foot! It was a very pleasant reunion with my old pal Pascal, who looked no different (except more prosperous) from the days when he and I used to take part in the same Variety Concerts in the provinces while I was still in my teens.

Soon after the Royal Albert Hall and that spring tour, I flew to the US and Canada to do promotional work for concerts at Carnegie Hall in New York City and Massey Hall in Toronto. The Mike Douglas Show was my introduction to the American version of the chat show. While in America I was surprised by what I can only describe as the professional autograph hunters, who patiently lay in wait for the 'celebrities' who appeared on these shows. After the Dinah Shore Show, as I finished signing my name for someone, he said: 'By the way, who are you, anyway?'

The concerts in America went well, but the publicity surrounding them was pretty heavy going. In two days in New York I did sixteen press interviews, one after the other, all in the one room – one of which was with Valerie Hendy, an old friend from Stanbrook days. Here she was now, correspondent for *The New York Times*. Her subsequent article portrayed my days in the cloister from a different angle.

MARY O'HARA JOURNEYED FAR TO REACH STAGE

During the summer of 1970, I spent six weeks inside Stanbrook Abbey ... to 'experience the rigors' without commitment...

I was assigned the task of dusting the visiting parlours from the 'outside' each morning... Sister Miriam dusted the parlours ... from the 'inside'. We never spoke but after a few mornings of pushing around the dust, we began to grin at each other through the wooden grille...

I worked up the courage to ask an American nun in the community to tell me anything she knew about Sister Miriam. It was quite a story...

We began to meet at a pond in the late afternoon...

Later that year, I wrote letters from Boston and sent books and Joan Baez's albums. Sister Miriam sent notes and scraps of lyrics and suggestions about poets I should read. Each summer I would go to

England to visit her. I always hoped she would play the harp and sing for me but she never did.

Since leaving the monastery, she has recorded two more albums... Frequent television appearances have ended her anonymity and strangers often stop her when she shops in London to ask for autographs... When reporters or admirers remark on the strange twists her life has taken, Mary makes jokes about second incarnations but sees a continuity in all she has done.

'I saw the service of God in the monastic life as an extension of love for my husband. I didn't confuse the loves, or try to replace one with the other...'

I arrived in New York a few days before the Carnegie Hall concert with the greater part of my luggage missing. Besides the stage dresses, all the music and spare harp strings were also lost. In fact, it was three weeks before my luggage turned up, and by then I had finished my tour and was staying with Ray and Joyce Byrne in their charming hideaway cottage outside Toronto.

With the dress I was fortunate. Once again Mary O'Donnell came to the rescue. By sheer accident I discovered that she was in New York. Mary designs for the fuller figure but I fell for a beautiful multicoloured dress which, with a few minor adjustments around the waist, fitted me perfectly, and I bought it there and then. I've had great mileage from that dress, wearing it for those concerts and also at the London Palladium, for the Royal Variety Show at which Her Majesty Queen Elizabeth The Queen Mother and Princess Alexandra were present.

Sometime during this period Sarah Hook took over from Lucy Broughton as my PA. Sarah had a well-developed comic streak, an attribute that is highly appreciated at any time, but especially on tour. Later we were joined by Sue Laity, an attractive ex British Airways hostess who subsequently became a fashion designer. Both were very practical, which I'm not.

My father was appalled when he heard the very high percentage of my earnings that Jo Lustig was taking but I believe the services of 'tough' managers like Jo Lustig are essential for various reasons. Not only can they strike a hard bargain with special knowledge, experience and negotiating power – and never turn a hair – but without them, unscrupulous and unethical people will not hesitate to take advantage of a performer if they know he or she does not have a worldly-wise agent or 'pushy' manager as a buffer, not just by securing paltry fees but by not paying the agreed fees at all if they think they can get away with it. My first experience of this sort of disreputable behaviour was Al Grossman in connection with my appearance on the Ed Sullivan Show in 1961. When he strongly suspected I was planning to withdraw from the music scene, he failed to pass on to me the agreed payment he received on my behalf. When I sent him a reminder requesting that he do so, his response was one of surprise. 'Did you not get the cheque I sent you?' After that, all further 'reminders' from me were met with a thundering silence. Eventually I gave up. It was only after Jo Lustig informed him that I was mentioning this despicable incident of the non payment in my autobiography that the cheque was sent – twenty-seven years later.

Possibly the worst case of non-payment concerns one Hal Shaper, a South African lawyer turned dodgy record producer. He produced an album of mine called *Spread a Little Happiness* that was advertised on TV by a company called Tellstar. Though Shaper and I co-owned the masters and the album continued to be released in various countries for twenty unbroken years, I never got as much as a statement, let alone royalties. Eventually, the master-tapes came into the possession of one Steve Brink of Prism Records. When Pat was able to prove to him that I owned the tapes, he was in a position to pay me a small recompense. Steve then went on to release forty traditional songs of mine on H&H Music. He and John Nice of Valentine Music stood out as honest people in the murky world of the record business as far as my work was concerned.

Then there was millionaire Bernie Solomon in LA who continued to release albums of my songs for over fifty years, ignoring all requests to stop. People of that calibre pick their victims, knowing they will not or cannot afford legal writs. Among my pile of mail, one day, I found a cheque forwarded by a stranger from Edinburgh who'd found it in a book she had borrowed from her local library. It was for an engagement I had in America a year previously and I remembered corresponding with the organisers about not having been paid. My poor mother-in-law spent days trying to trace the cheque to no avail. I must have used it as a marker when I was on tour because to me it looked very much like a receipt. Don't ask me how that happened... So, in my case, a manager was a necessity.

Most performers welcome the boost to their confidence that positive responses provide. Twice in my life, I have admired someone else's work so much that I felt compelled to write to tell them so. One was actress Fiona Shaw and the other RTÉ film-maker Bob Quinn. Recently the following arrived in my email:

Letter sent to my web page:

Hello Mary

I don't know if this will actually get to you, but I just wanted to write and say thanks for all the great music! I'm sure you have gotten thousands of letters like this over the years and so sorry to bore you with more of this, but I just discovered your website and am enjoying all the information and videos on You Tube, etc.

About 10 years ago, a friend of mine gave me a big stack of records that he didn't want and, among them was your record called Mary O'Hara's Scotland. Thinking what a joke this music might be, I put the record on one day out of boredom, while cleaning my house or something equally mundane. But after hearing a few moments of it, I had to absolutely stop what I was doing and listen to the whole record several times. I have since then, bought many of the available CDs of your wonderful music. The odd thing about this is, that I work in the music industry here in Nashville, Tennessee, where I play guitar, bass, violin, cello, saxophone, etc. (none of them really well, but enough to make a decent living) and also mainly engineer in the recording studio, etc. I help people make records, in many different ways, many different types of music, and constantly deal with the artistic visions of the people I work with and try and help them realize their musical aspirations, etc. I also play in bands that make records and tour and have adoring fans and such, so I know what it is like from either the stage or the audience. When I hear your music play I nearly burst into tears every time. It is from another world and time, and is truly amazing at how it transcends the ages and touches the listener deeply. It's truly wonderful, and I'm so glad the internet is here to give many more people the opportunity to hear your music and learn about it and enjoy

it. Thank you so much for all the great music! I hope you are doing
well and All the Best wishes. Thanks again for such beautiful music.

George Bradfute
Nashville, TN
29th March 2008

Such messages serve a very useful purpose. It is so easy to think that
whatever we do in life is a waste of time. This email, that came via
my web page as I was putting the final faltering finishing touches to
this update of my autobiography, encouraged me to persevere.

Dear Mary,

I'm a retired Anglican priest whose Irish forebears farmed in Ireland
until the famine of 1846.

    Your lovely book *The Scent of the Roses* fell into my hands earlier this
month having been left on the free shelf in our apartment building
where items get passed on. I want to thank you more than words can
begin to say even though I am now only up to the monastic chapter
in your life. But I want especially to thank you for introducing me to
Richard and sharing your exceedingly rare courtship and marriage and
its even more rare delineation made so by the rarity of gifts like yours
and those of Richard. I have been revamping a poem of 50 lines on
water for much of the past year, one that saw the light of day in 1952
awash as it was then with the 'imperfections of youthful endeavour',
the more so since I had taken my degree in mathematics. But to read
Richard's poetry in the pages of your exquisite autobiography and then
to find them on the internet has been a real gift. Again Mary, thank
you very much. Pax.

Signed: Peter A.N.
12th October 2010

Eventually the pile of unanswered letters got so high that it was no
laughing matter. A friend who was visiting me, announced one day:
'Mary, I've solved your unanswered mail problem.'

I was delighted of course. It was only much later I found that she
had burnt the lot. I was shocked but it was too late to do anything
about it. Perhaps it was the only sensible solution at that time.

One September afternoon in 1978 I was on Lord Montagu of Beaulieu's estate in Hampshire filming a scene for television, when Éamonn Andrews popped out of nowhere to announce: 'Mary O'Hara: This Is Your Life.'

I was driven to the Southern Television studios in Southampton to be confronted with some of the key people in my life to date. It proved to be a programme punctuated with laughter and tears. My father was brought from Dublin; Dermot (whom I hadn't seen since Christmas 1961 in Nigeria) from Calgary in Canada; Florence, my first mother-in-law, from Washington, DC; Lesley and Gavin Scott-Moncrieff and David Murison from Scotland; Déirdre Kelleher, Gay Byrne and his wife Kathleen Watkins, Seán Óg Tuama, Val Doonican, Joyce Grenfell, Richard Afton and Lady Lily Mackenzie – all in turn greeted me with affection and sometimes emotion. My sister Joan, Joan Baez, Sister Angela and Sister Petra from Sion Hill, unable to be with me in the studio, sent their greetings via television film. There were inevitably some gaps. Lord Moyne and Pat O'Toole, significant people in my life and in my return to music, were not present. Nor was there anyone from those Oxford days with Richard. I knew Dudley Moore was in town and would have been delighted to come on but I suspect they did not want to risk what they considered to be any 'sadness' creeping in. However, it was a moving experience, and at the end of the programme a smiling Éamonn handed me the big red book engraved with the words: 'This is your Life'.

The programme was broadcast on 4th October 1978. In a way it turned out to be only a small landmark in my life. I did not know at the time but there was a lot more to come.

CHAPTER 15

Travels With My Harp

ARLY 1980, my three-year management contract with Jo Lustig
was coming to an end. I would have gladly got out of it earlier
but, as there was no let-out clause, the amount he was naming
for releasing me was astronomical.

Pat had been instrumental in persuading me to take on Jo Lustig
as manager in 1977 and when that alliance started to fall apart, I went
back to Pat for advice and, I suppose, reassurance. He too felt bad
about the management situation not working out. By then Pat was
fully immersed in his own studies at the University of Toronto but as
the crisis with Jo developed I made frequent calls to Canada, only to
find that Jo had beaten me to it. Pat and Jo got on well and had much
respect for one another. Pat understood the mechanics of management
and the economics of touring much better than I did and he was disappointed that I did not make more effort to patch things up with Jo
but, as always, he supported my decision and set about helping me
find a new manager.

To succeed Lustig, I found John Coast, a handsome, dignified,
cultured man, who managed people like Nana Mouskouri and John
Vickers, the opera singer. He could not get involved, of course, till
I was contractually free but that did not stop him attending my
performances and contacting promoters. After attending a concert of
mine for the first time, he remarked to Pat: 'It's like having a Rolls-
Royce in my garage and I'm not allowed to drive it.'

Shortly before my Lustig contract ended in February 1980, Jo
approached John Coast saying he had some lucrative work for me in
the pipeline and offering to split commission – a not unusual practice
when people change managers. John was keen to take up this offer,

as was Pat but, at this time, my inclination was to have a clean break. To everyone's dismay, I declined the offer. The talk of a film about my life was put on hold, which was no harm. Naturally it took some time for word to get round that my new manager was John Coast and, since I didn't agree to their sharing commission, no engagement could be booked until the day after the Lustig contract expired. Therefore, whenever anyone wanted to book me, understandably it was my ex-manager Jo Lustig they contacted and instead of letting them know that he would no longer be my manager at the date requested, he simply gave them to understand I was unavailable, or worse, that I refused the work.

Immediately after my contract with Lustig expired, I was in London opening a book exhibition for the Irish Tourist Board. Normally management organised such matters but I had acquaintances at the Irish Tourist Board who had my number. After my talk, a young man approached me, introducing himself as Glenn Gale, a journalist with the London *Sunday Times*.

'At last I've managed to catch up with you. May I try to persuade you yet again to change your mind and do 'A Life In the Day Of' for us?' he said. 'When my editor saw you were to be here today, he asked me to come along and discuss it with you in person.'

Taken aback, I replied: 'I'd be delighted to. I read it regularly. But there must be some mistake about my not wanting to do an interview.'

'We've been trying to reach you via your manager, Jo Lustig?'

'Ah, that explains it. I've a different management now and have had for a while.'

He described how for quite some time they had been telephoning Jo Lustig seeking an interview with me for the back page of their colour magazine.

'People would give an eye-tooth to appear in this feature,' he said – as if I didn't know.

'We were prepared to come to your house or wherever you were and bring a cameraman. We are very selective.'

'We were told you refused to do interviews any more; that you had become a recluse in your country cottage; that you did not talk to journalists, etc, etc.'

'What's more, we were offered someone else in your place – another female singer from Ireland, an Irish Catholic girl, 'in the same vein as Mary O'Hara', we were told. She lives in Ireland and we were offered

airfares to go over and interview her. But my editor insists that it is
Mary O'Hara our readers want, not Dana.'

I happened to know Dana, a particularly nice person. I had read
in the press that Jo had signed her on as a client shortly before my
contract with him expired. In fact, a few years later she appeared as
a guest on my ITV series 'Mary O'Hara and Friends' – both of us by
then with new management.

'If you ever have any problems with this fellow, let me know and
I'm willing to be a witness,' the journalist promised after he'd finished
interviewing me some days later. Fortunately I never had to take up
his offer but I did write a letter of complaint to Lustig asking him to
please stop pretending to be still my manager. Needless to say, he did
not respond.

What proved to be the first instalment of my autobiography,
The Scent of the Roses, was published in 1980. Behind the scenes and
unbeknownst to Lustig, I had been quietly working on it over the
previous year. I had wanted to give Jo Lustig due credit, but for legal
reasons, I was advised it would be best not to mention him at all in
the book – which, in view of the book's later success, possibly annoyed
him. But that was not the primary intention of the omission. I do owe
Jo Lustig a lot. I will always remember how kind he and his wife Dee
were to me when I first met them. If the correspondence in my filing
cabinet can be relied upon, Jo never forgave me for not renewing my
contract with him and ever afterwards used whatever influence he had
to belittle my work but, from the start, I made a conscious effort to
avoid any remark critical of Jo, no matter how provoked by journalists to do so. I consider myself fortunate. One hears of performers
whose careers were prematurely blighted by a bad relationship with
their managers.

Now having the means to buy a place of my own, and after some discussion with close friends, I realized that my five happy years living
in the Gardener's Cottage had come to a natural close. My extremely
generous friends and patrons, Bryan and Elisabeth Guinness, were
clearly sorry to hear of my decision. Indeed they and those of their
children who were still living in Biddesden House at the time had by

then become almost like family to me. And of course we've kept in touch down the years.

When I saw a picture of a 17th-century thatched cottage for sale in the window of an estate agent's office, I was hooked. Some while after I'd settled in, *Woman and Home* asked me to write a piece for their magazine and I reproduce excerpts from it here:

... When my little cottage was built in 1667 – by people escaping London after the Great Fire – neither Tolkien nor his hobbits were yet heard of, but the moment I saw a picture... I knew it was a hobbit house. No trouble naming it: Rivendell, from *The Lord of The Rings* (I thought it a bit much to call it Bag End). It stands amid some trees and shrubs on a two acre plot of land on the edge of a quiet Hampshire hamlet...

One of the main attractions of the new cottage was, and is, a mature garden, the legacy of who knows how many previous owners. Clearly they were skilled and loving gardeners. My knowledge of gardening is very limited but I'm learning and it's hard to describe the sheer pleasure that the garden here at Rivendell Cottage affords me...

My harp is now quite old but it should have no difficulty settling comfortably into these 17th century surroundings. It started life as a sycamore tree in a Scottish woodland and I like to think that the love with which, surely, Henry Briggs made this harp lives on in it and is activated whenever it is played. As D.H. Lawrence puts it:

> Things men have made
> With wakened hands and
> Put soft life into, are awake
> Through years with transferred
> Touch and go on glowing
> For long years. And for this
> Reason, some old things are
> Lovely, warm still with
> The life of forgotten men
> Who made them.

My first tour with my new manager, John Coast, took place in autumn 1980 and under his management I continued doing autumn and spring tours in the UK. In 1982, I was having another major UK tour. Much planning went into the scheduling of the concerts in order to minimise unnecessary travel and long distances. Everything was arranged so as to minimise 'wear and tear' on me. Then Pope John Paul II decided to visit the UK. He was scheduled to address a mammoth meeting at York Racecourse and the organisers of the papal visit invited me to sing at this event. It was indeed a great honour to be asked to sing for the Pope in front of half a million people, the largest audience I ever sang for, but the diversion and long drive to York played havoc with the meticulous arrangements so painfully arrived at during the pre-tour discussions with my management. I did my best to persuade John Coast to plead 'clash' of engagements and get me out of being involved. However, the organisers of the papal visit persisted. For me singing at York was breaking one of the basic rules I had worked out with my new management. Eventually I agreed to do it.

I don't remember much about the performance itself or what the Pope said or did except that afterwards I was given a commemorative token. Besides another hymn chosen by the organisers, I sang my own setting of the Magnificat (in English) which I had done while at Stanbrook. Then I continued with the interrupted tour.

The year 1980 was particularly hectic for me. Apart from the concert tours, TV appearances, book signings and recording a new album, I appeared at numerous public and civic events where I met some memorably interesting people, themselves in the public eye. One such event that stands out was at the Savoy Hotel for the annual Woman of the Year Luncheon at the end of which I had been invited to make a speech. Though during my performances I sang and introduced my music, sometimes before fairly large audiences, I still had a dread of 'giving a speech', knowing that in the audience would be numerous people much more skilled and more practised than I. Before the luncheon, the Duchess of Kent engaged me in a lengthy conversation and showed a genuine interest in my doings, past and present. After the meal, the speech now safely over, Arianna Stassinopoulos came up to me and introduced herself to say how much she appreciated my speech and would I like to join her and a few friends for tea in the hotel. Indeed, she needed no introduction as I had always admired her and her writing. A few days later we had lunch together at her flat. I won't conceal the fact that I felt flattered that my then most recent album *The Scent of the Roses* was gently playing in the background.

I still have the recorder her charming, if intriguingly eccentric, mother gave me as a present that day.

Shortly before the publication of my autobiography, I was approached to record the album *Tranquility*, which quickly went Platinum. Jed Kearse, the producer, was instrumental in my exploring yet another avenue of song. He explained that he wanted this album, which would be TV advertised, to be wide-ranging and he sent me a long list of songs that included classical titles he felt confident I could successfully tackle. For example: 'The Shepherd's Song' (*Bailero*) from Songs of the Auvergne, Handel's 'Where E'er You Walk', Gluck's 'What is Life to Me Without Thee', etc. For those light classical songs I needed a lot of practice with a pianist. Dave Gold, my MD/pianist, admitting that this was not his field, found someone to replace him. This turned out to be Jo Stewart – a veritable god-send. Her partner, John Franchi was already my flautist. Employing Jo coincided with my change of management and she soon took over altogether from Dave Gold. I reorganised my backing group, cutting the number from five to two (piano and flute). She could conduct; she made many fine musical arrangements and we worked very amicably together for the next few years. She toured with me and co-produced my next album, *The Scent of the Roses*. Since my way of touring did not automatically guarantee full-time employment for my musicians, it was agreed that I'd always give Jo ample notice of any forthcoming work and that she would do likewise to me, if for any reason she was unavailable to work with me. It was her responsibility to find a suitable replacement and also select and rehearse a flautist. This arrangement worked well until one day, virtually on the eve of a Canadian tour Jo was offered an enticing contract with the prospect of a West End run and she pulled out of my Canadian tour at very short notice, leaving me stranded with only a few days for me to find a replacement. Frantically I rang all my musical acquaintances up and down the country. Fortunately, I didn't need to go further than the second audition to find Matthew Freeman, a superlative, classically-trained musician who was equally at home with modern MOR songs. Matthew, Pat and I became good friends and he stayed with me until I retired from singing in 1994. He toured with me in the UK, USA, Canada, Australia and New Zealand. On my ITV series, 'Mary O'Hara and Friends', I insisted that Matthew conduct the City of London Sinfonia and co-produce as well as conduct the orchestra on an album of the televised series (*Spread a Little Happiness*). From there he progressed to conducting the London Philharmonic and orchestras in Europe. Of late he has been involved with the hugely successful Abba revival. When we first met, Matthew had regularly worked as an accompanist with Ian Adam, a singing teacher, whom I first met after the private recital I gave for the Queen Mother. Adam trained Sarah Brightman and many older established actors who suddenly found themselves faced with taking on a musical. Whenever I embarked on new material with Matthew, I enjoyed the benefit of the vocal exercises he had picked up from Ian Adam and passed on to me until eventually, in my early fifties, I started taking singing lessons directly from Ian Adam.

After 1980, Pat in effect became my overall manager, mediating with tour managers and others and removing the need for me to involve myself in any way beyond getting on with music-making. Between 1980 and 1994, there were many challenges and exciting things happening. Apart from concert tours, TV programmes and recordings, I was commissioned to produce two more books: *A Song for Ireland* (1982) and an anthology on the subject of love, *Celebration of Love* (1985), both of which I found, with Pat's invaluable help, relatively stress-free to write. Under his guidance, my approach to writing had improved – for one thing, I had become better organised – and let me say here, I could not have tackled the book *A Song for Ireland*, without Pat's input. He was more or less the architect of that book and above all was responsible for the historical content, he being a historian, among other things. After the initial hesitancy, I tackled the anthology project with relish. It's a lovely sort of indulgence to be allowed to pick and choose from works of some of one's favourite authors. Both books, like the autobiography, did well, making various best-selling lists. Surrounded now by more sympathetic people, touring also became easier.

I liked to be at the hall two hours beforehand for my usual routine – do the sound-check, partake of the light meal, put on the war paint and change into full battle-dress, all in the quietitude of my dressing room – but things didn't always go according to plan. Milton Keynes is a new town, full of roundabouts. It is as if the architect had just dis-covered new geometric shapes called 'circles' and scattered them about willy-nilly, just for the fun of it. Which is alright if you don't have a concert in town and your driver has studied his map beforehand... Anyway, it was the final concert of one UK tour; we were booked to fly to Australia next morning and I had some last minute packing still to do. I did not want to delay after the concert ended and, for that reason, we decided there would be no encores. After driving round what seemed like dozens of roundabouts, it was becoming clear that we were getting no nearer the hall and that I'd be late for the sound-check. To make matters worse I was dying to spend a penny. At last, in the fading light, when I saw a likely spot, I said to Pat: 'Let me out here.'

Pat obliged but while I was in full flow, I heard approaching foot-steps. In the rush to escape notice, my knickers got wet. Eventually we found the hall. I ran to the dressing room, rinsed the knickers, hung them on the radiator and went immediately to the sound-check. As usual, Pat gave the sound people my list of songs and explained to them why there was to be no encore.

'Bring up the house lights as she goes off stage. We have to catch a plane early in the morning.'

It was a full house and Jo Stewart and John Franchi were with me. As usual those days, the order was: songs with the harp in the first half and after the interval the musicians would join me. Pat saw me onto the stage and the concert got under way. He then locked the dressing room and headed towards the manager's office at the other side of the building, as complicated to reach as navigating the round-abouts into town earlier. As he was talking to the manager, he heard, over the tannoy, a harp string breaking and me telling the audience to amuse themselves for a couple of minutes while I fetched a string from the dressing-room to replace the broken one. Easier said than done.

While Pat was rushing to reach the dressing room, and getting hopelessly lost in the bowels of the building, I managed to get off stage but in the dim light couldn't find the dressing room door. It was one of those dark seamless walls where you needed radar eyes to iden-tify the concealed doors. The audience had become highly amused at my antics. When at last I located the correct door, it was, of course locked. After some quick thinking, I climbed back on stage empty handed. I apologised to the audience, who were still enjoying the situation.

'I'll rearrange the programme. We'll have all the songs with harp after the interval and the musicians will accompany me during the entire first half.'

Jo rushed out with her bundle of music sheets, placed them on the piano and sat down to play the first song. A few bars into the song, there was an almighty crash when all her music cascaded to the floor. The audience warmed even more to all this. We got through both halves without further incident. At the end, with prolonged applause and everyone standing, I decided I had no choice but to go back on for an encore, which in this case was 'All Through the Night'. Nobody, of course, thought of telling the sound people of the change of plan. There was Jo's beautiful piano introduction and I had just sung 'Sleep my love and peace attend thee', which I would have followed with 'All through the night...' when, over the tannoy came the words, 'The bar will be open till eleven o'clock.' We all collapsed with laughter, me included. I attempted to start again, the beautiful introduction on the piano, the same 'Sleep my love' etc, but as I was about to sing 'All through the night' I got a fit of the giggles. The audience loved all this and joined in the laughter. It took another failed attempt or two before I could steel myself not to laugh and to finish the song. And then another encore. The thought of the early flight seemed inconsequential. It was midnight before I collected my, by then, dry knickers and headed for home.

The middle of March, around St Patrick's Day, is a busy time for many Irish musicians. The Irish Diaspora is large and widely spread and it is the time of year when many pine for home, that 'Old Ireland' image so celebrated in song. People, mostly those who were born outside Ireland, want to celebrate their Irishness. In America in particular, and to a lesser extend in Canada and Australia, it is a time for green beer and 'kiss-me- I'm Irish' T-shirts. My type of music did not sit well with this type of nostalgia. So, I kept a low profile around that time of year. However, for a couple of years in the late 1980s, I agreed to headline a half hour in an 'Irish Evening' that performed in a few cities in the English Midlands. My routine was to have my material timed and ready, do my spot and then leave.

At the end of an evening Pat liked to have a word or two with people as they left, hoping perhaps to pick up some useful tips about my presentation. Generally he is rewarded but on this occasion, a surprise awaited him. Enquiring of a smiling buxom woman which section of the show she liked best, hoping perhaps to hear her say 'Mary O'Hara'.

'Oh, Fr Michael Cleary,' She beamed.

Disappointed, but undaunted, he asked: 'What do you think of Mary O'Hara?'

'Ah, sure that one! She can't sing for nuts.'

Nowadays one has to rely unavoidably on technology and technicians – it was much less so when I first started out. Perhaps it is too much to expect every 'balance and control' technician to be sensitive to chiaroscuro – the nuances of light and shade, loud and soft, the dynamics of an individual's performance. To give a straight-forward example: in the song 'Greensleeves', I chose to sing each verse *mp* and each chorus *f*. But too often, what I heard on the finished product was the volume of the verse brought up and the chorus brought down. I recognise that at times my soprano voice posed a problem with dynamics that would not obtain with a mezzo. It's a poor excuse to say that the equipment sets the parameters automatically. How often I requested in vain of the sound technician: 'Please don't interfere with the dynamics.'

This may be a good place to mention how much importance I always attached to programming songs, whether on an album, in a fifteen-minute broadcast or in an entire concert. Each song has its own mood, which must be respected by the song that precedes it and by the song that that follows it – all of which calls for thoughtful planning. Compilations neglect this factor and bundle songs together, any old way. A balanced variation may sum up what I mean.

A perennial hazard was charity performances, generally organised by eager amateurs. Once I had a Polish choir as guests on my ITV television series and afterwards someone persuaded me to take part in a concert in London for a Polish charity. The well-meaning organisers forgot to make arrangements for a dressing room and I had to use the public 'Ladies' with my PA mounting guard while I changed. Another

time in 1975, I gave a recital for free to oblige a friend who was organising the Isle of Man Festival. The concert went well but I remember
being dropped unceremoniously outside the airport entrance and left
on my own to drag my harp and suitcase to the check-in as best I
could. I could not help contrasting the treatment then with that of
three years later, under Lustig's management, this time in a much
larger venue with a four-figure fee... They couldn't do enough for me
and for my entourage. Can it be that the more you charge, the more
you are appreciated?

Touring with Pat (who became my husband in 1985) and my MD
Matthew Freeman was great fun. Matthew was always cheerful and
reliable. People liked him, especially the girl flautists. Once we drove
from Eugene, Oregon, giving concerts in Victoria, Vancouver; up over
the Rockies to Kelowna, Kamloops; down the other side to Calgary,
Winnipeg and all the way to Chicago. It was in the middle of winter
and the roads over the Rockies were frozen. I pulled a muscle in my
groin while cycling near Kelowna, but, mercifully, after a break of a
couple of days it sorted itself out. I managed to do the concert anyway. In Vancouver, Matthew bought an electronic keyboard and we
whiled away the long hours driving in the snow, amusing ourselves by
making up songs and singing them. Pat drove. Here's one I made up
which I sang in a Country and Western accent:

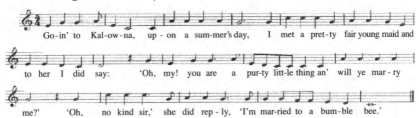

After a concert in Vancouver, as I'd finished signing things and was
about to leave, a woman, who had been standing at some distance,
said: 'While you were on stage I've been watching your aura.'

Apparently, it was very visible to her from the audience side.

'Oh yes,' I said, in a non-committal way.

'Have you got anything wrong with your left lung?'

'No,' I said. End of exchange.

'How's your aura?' became a popular greeting between us for the
rest of the tour.

The incident went completely out of my mind. Then, months later back in the UK, I was having a medical before a lengthy concert tour of Australia and the specialist remarked: 'You have a slight weakness in your left lung. Nothing at all serious. I only mention it because you are a singer.'

After that we stopped making jokes about auras.

One of the first things I did when I signed with John Coast was to wonder about the possibility of touring in Australia. My memories of that first 1959 Australia/New Zealand tour were so good that the possibility of going there again held great appeal for me. When Coast contacted Clifford Hocking, the music industry's best known and most highly regarded impresario in the antipodes, he was delighted, having been given to understand time and time again by the previous management that I was not interested. He had given up trying. I did three tours with him, the second of which included piano (Matthew Freeman) and flute. For the final tour, he invited Pat and me to use as a base his Melbourne home, a restored colonial property, tastefully furnished and full of books and paintings. Last time we heard from him, it was on a postcard, which read: 'I'm on a Russian cruise ship in the middle of the Pacific. And they have the good taste to be playing Mary O'Hara.'

In 1982, I was in London recording a book of children's stories for the Tempo Storytime Series 'The Scallywag Gang'. This was owned by Ann Miles of Warwick Records, who earlier had produced my TV advertised *Tranquility* album. The three of us got on well. Taking Pat aside one afternoon, with an air of confidentiality she said: 'Mary should make an effort to be reconciled with Jo Lustig because he has something on her which, if released to the press could destroy her future in singing. You should try to persuade her.'

Pat said that he had been arguing for a reconciliation for a long time – not because he thought Jo Lustig or anyone else had any information that could discredit me but because he had always liked Jo and regretted the split.

'Oh, but he has,' said Ann, which startled Pat

'Well, let him publish then, if that's what he wants,' said Pat.

Afterwards Pat and I discussed what it could possibly be but could think of nothing and banished it from our minds.

Around that time, I had a call from a journalist on one of the

London tabloids, a gossip columnist, if I remember correctly. He had a dossier, he said, with interesting information and pictures of me and Sarah Hook, my PA. Where he got this file, he wouldn't say. I asked Pat to listen in on the other line. The journalist was pleasant enough but the focus of his whole investigation was my relationship with Sarah. How much I liked her, would I miss her, why was she not married, etc, etc. His final question was: 'Can you imagine life without Sarah?'

I laughed and said: 'Of course.' And there the conversation ended.

This inquisition puzzled me but the man was pleasant and I was willing to put it down to one of those trivial episodes that sometimes happens with journalists. I asked him, by the way, how he got hold of my private home number but he wouldn't tell me. When I came off the phone Pat said: 'Did you realise what that was about?'

'No, but thought it a bit odd.'

'He had a file or dossier which suggested an improper relationship between you and Sarah. This must be what Ann Miles was talking about.'

Three years later, when Pat and I got married, Michael McDonagh in London handled the publicity, mainly in order to keep the press at bay. His job was to hand story and pictures to the Dublin and London newspapers and all of them ran front page stories on our wedding. I was on tour at the time in Canada and when we returned to the UK there was a call from Michael. He told Pat that some of the journalists remarked how fortunate they were not to have fallen for the dossier Jo Lustig had passed on to them. Michael also had a copy of the dossier. Many of the photographs in it were taken by Sarah Hook during the filming for the TV advertised album *Tranquility,* one of which was later used for the cover of the autobiography and the album of the same title. Sarah and I got on very well and frequently indulged in a fair amount of larking about together. We were simply great pals at the time.

Overall, I found press people reliable and often surprisingly kind. Sometimes those who knew me would ring up to confirm a story's authenticity. But it stretches credibility when, for example, one reads an interview (in the Nigel Dempster column), given supposedly in my cottage, verbatim quotes and all, when in fact I was three thousand miles away at the time. It sows doubt about what one reads in the media about others.

After I bought Rivendell my father, a civil engineer and architect, to my dismay at first dismissed the dwelling as 'mud walls and grass roof'. (I suspect my father expected me to invest in something more like a manor house.) One Irish newspaper had no problem with the mud walls and, in bold capitals, described my new venture into the property market:

MARY O'HARA, FORMER NUN, HAS TURNED HER BACK ON
A VOW OF POVERTY AND BOUGHT A MANSION NEAR
NEWBURY, ENGLAND'S RACING CAPITAL.

It said it all, no matter that Benedictines don't take a vow of poverty. And I'm not even remotely interested in racing.

Occasionally, a newspaper got it wrong, whether deliberately or otherwise. Pat's policy was to ignore such provocations. His philosophy: in the long run, truth prevails.

An assortment of people came backstage after every concert and occasionally someone wanted to suggest ideas about work. Sometime in the very early 1980s, after a performance at the Grosvenor Hall in Belfast, Pat came into the dressing room to prepare me. 'There's a BBC television producer coming in to discuss possible projects with you. Now, remember the four important points.' I was very conscious of Pat's four points.

Having closely watched how I operated, he had noticed how fond I was of using the word 'No' in relation to any new undertaking and how averse I was to anything that seemed to suggest a departure from the familiar pattern of my work. I tried to wriggle out of doing things about which I was unsure. Consequently, when Pat and I at first started working together, he sat me down one day and placed in front of me a piece of paper on which writ large were four points:

1. Don't yawn when someone has come to discuss a new project.
2. Don't say NO immediately. (Wait a bit and give the impression you are interested and at least considering matters.)
3. Don't suggest someone else who can do this better than you.
4. You can safely say YES to most things. They probably won't happen anyway.

So, that night, with a bomb scare keeping everyone on their toes, Alan Tongue introduced himself. Our short discussion was the beginning of a long friendship and of working together on many TV programmes, including the BBC TV series 'Minstrel of the Dawn' filmed at great houses in Northern Ireland. On each programme I had several guests and had the opportunity to experiment with different formats of presentation.

This boosted my confidence and came in useful later on when ITV approached me about doing two series of television programmes for them called 'Mary O'Hara and Friends'. All the programmes were shot in the studio in Southampton, an hour's drive from my home. While I still continued with my writing and with concerts, these two television series were the core of my work in the mid 1980s. As well as tours in the UK and Ireland, I toured Canada several times and also Australia and New Zealand. I gave another concert at Carnegie Hall and at many other major concert venues in the United States. Labrador City in northern Canada was definitely the coldest and not far behind was Whitehorse in the Yukon where organisers somehow managed to fit four hundred people into a three-hundred-seat gymnasium.

But if asked what was the most spectacular venue I've ever performed at, the answer would undoubtedly be the ancient, open-air Herodaticus Theatre at the foot of the Acropolis. In August 1989 I was invited by the Greek composer Yannis Markopoulos (of *Who Pays the Ferryman?* fame), to take part in the Athens Festival. There I sang not only two of his songs in Greek, accompanied by his orchestra but also *'Róisín Dubh'* (*a capella*), *'Óró Mo Bháidín'* and other songs with the harp – as far as I know the first, and possibly the last time Gaelic songs were heard in that ancient setting. I was staying at the Hilton Hotel. My diary has this entry: 'Apart from performing there, the best thing is the view of the Acropolis from my hotel window. It's not just spectacular, it is very moving. I don't recall this reaction to any other view ever. The Acropolis stands there in full view. I was hugging its base yesterday when we were filming for TV my part in the Yannis Markopoulos Festival of Athens Concerts there.'

In the mid 1980s also I was pleased to be able to give an all-Gaelic concert at the National Gallery in Dublin. The performance was recorded and released as an album/cd. For most of my singing life, I could only sprinkle the occasional Gaelic song here and there in my programmes. It was very satisfying to be able at last to give a two-hour performance in nothing but my own language – Irish Gaelic and Scot's Gallic.

In 1990 the celebration of Easter in the Orthodox Church and in Western Christendom coincided and BBC Radio 2 flew me to the Holy Land to take part in a special broadcast. The most memorable experience for me was facing the Wailing Wall with my hands on the lowest stone thought to have been there in Jesus' time. Who knows, perhaps the very stone I touched was touched by Him. I was also profoundly moved by the thought that the wall must surely be soaked with thousands of years of prayer.

The year 1985 turned out to be very significant for me. It included two rather dramatic accidents, and marrying Pat, which was no accident.

Mid UK tour on an unusually mild day in February, as was my wont on many concert days, I'd borrowed a bike from the hotel and cycled off through the lovely countryside on my own. Eventually, nestling against a friendly hedge in a field, I got lost in my book (a Daphne Du Maurier). Realising it was time to head back to the hotel for lunch, I got on my bike and glancing at my watch as I cycled through the last sleepy village, I saw I needed to hurry. I stood up on the pedals and remember no more. Weeks later this memory came back to me unbidden. I was in total darkness hearing a man's voice saying very urgently: 'Don't move! Don't move!'

Darkness again. My next memory is of a man's very agitated voice, possibly as I was coming out of the anaesthetic? I later found out that I had been discovered unconscious on the road by a passing motorist who rushed into the nearest house for help. Mercifully, a nurse lived there and when she saw the state I was in, fearing my neck was broken, she cautioned that I should not be moved and immediately called an ambulance.

When a very worried Pat and his two assistants saw I was not back for lunch, they drove out looking for me and saw the ambulances. The 'SOLD OUT' notice in front of the theatre in Darlington was swiftly changed to 'CANCELLED'. The remainder of the tour was also cancelled. I was kept in hospital for a week.

Pat's state of mind can only be imagined. My injuries were severe but not life-threatening. Facial injuries (for several weeks the right side of my face looked like the Elephant Man), teeth knocked out, injury to my eye and cheekbone, a ruptured ligament in my left thumb. Micro surgery corrected the latter. I was told that if this had happened ten years earlier when this type of micro surgery was unknown, I would have been left with a useless thumb – not good for harpers. As it happened, use of the thumb was forbidden for just six months so David Snell played my harp accompaniments in the TV series that followed.

Pat's dilemma, as my manager, was made worse by his having to cancel the USA/Canadian tour he had set up for March/April with the bookings already going very well. Although he never even as much as hinted at any of this, I'm sure it was quite a nightmare for him all told. His sole concern was that I would fully recover. The following letter to June Scott, my flautist for the cancelled tour, hints at some of the problems:

15th February, 1985

Dear June,

Enclosed please find cheque for £640 for the recent tour. I have been so busy cancelling overseas engagements that I have not managed to chat to Matthew Freeman yet. He is in shock, like the rest of us, and hopes Mary's ITV series will not be affected.

The venues missed in Scotland and others are already enquiring about a July tour, so I may be getting in touch with you again shortly.

Stay well and avoid bicycles.

Please let me have a receipt sometime.

Sincerely
Padraig O'Toole

There was an unspoken fear that my face would not be sufficiently healed for the cameras in the upcoming second TV series, 'Mary O'Hara and Friends', scheduled to start in May. Everyone was on tenterhooks. My recovery, thank God, was rapid and thorough; the only legacy being some small irregularities in the structure of my face and in the top row of my teeth, which only I would notice. The filming of the TV series went ahead as planned, as did the TV-advertised album (*Spread a Little Happiness*) based on the TV series. Once this was over, we had two weeks on a Greek island.

I had known Padraig O'Toole since 1975. He grew up speaking only Gaelic on Inis Mór, one of the Aran Islands, off Connemara and Clare on the west coast of Ireland. As a youth he had spent summers fishing, working on a lighthouse and labouring on building sites in the East End of London. He graduated with a Double First from the National University, entered a seminary and after ordination set out for Africa. When I first met him, however, he was in the process of leaving the priesthood and claimed to have no intention of ever again committing himself to either an ideology or a person. His declared aim was to wander the globe and his urge at that time was to work in South America as a VSO (Voluntary Service Overseas). To prepare himself for this task he had decided to study adult education at the University of Toronto under the noted South American educationalist Paulo Freiri, who regularly taught there. As it happened Freiri died unexpectedly and Pat never got to attend his courses but he got to know other people such as Marshall MacLuhan who inspired him to continue with his studies. As a result he went on to complete a doctorate in management at the University of Toronto. For a time he was unsure about what he wanted to do with his life but a commitment to marriage was not part of his plans.

One thing I've always admired about Pat is his patience. He has very good interpersonal skills and, if he takes an interest in something, it has always amazed me how fast he acquires competency. He is quick thinking and, if needs be, can make very quick decisions, whereas I'm a procrastinator. Furthermore, he is enviably ingenious. Once after a Carnegie Hall concert, I was stuck with my musicians for two days at New York's Kennedy airport because of a heavy snowfall. The backlog on the main transatlantic runways stretched for days. Pat arrived and within minutes he had got air tickets. How did he do it?

'Well, I asked the girl at the desk if there was any airport to which nobody wanted to fly.'

Within an hour or two we were on our way to a mining town in the opposite direction to London and in no time we were able catch a flight from there to wherever we were aiming for.

After Pat had completed his doctorate at the University of Toronto, he was still unsure of what direction he wished his life to take – having by then left the priesthood. While at Toronto he had travelled most of Canada doing research and his professor, Alan Brown, was very keen for him to stay in Canada and take up lecturing. Brown later stayed with us at Rivendell. 'Pat', he told me 'can write engagingly about the most boring of academic subjects.' Pat however was restless and wanted to take a year off to travel.

At this time my own work had expanded considerably. My autobiography *The Scent of the Roses* had generated considerable interest. It was six weeks on the *Sunday Times* top ten best-selling list in the UK and number one in several other countries. I had contracts for two other books, with several TV and touring contracts in the pipeline. This provided sufficient challenge for Pat's research and organising skills – as well as satisfying his urge to travel without commitment. The partnership worked well and, after almost a decade of knowing one another and six years of working closely together, the decision to get married was not difficult. We loved each other.

Pat would have liked to have had the marriage ceremony in his home place of Aran. But for me marriage was a very precious occasion and I wanted to keep it very private and involve the minimum number of other people. I managed it with my first wedding to Richard. I wanted it that way for my second wedding to Pat. Because the Catholic Church wants to make sure that there are no obstacles to people marrying, we had to wait six months before the church ceremony could be organised. I was scheduled to tour in Canada by then so we arranged the wedding for 17th September 1985. It was to take place in the town of Bramalee, just outside Toronto, on a day between concerts. I had a concert in Stratford, Ontario, two hundred miles away, the previous night and a book signing in Toronto the following morning. Since Pat has a 'thing' about not wearing rings, medals, or chains, it was at the last moment he agreed to a wedding ring for himself, so it was only on the morning of the wedding, en route to Toronto, that we picked up the two rings in a jeweller's in Stratford. Due to the last minute rush we did not try on the rings till we were nearing Toronto. They didn't fit. To further complicate matters, Pat had left his new suit hanging behind the door in England.

Giving me away was Ray Byrne, our very good friend and a brother of Gay Byrne of RTE. We left for the wedding from Ray's house. We were dead late but this bothered nobody – except Ray who was a stickler for time, but he magnanimously veiled his irritation. Other guests were the Best Man, Matthew Freeman, Joyce Byrne (Ray's wife) as Matron of Honour and Dr Russ Kempton, our Canadian friend who came down from the Canadian far north for the occasion. The Parish Priest and another priest friend completed the party. It was a very joyous occasion with much laughter brought about over the ill-fitting rings and the borrowed suit. A month later, after a concert tour in Canada, we were able to have our honeymoon in Puerto Vallarta, Mexico, where we had our wedding rings properly fitted. Pat valiantly wore his for a while. Ross had booked a room for us in a small private hotel and during breakfast next morning, the owner played classical music on the piano for us.

Recently our Dutch friend Jean Heitz sent me this joint letter written to her from Canada at that time. It gives a flavour of what was happening as we started into a prearranged six-week tour under the aegis of the Saskatchewan Arts Council of Canada. The honeymoon was postponed until this was over.

Motel Prairie Palace,
Eston, Saskatchewan, Canada
30th September 1985

Dear Jean & Flip

You'll hardly find this place on any map but it is sited among millions of acres of wheat and oil wells. The town itself, I believe, has a population of 3000 people. We drove for 100 miles today but saw not a soul but machines moving in the distance. The tour (4 concerts of 30 done so far) is going well…

The wedding went very well – a bit like a comic strip. It was a build-as-you-go project. It kept being postponed with the few attendants more prepared for the event than the central figures. I wore a new suit (borrowed from the celebrant because I forgot my own suit hanging behind the door at Rivendell). The rings were bought that morning in a bit of a rush in Stratford (a couple of hundred miles away) and they did not fit the fingers. The press were on the phone to the church long before the wedding took place – all because we were so much behind time.

Anyway, Mary is behaving very obediently since she became Mrs O'Toole. She's even singing better... It looks like we're having 20 different wedding receptions. They had a pre-wedding cake for us in Chicago.

It has been cold here in Saskatchewan but the sun itself is nice and hot. Today en route here, we spent three hours absorbing the quiet of an elbow of the meandering Saskatchewan River.

Must now go again for a little bit of Prairie air – I'm told!

Love
Pat

Dear Jean

I see Pat has filled you in with the latest. Today's outing was memorably lovely – after the days on end in hot air-conditioned hotel buildings. There was snow in some towns we passed through. The sun shone and I got a bit of a tan, believe it or not. The warm sun, the pure fresh invigorating air; the beauty of the river and the surrounding hills; the sheer unalloyed silence; and – very important – the delicious raw apples, nuts, grapes, brown bread and spring water for lunch made the day an interlude worth remembering. Pat is holding up tremendously well to married life – it's not new to me, remember! I must admit though that concerts and concern for them occupy prime place in my mental world. We can only unwind when the tour is over and we reach Mexico. Chicago was much more hectic with two concerts squashed together, Saturday night and Sunday afternoon. Long air flights before and after. Much more relaxing travelling this way by car along quiet spacious highways with none of the frantic hassle of England's motorways. We are settling into the tour very happily. The Arts Council's committee people in each town are extremely friendly and kind and entertain us with tasty morsels in their civilised homes after concerts...

End of space looming – and I'm endeavouring to lure Pat into the open once again before the light fails.

Will write again soon
Warmest love
Mary

The rescheduled tour of North America, went very smoothly – until during the first song of the tour's last concert which was in Saskatoon, I fell off the stage into the orchestra pit and, once again, was whisked off to the local hospital, unconscious, in an ambulance. This time

I was only kept overnight. The setting of the two mishaps couldn't be more different – the first on a country road with not as much as one spectator and the second on stage before an audience. Neither of these accidents had any long-lasting effects on my singing career, thank God.

Ever since I settled into The Gardener's Cottage and later Rivendell my father, who lived on his own in Dublin, would come over to me a few times a year and stay a couple of weeks at a time. This suited us both very well. In the late 1980s, however, when it became evident that he was no longer looking after himself properly, he came to live with us permanently, something for which he'd been angling for a long time, but which I'd hitherto resisted fearing I wouldn't be patient with him and that his presence might be divisive, now that I'd remarried. It should have been a very happy set-up all round because, of all his children, I had been the closest to him. But having him around permanently was a mixed blessing. He was in his element when we had friends for a meal or to stay. It gave him an attentive audience. He was a very good raconteur and had a rich life experience on which to draw. An erudite man, he loved books and could quote several of his beloved (late Victorian, mostly) poets verbatim and at length to fit any occasion. He got on well with everybody, particularly women. After my mother died (he was then fifty), I know of women who would gladly have married him, one even got engaged to him. I never met her because I had gone to live in the States with Richard. I didn't even know about the engagement until my brother-in-law casually mentioned it in a letter. I remember being quite upset simply because my father hadn't told me. He was working with FAO in the Arabian Desert when he got my telegram about Richard's death. Significantly, he immediately broke off his engagement.

My father valued his independence. No longer living in his flat in Ballsbridge within walking distance of Dublin City Centre, he had given up driving, so I suspect he felt fettered living with us in the middle of the countryside. Pat and I were not always around. If he loved anything more than his books, it was horses and horse-racing. Very soon after my mother died, he started to indulge once more in his favourite pastime: attending race meetings. He came to own horses

and I know that at least one was a winner at Cheltenham. In his old
age, when he wasn't reading or taking a walk, he watched the races
on TV. We took him to Greece and Turkey on holidays once but we
felt he'd have been happier back home watching the races, though he
was not the type ever to complain. Even when I was not on tour,
I couldn't, and to my shame, often wasn't willing to give him more
of my time, which I now regret. There were occasions when it was
difficult for everyone. He died in 1988 and was buried, as was his wish,
beside my mother in Dean's Grange cemetery in Dublin. It is only
when your parents are dead that you wish you had given them more
of your time while they were alive – asked them more questions and
listened attentively to their stories. An abiding childhood memory is
of my father singing as he went about the house. Which brings me
to his first-born, the most multi-talented of his children: my sister
Joan.

By all accounts she had achieved high acclaim in her chosen profession as a theatre actress, principally at the Abbey Theatre. In her
later years and up until the time of her death, she also had become a
household name in Ireland playing the role of Eunice in *Fair City*,
a popular RTE TV soap.

In 1978 I had three nights at the Gaiety Theatre in Dublin. After
the first concert Joan came backstage – she had never seen me in
concert before – her first words were: 'Mel, I'm at your feet!'

Those words of hers meant as much to me, if not more than Paul
Hume of the *Washington Post*'s summing up of the recital at the Phillips
Gallery (1957): 'Mary O'Hara has raised the art of folk-singing to a
new high level.'

Consciously or not, I suppose I'd always sought Joan's approval.
It was rarely forthcoming. In a press interview in 1997, she mentioned
her unhappy childhood and acknowledged how she deliberately kept
her distance from her siblings: 'I usen't to speak to them, they were
afraid of me...'

For a while after her marriage, we became close, but, sadly, the
rapport did not last; she began to distance herself again.

In the final months before she died in 2007 I was able to go over
to Dublin and spend long hours with her in hospital. One day she said
to me: 'Mel, you were very lucky with your two husbands.'

'Yes, Zone,' I said, 'very *blessed*.'

August 1986 at Rivendell.

'Legs O'Hara' and 'Legs O'Toole'.

In Chicago for concerts, late 1980s.

Mary and Pat with Leon Uris, at Claridges for the launch of his novel
Mitla Pass, *25th April 1989.*

Mary with old acquaintance Tim Pat Coogan, Irish writer, journalist and former editor
of the Irish Press. *Also at the launch of Uris's book.*

Chicago, May 1987.

Mary and her father at Rivendell in the late 1980s.

Mary meets the Duchess of Kent at a Royal Gala at the Theatre Royal in Norwich, early 1990.

Chicago 1990, after a concert.

*Mary's first camping
experience on the
slopes of Mount
Kenya, almost on
the equator but
very cold,
October 1996.*

*The Land Rover after it
crashed over the bridge
on the way to Mombasa.
Repaired, it gave good
service later in
Tanzania.*

*Reuben, Mary, Muthone,
Muthone's daughter
and Elijah the cat at
23 Chalbi Drive
Hospital,
Dar es Salaam.*

*Takawiri Island on
Lake Victoria, wearing
nets because of the flies.
Coming here the
overcrowded boat hit a
fishing vessel and they
thought they'd be spilled
out among the crocodiles.*

Sailing down the east coast of Africa, 1997.

Camping in the bush (Olduvai Gorge, Kenya) with some of Pat's students, 1999.

Any Nits? With 'new' best friend Rafiki, and Rory Moss.

During one of the frequent power cuts in Dar es Salaam, 2000.

The cast of Harp on the Willow, *including Marina Prior (2nd from right) who played Mary, Sydney, Australia, 2004 and again in Melbourne 2007.*

2009: Mary after giving a talk in Ottawa at the Northern Lights Harp Festival organised by Susan Sweeney Hermon. Susan (left) with Janine Dudding, the other member of Acacia Harp Duo

Mary and Pat after one of Mary's talks in Halifax, NS, with friends Ed and Maggie Murray.

During filming of the video Mary O'Hara at Home, *summer 1990.*

A 2011 photo of Mary and Pat.

You never knew what Joan was going to come out with next.

'Mel,' she said rather shyly the next day, 'if you die before me, can I marry Pat?'

I had known for some years that she had returned to the practice of her Faith which was a source of great strength to her and we often talked about the power of prayer. As the days went by, now and then, I instinctively told her gently that I loved her and one night, opening her eyes, she said through the oxygen mask: 'And I love you too Mel.'

I was on my way to see her the next time but she died before I got there. Joan had a highly developed sense of the ridiculous which, I think, kept her sane. A saying of hers I will always remember: 'You can't get to heaven without a sense of humour.'

Pat has always loved teaching and I guessed that if I ever decided to give up singing, he would return to the classroom. We agreed that if I could find a congenial manager, Pat would return to his books. We found such a person in Johnny Manns, a happy-going person, who was not pushy or ever felt a need to control people. We sat down and discussed my requirements, likes, dislikes and reservations. He then booked engagements, mailed me the contracts and telephoned to discuss any perceived problems. From there on, he trusted me to carry out the engagement. We had a very amicable relationship and all went smoothly. And so in 1986 Pat did return to the classroom and at the same time he started a Masters Degree in Information Technology at Reading University. He felt quite happy leaving my work to Johnny and me and had no need or desire to get involved. His teaching schedule meant he could not accompany me on tour any more and this took much of the fun out of touring. Matthew Freeman also, was by now getting a lot of work as a conductor, both in England and abroad and was not always available to accompany me especially on lengthy tours, which I gradually ceased doing.

It was important to me that Pat felt fulfilled and the idea of my winding down my singing career was not an unwelcome prospect. I could not part-retire from singing. It had to be completely or not at all. In 1992, after taking part in the bicentenary celebration of that famous Last Meetings of the Harpers in Belfast in 1792, I decided to bow out of singing altogether while my voice was still at its best.

I had seen too many singers whom I admired tread the boards for too long after their sell-by dates. I informed Johnny of my decision. He just said that it was a pity and, typically, did not try to dissuade me. The arrangement was that I'd fulfil my current six-month schedule but he was not to book any more new engagements after a certain date. With Pat now involved in full-time teaching, it was left to me to make sure all my engagements were written into my diary.

One day I looked up my diary to book an appointment with my hairdresser and to my horror found I was also booked that same evening to do a concert in Brighton, a few hours' drive away. Matthew Freeman my MD and pianist could not be reached, nor could my flautist. I had my harp, of course, and, as it was a Saturday, Pat was able to drive me to the venue – at top speed. In the course of the journey I rearranged my whole concert programme cutting out the songs that required piano or flute. By now, I had a very wide and varied repertoire that could be called up at a moment's notice. I arrived at the hall just in time to do a quick sound check, which was easy as it was just me with my harp. I had to forego my customary routine before a performance but the two-hour performance itself went very well.

Friends suggested that I do a 'Farewell Tour' or perhaps give a 'Farewell Concert' at the Royal Festival Hall or Albert Hall in London but I was totally against any such fanfare. I wanted to slip away quietly, very quietly. Johnny did not object nor did Pat. I did not want any announcement or extra fuss made about what was to be the last singing performance of my career, which as it happened was some-where in Wales. The date had been shuffled about at some stage, and, as in the case of the concert mentioned above, Manns' office forgot to send the amended paperwork. At some stage they must have phoned me to let me know the new arrangements, but the change never found its way into my diary, with the result that when the day came I was nowhere be found. In fact, all that afternoon I was with a friend at a Garden Centre and consequently out of reach (no mobile phones in those days). I was told afterwards that the venue was sold out. It was all very embarrassing. Johnny was very good about it and took the blame.

That was how, in 1994, I retired from singing. Nothing spectacu-lar. In all probability I could have gone on singing with my voice still at its best, but for who knows how long. I decided not to take the risk. What I could not possibly have known at the time was that my retirement from singing was just the beginning of a new life – a life full of undreamt-of adventure and unexpected challenges.

CHAPTER 16

Africa Casts its Spell

WONDERFUL and wonder-filling East Africa! Six years of adventure, discovery, enrichment and mind-broadening. Even a few death-brushing experiences did not spoil the general enchantment. And this is how it came about.

It was early in 1996. Pat was still teaching and each school holiday or half term I'd pick him up from school and we'd fly off to Spain or Greece. Pat, who was now a Deputy Head, was finding work more of a chore and each Friday he'd arrive home exhausted and discouraged, which was very uncharacteristic. This time he suggested we try the east coast of Kenya and there was no dissent. We both relished the prospect of sun and sea in a part of the world we hadn't yet visited. Africa hadn't lost its lure for either of us: Pat remembered with affection his eight years working in Nigeria starting in the mid 1960s, which took in the Nigeria/Biafra Civil War; I had positive memories of visiting my father in Ghana, then known as The Gold Coast, when I was a teenager.

Imagine a cold and wet, dreary afternoon in February in England. I'm downstairs sorting out the supper and Pat is upstairs settled into his study, unwinding after a tedious week of teaching. He was engaged, as was his wont, in his customary weekend pursuit of reading the *Times Educational Supplement* while sipping a glass of red wine with the week's unopened mail by his side. This time he also had a bundle of holiday brochures about Mombasa, a tourist resort on the shores of the Indian Ocean. I knew that he would not be interested in much else until he had finished reading his TES and was surprised to hear him calling down to me: 'Mary, what about two years in Kenya instead of two weeks?'

Without any hesitation, my response was: 'Why not?'

He had spotted ads for 'Head of History' at two different schools in Nairobi. I am not of a practical bent of mind but I have to believe Pat when he tells me that my next question was: 'But what about Rivendell?'

Pat suggested we sell it or let it – and let it we did. I was really excited at this prospect.

Pat had not taught history since his young days when he lectured in History and Agricultural Science at a Teacher Training College in Nigeria. The advertisements required the usual 'recent photo and hand-written CV' – something Pat hadn't attempted for several years – but both schools waived these requirements. He listed his qualifications and experience and we waited in a state of pleasant anticipation, hoping that at least one might reply. In fact both replied. Each school, having seen his CV, independently suggested that he might consider applying for the post of 'network manager' or 'IT co-ordinator', posts not yet advertised. They emphasised that the post of 'Head of History' was still available. Pat is very keen on IT, having already been IT co-ordinator in two schools in the UK. Both Nairobi schools called him for interviews, which were to take place in London in the same week. By the time of the interviews Pat had resigned his Deputy Headship and was doing supply teaching. One month he might be teaching Desk Top Publishing to a class in Basingstoke, another couple of months 'A' Level Religion in Reading, or Design Technology at some other school. He was finding his new situation very stimulating but still, the prospect of Africa sowed restlessness and a desire to travel – in both of us.

When Pat returned home from the interview with Mr Onslow, the Headmaster of Peponi School, Nairobi, he looked genuinely pleased and had been struck by how similar Onslow's philosophy of teaching was to his own.

'I'd really love that IT post,' he said, 'and I like that Headmaster. The problem is that he has several interviews set up and only at the end will he make a decision. It'll be a couple of weeks before he can make a decision.'

'But what about the other interview you've set up?'

'I'll take my chances and go ahead with it.'

We were both somewhat disappointed and now in a state of suspense. What if the other interviewer offered him the job...

Next day, mid morning, the phone rang and it was Mr Onslow asking to speak to Pat. I explained that he was teaching in Basingstoke
and would he like to leave a message.

'Yes. If Dr O'Toole is still interested, he can have the job.'

I telephoned Pat at once and he was over the moon – as was I.
That's how we both ended up in Africa in July 1996. That evening we
started planning, thrilled at the prospect of two years in Nairobi,
endless sunshine, long school holidays, going on safari, visiting game
parks.

The city of Nairobi sits sprawled on a six-thousand-foot-high plateau
and though it almost straddles the equator, it can still be quite cool
in July. We landed late afternoon on a sunless day. Mr Onslow picked
us up at the airport. Our first impressions did not disappoint – jostling
crowds, alive and colourful, novel sounds and smells, people dashing
between cars, just missing being run over as Mr Onslow drove at speed
zig-zag fashion over pot-holed roads.

Though we had already rented a bungalow on the edge of town,
we spent our first night as guests of the Onslows in their colonial-style
home with its very pretty English-style garden. We spent our siesta
looking out of the windows and listening to the strange sounds coming from the garden. We spotted strange birds and a colony of tiny
striped mice playing in the flower border just below our window. We
never came across these mice again during our stay in Africa. We felt
as if we were on a different planet. But we were soon brought back
to earth when the Onslows dropped us off at our rented house in
Lavington, a respectable suburb of Nairobi but also bordering a
notorious slum.

Our smallish three-bedroom bungalow, rented from a Kenyan, was
squat in the middle of an acre of land with flowering shrubs and a
banana tree outside the front door. It was surrounded by a fifteen-
foot-high concrete wall and was guarded night and day by four huge
dogs, a cross between an Alsatian and a South African Ridgeback.
A watchman unleashed the dogs during the night and they looked
(and acted) as if they'd eat you alive if you so much as dared to put
your toe outside the door. A second watchman took over at 6 am,
chaining them to trees, so that we could freely move about outside.

Their barking was quite formidable and constant. My suggestion to
get rid of them was viewed with both horror and incredulity; our continued safety depended on them, I was told. It was the first of many
clouds to come looming over Paradise.

On our second day in the country, we were taken on a tour of
Nairobi National Park and, as if on cue to greet us inside the gate,
we were met by a group of stately, elegant giraffes – much more
welcoming than the baying dogs at Lavington. We spent the day in
the park, catching sight of a multitude of exotic birds and wild
animals – a fitting introduction to Kenya that we could not fault.
Weekend camping trips were a feature of Peponi school life and we
soon found ourselves with a bus-full of excited students heading in
the direction of Mount Kenya for my first camping experience. This
included swimming in a river and mountain-climbing up the *very* steep
oddly-named Delemere's Nose. This proved to me that my new hip
was fully functional, which reassured me that I could now go back to
my beloved tennis – which I did with gusto.

After that first taste, here I was, aged sixty-one, hooked on camping. From then on we went camping on our own almost every weekend. Friday afternoons, I'd pick up Pat from school and head straight
for our destination, by the shores of Lake Naivasha or Nakuru
National Park or farther afield. My most vivid memory was of camping all on our own, probably where we shouldn't have camped, and
being woken up at 3 am by the sound of a group of hippos munching
grass all around and right up against our lone little tent. I nudged
Pat, sound asleep in his sleeping bag, and together, almost not daring
to breathe, we listened intently to the 'munch, munch, munch' sound.
Eventually as the midnight feast seemed to have ended, we dared to
peer through the window of our tent and there, under the full moon,
were four huge hippos heading back towards the lake.

Pat had quickly settled into his teaching at Peponi. He was hired
as IT co-ordinator but because Kenya, at the time, was suffering from
prolonged power cuts, he found himself teaching Physics and Maths
until such time as the school could import an electricity generator
from England. Physics he loved but knowledge of the subject had
advanced considerably since his time in college and this meant his
burning the midnight oil to catch up. It also meant that for the
first few months or so, even our camping trips were overshadowed

somewhat by his need to study. It was the type of challenge Pat relished. It seemed incongruous to sit in our tent by Lake Naivasha with
Pat preparing his lessons and studying physics text books by hurri-
cane lamp.

Soon, however, Pat felt he had mastered his subject sufficiently, so
no more textbooks when camping. The electricity generator arrived
from England and he resumed his original job of Head of IT.

During most week-days, while Pat taught at Peponi, I went about
my own routine. Much to the concern of everyone, especially our
house-girl Muthoni, I decided one day to explore the slum adjacent
to our house. It seemed quite a natural thing to do. Muthoni insisted
on accompanying me but first she counselled me to dress simply and
remove bracelets, rings, earrings, and any other sign of wealth. A bit
extreme, I thought, but later she explained that there had been times
when she herself had been robbed of the clothes she wore as she walked
home after work. People in the slum were very pleasant and even talkative but inevitably my visit turned into a kind of procession of happy
little children, laughing and dancing round this novelty in their midst.
Soon, friends dissuaded me from making a habit of this.

After that, my regular walk most mornings was in the other direction from the slum, to a Catholic college that had an excellent library.
I chose to avoid the main road, using instead the quieter, more picturesque route, used only by Africans. Practising my Kiswahili, I much
enjoyed the courteous exchange of greetings with passers by – always
initiated by me – while we kept on walking. I trod well-worn foot-
paths, crossed neat, though wobbly little wooden bridges over mur-
muring streams; crossed the odd tarmac road on to some wide leafy
avenues lined with jacaranda trees, part of the more affluent suburbs
of Nairobi. People got used to the sight of this friendly white woman
walking on her own. The fortified properties along the route, with
their high walls, iron gates and armed watchmen, had owners,
whether African or European, who usually went about in their 4 x 4s
and simply did not walk. Some of the people I met probably worked
in those houses or maybe wished they did. Only once was I asked for
money. I was crossing a narrow, rickety little bridge, when three
youths stopped me: spreading my hands indicating I had nothing on
me, they took my word, allowed me to pass and we continued on our
different ways. Other than that, the only people who stopped to talk

to me were young people looking for work. Many spoke good English. Beatrice explained she was Luhya, from Western Kenya near Lake Victoria. An abused wife with a small child, she ended up working for us, much to the annoyance of Muthoni, a Kikuyu who never tired of pointing out we did not need another worker, least of all a Luhya. Eventually Pat arranged a typing course for Beatrice and she moved on. Last time we heard from her she was in America and doing very well.

One other recruit from this period was George, a very bright young man with a positive and sunny nature. He had only basic schooling, something that he wanted to remedy. He considered himself a Maasai and was very proud of the fact, though I discovered later his mother was Kikuyu. He too came to our house and learnt to cook and write and speak better English. He greatly loved his Maasai tribal culture and liked nothing better than to demonstrate the Maasai dance which, in our ignorance looked to us like a competition to see who can jump the highest. Once, I feared he might decapitate himself. Oblivious to the ceiling fan that was turning full blast, he did a voluntary demonstration for our visitors; forgetting himself in his enthusiasm, he jumped higher and higher. After that, any dancing was done outside. Eventually we paid a friend to give George a job as night watchman at a mission station at the foot of the Ngong Hills outside Nairobi. He acquitted himself well, we were told, putting to rout a whole group of armed robbers that one night invaded the compound. Nobody is his right mind confronts an armed Maasai in full battle attire. Dear George was destined to make several benign appearances in our lives during our next six years in Africa.

I was shortly to see another side of Nairobi life. Anyone visiting the city cannot but notice the multitude of street children wandering about. I was therefore very interested and curious when a Lavington neighbour, Shariffa Keshavjee, a wealthy Asian Moslem woman, asked me if I'd be willing to teach songs to some street children. Shariffa was in the process of founding what has since become the very successful Hawkers Market Girls Centre in Nairobi. Still at the initial stage of the project, Shariffa and her group of women friends were organising classes for girls between the ages of five and ten and they wanted to enter them for a singing competition. She had heard I was a retired singer. I drove to the school a couple of times a week and taught the children songs. I am not sure how appropriate the songs were or whether my pupils won any competition, but it would be difficult to find anywhere a more welcoming and enthusiastic group of pupils. In spite of their sad situation, they were always cheerful and happy. They showed such gratitude and delight at my visits. Next time I bumped into Shariffa was in London April 2010 when I was opening an exhibition run by the Society for Art of Imagination at the request of its founder, Brigid Marlin, (my would-be-blackbird friend of College of Art days). It was then I heard how well the Centre continues to prosper.

Rather than sell our old car in England, we shipped it out to Nairobi but it took much longer to arrive than we had anticipated. In the meantime Mr Onslow very kindly lent us an old Landrover. It was half-term when word came that our car had finally arrived at Mombasa and we looked forward immensely to our two-hundred-mile trip to the coast to collect it. The Nairobi/Mombasa night train is legendary. It is downhill six thousand feet. The train, we discovered, had seen better days but we were assured that nothing much could go wrong on the trip down-hill as all they had to do was to release the break. In the morning we arrived at Mombassa, a humid, teeming city. We had arranged to meet the man responsible for shipping our car at a local hotel for coffee, or as it turned out, beer and when I heard the phrase 'a little problem' I was by now sufficiently knowledgeable about Africa to know that 'little' meant 'big' and that we would not be getting our car that day. And so it proved.

Pat had pre-booked a few nights at Nyali Beach Hotel, a fashion-able, well-established place overlooking the ocean. Our stay there was idyllic. Swimming first thing in the morning in the vast pool and later in the Indian Ocean; friendly Africans, delicious food. Our expect-ations were high and we were not disappointed. It only added to the enjoyment to find little vervet monkeys had, in our absence, come in and been rifling through our belongings in the bedroom. This was the first of many experiences that made our coming to Africa worthwhile.

Though we expected to be driving our car back to Nairobi, all the signs were that it would not be ready. So, when Pat saw a direct 'non-stop' bus service advertised in the hotel, we booked two seats. Travelling by bus was considered to be by far the cheaper end of the market. It was said to be dangerous and unpredictable; but that did not put us of. We arrived at our bus terminal for a 7 am departure but were told that the bus was full. It made no difference that we had our tickets and our receipts. Information was scarce and very reluctantly dispensed but we sat on a bench and simply waited. By ten o'clock we were summoned to the bus to find that it was only half full but we were glad of the seats and sought no further explanation. The driver was young and cheerful, drove fast, and was apparently pro-grammed to refuse to acknowledge the existence of potholes. For me a highlight of the return journey was our first sighting, ever, of baobab trees. Until then I had assumed the baobab was purely fictional, never having come across it anywhere apart from the mention of it in *The Little Prince* by Saint-Exupery. Now, here they were, in all their awesomely huge other-worldly-looking splendour, with their strange, relatively short, non-spreading branches, making the trees look as if 'their roots are up in the air', as someone has put it. Acres of them were growing together or solitary, close to the roadside with locals standing or sitting under and around them taking refreshments. About half way on our journey we were further fascinated to find the roadside lined with troop of baboons, clearly waiting for the bus to pass and pounce on the dozens of bananas the driver tossed out the window towards them. No slowing down. A regular ritual it seemed. Still relatively new to wild-life we simply emailed our friends, thrilled to be telling them about this episode and referring to the baboons as monkeys.

Shortly after leaving Mombasa, our so-called 'non-stop' bus to Nairobi swerved here and there, taking in both sides of the road and picking up anyone and everyone heading in our direction. At one place the driver stopped to pick up a bag of green leaves, which Pat recog-nised as Khat, a marijuana-type stimulant taken by long-distance drivers in Kenya to keep awake. Every so often we saw him dip his hand into the bag, chew a leaf and offer another to anyone interested. About four hours into the journey, the green leaves began taking their effect and the driver became ever more cheerful and erratic. As evening approached, the driving became even more hazardous. Our driver and drivers of on-coming vehicles, racing towards us at speed, vied with one another to see who would reach the pothole first. The rules of the road were suspended and whether one drove on the left or on the right was dictated by the location of the potholes. It was only as we approached Nairobi and the dual carriageway and the police road-blocks that he calmed down. By the time we entered Nairobi, he, by now on first-name terms with us, insisted on taking us directly to our house in Lavington. Were we relieved to have reached the safety of our barking dogs.

It took two more trips to Mombasa before we finally took posses-sion of our car. On one occasion we took a taxi along the coast for about thirty miles and stayed at another fine hotel with a sprinkling of holidaymakers from Europe. It was a bad season for tourists and the locals who depended so much on tourism pleaded great hardship. We struck up a conversation with two fellows who eked out a fragile living taking tourists out to the reef in a battered-looking outrigger with a large sail. It was made from a hollowed-out tree which the locals called *ngalow*. They told us how bad the season was and how desperate they were for money. Pat and I discussed this and came up with a plan. We had arrived by taxi and intended to return to Mombassa by taxi. What, we asked ourselves, if we added a bit more money and our two new-found acquaintances sailed us down the coast to our old hotel? It would take four hours' sailing they said. They jumped at the suggestion and next morning, as others were returning from their morning swim to have breakfast, Pat and I marched down the beach with our minimal luggage. Several people we met volun-teered the information that we were daft.

'They will take your money and dump you overboard,' one opined, while shaking his head.

The boat was too narrow to take our bag lying flat. Also the large sail seemed a lot more tattered than the one we remembered from the previous day. The boat likewise looked slightly more bedraggled. Anyhow, nothing daunted, in we got and off we went. The boat zig-zagged its way safely out towards the reef and just as our confidence was returning and we were about to cross to the deep water beyond the reef, the long pole that the younger man used for pushing got stuck in the crags. The boat sailed on without it, towards the high waves. Of course, we needed that pole and as the boat turned side-ways to the breakers, our navigator jumped overboard to retrieve it.

There followed a period of navigational uncertainty as we tossed and turned and for a while I was not sure if my swimming skills were sufficient to save me. We had no life jacket but Pat, brought up by the sea, had instilled into me that in such situations you automatically cast your eye about for whatever floats, whether a bottle of drinking water or a suitcase. The captain, for so he must have been, finally managed to drag his navigator – for so he must have been – and his pole aboard and, everyone all smiles, we made a successful passage over the reef. I know nothing about sailing but Pat does and he assured me that he was impressed. Once outside the reef, if it was not always plain sailing, it was certainly one of my most pleasant days at sea ever. Our boatmen had good English and chatting about the conditions of their lives made the hours slip by unnoticed. The promised four hours was more like six but we were not surprised. Had there been fewer holes in the sail, I'm sure we could have shaved several hours off our voyage, but who would want that? It was money well spent.

The most attractive feature of our house in Nairobi was the large garden, which we soon discovered we shared with a tortoise. Nobody knew how old he was. That and his habit of disappearing without trace for days earned him the name Moses. He just came unannounced out of nowhere. He never needed anything, never made demands; sometimes he would make his regal way in one door and out the other, ignoring whatever was going on around him. We only started to enjoy our garden fully when we managed to persuade the owner to remove the three fiercest dogs. We kept Bahati, Swahili for 'lucky', the youngest dog, and not yet grown into full fierceness. He didn't 'eat us alive'. He stole our hearts. Consequently, he was probably not a very good watchdog and one dark night, thieves came and stole all the manhole covers. Relaying the incident to his colleagues at Peponi next morning, Pat observed the 'we told you so' nodding of some heads. It was comical to watch Bahati trying to play with Moses but he never got anywhere.

For months Muthoni, our house-girl, had been pleading with us for a kitten but I was firmly against the idea. I felt we had enough on our plate and could not handle being manipulated by yet another animal. Then one day someone threw a tiny under-nourished little kitten with disproportionately huge eyes over the high wall that separated us from the slum. Muthoni presented us with it, more or less as a sign from above, a *fait accompli*, now safely snuggling in her ample bosom. We named it Elijah – the rest of our African staff, apart from Muthoni, had lovely biblical names – and for the first few days she claimed to be keeping it alive with her own milk. We watched Muthoni gradually introduce huge dog to scrawny kitten and, in disbelief, we looked on as she trained them to eat from the same plate. Shades of the lion lying down with the lamb. If Bahati ruled us, Elijah ruled Bahati. He became besotted and never gave up trying to play with her. Soon Elijah grew stronger and liked racing up a tree to peer disdainfully down at Bahati who waited adoringly below, giant paws around the trunk but unable to join her. We'd sit on the lawn for ages watching these two very different animals playing – Elijah lazily tolerating Bahati as he gently pulled her this way and that. She made the odd wild swipe at him and then Bahati would dash off to the far corner of the compound to investigate what Moses was up to – which was nothing much.

We had been living in Kenya for several months before we had the pleasure of seeing our little red imported Volkswagen GTI (fondly referred to as Marco, the Dragon), parked outside our Lavington home. But that was only a first move. For every necessary registration, Kenya has in place a well regulated system of bribes. Though Pat was in possession of all the documentation, each visit to a government office turned up new requirements, until one day a kindly official pulled him aside and briefed him on the facts – as if anyone could be in doubt. At this stage, the job of getting the car taxed was handed over to me. It was now my turn to deal with officialdom. This involved several long waits in several long queues and for several days. In my naivety it never occurred to me that I was expected to give a bribe. That way the business would have been expedited. I never caught on to this. I simply turned up again the following day, as instructed, and patiently joined the queue – more often than not, the lone European in a line of Africans. In the end, the same individual who kept telling me to 'come back tomorrow' resignedly handed me back the form, now officially stamped. I think he just took pity on me, a poor benighted *mzungu* ... Perhaps he despaired of my ever figuring out the system.

Finally Marco could take us camping. And then we found that what worked well on the smooth roads of England was a disaster on the rougher terrain of East Africa. Travelling in Kenya could be arduous, often adventurous but never boring. One had to be prepared for the unexpected, be it the bridge down or the fatal accident. Cavernous potholes seemed to open up suddenly out of nowhere. Pat saw to it that we never left our house without the necessary emergency equipment – tow-ropes, spares, blankets, first aid, HIV kit. Timing was the most difficult to gauge for one tried to reach the destination before night-fall, the hours when robbers were most likely to strike. If anything this added to the general excitement. Pat who is very interested in development, liked to divert by going to out-of-the-way places to inspect projects he had heard about. I often wondered why so many of what must have been at one time very promising ideas had become such failed projects, derelict in every sense. Kenya is a rich country, so full of potential and yet so poverty-stricken. It took a while for me to understand the reason, which is of course corruption.

Shortly after our arrival we purchased a second-hand Landrover, ideal for camping and especially fitted out to contend with the pot-holed roads of Kenya. We bought it from Eamon Ceant, one of a team of Irish government foresters who had worked in Kenya for several years in a project of reforestation financed to the extent of several million pounds annually by the Irish Government. I asked him why they were selling out and he shook his head sadly: 'A government minister wants to appropriate the land.'

But that wasn't the complete story; the Kenyan government also wanted the 'Aid Grant' paid directly into the minister's account and, failing this, was prepared to let the whole enterprise collapse. This was a familiar story and explained most if not all of the failed projects we often came across on our travels.

Pat's brother, Michael, who visited us in Nairobi, had an electronics factory in Ireland. He outsourced work to areas with cheap labour and Kenya, with its thousands of educated unemployed youth, seemed an ideal place. Michael was asked by the Irish government to train some young Kenyans for a joint inter-governmental project to be established in a very deprived area just outside Nairobi, not far from where we lived. About twenty young Kenyans spent six months in Ireland and, according to Michael, a better group of trainees you could not find – intelligent, hard-working, dedicated and competent. The factory was built and stocked and started up by Irish government money. The newly trained recruits were installed and everything seemed to work. Then it reached the time for the Kenyan government to pay its contribution of several million; it was paid into a ruling party politician's account. An idea that looked good on paper collapsed. Multiply this experience by several hundred and even I with no financial acumen can see disaster looming. Often it beggared belief what named individuals in the government and police were getting away with.

In their opinion this was meeting the donor nations' demand for 'transparency'. But Michael also explained that donors were not totally blameless in this matter. Governments in the EU, for example, had undertaken to spend a certain percentage of their GDP annually helping under-developed nations and towards the end of each financial year there was a rush to off-load substantial sums of money because unspent budgets meant egg on some anonymous functionary's face. It may be that some Aid projects are hurriedly researched and not carefully enough set up. This was redolent of giving concerts in American universities where students had already paid for entertainment as part of their annual fees and the authorities made no effort whatsoever to publicise outside the university.

I never read the daily newspapers till we went to Kenya where for the first time I began to take an interest, not only in the daily news but in politics – something hitherto very foreign to me. Gradually I came to understand the myriad forces and personalities that were at work. The media portrayed politicians and all organs of state, especially the police, in a disturbing and negative light. The populace, battered from all angles through misgovernment, had nowhere to turn. They were to be pitied.

As in the case of Marco, the Landrover too was shortly to be christened. We called him 'Lazarus' for, like his biblical namesake, he was destined to have more than one life.

Driving is something I've always enjoyed. However, driving anywhere in Kenya is hazardous. It surprised me that some Europeans thought me brave to venture out on my own but I took it all in my stride. Apart from potholes, which were ubiquitous and a risk for all drivers, I very soon learnt that the rules of the road were blithely flouted by most young African drivers, forcing one to be extra wary. The biggest offenders were the drivers of the *matatus*, the local name for the passenger buses that ply the streets of Nairobi. These ramshackle vehicles were always crammed with people and they flitted hither and thither in search of passengers, pouncing with speed upon any prospective traveller with a ready fare. As a form of transport, the *matatu* is cheap but it is prone to accidents and if you carry anything of value, avoid using it. Nairobi traffic seemed permanently gridlocked and thus encouraged a certain amount of aggressiveness.

While vigilance still remained paramount, travelling in Lazarus now opened up for us a new vista on Kenya. Not only did it afford us a safety greater than driving in Marco but, once ensconced inside it, in a double sense, we could look down on other smaller vehicles and therefore felt that much less vulnerable. It was ideal for camping in the wild. Gradually we started exploring the more distant countryside, places within a couple of days' reach of Nairobi.

One of our first memorable trips was to Lake Baringo, about two days' distant. Many of the lakes in this part of Kenya are saline and some soda but Baringo is freshwater and has crocodiles, hippos and several hundred species of birds and fish. Because we diverted in order to visit Crater Lake with its waters green as liquid paint, we arrived at Lake Baringo after dusk, later than planned. We did not feel it safe enough to start setting up our tent. A friendly boatman persuaded us to accompany him to an island on the lake that he claimed had accommodation for visitors. Under the cover of darkness, the rhythm of the oars, mixed in with the other tropical noises, sounded eerie, even magical, and the island itself, when it finally came into view, looked tall and ghostly, a cragged cone rising steeply out of the waters of the lake. We followed the boatman to the top, up winding paths lit with paraffin lamps. High up, out of reach of the flies, we found awaiting us a cool breeze and the loveliest of sleeping quarters. There was even a hut that served supper. It was difficult to believe that our exalted perch was one thousand metres above sea level and almost on the equator. It was exciting to wake up in the morning, the sun shining through the curtains and see from our bed the lake shimmering far, far below us. We saw crocodiles there in the distance and hippos. We breakfasted in another hut perched on an overhanging ledge. As it was Sunday and we needed to reach Nairobi before dark, it was with some reluctance that we meandered towards the jetty about mid morning. To our astonishment we saw a young man swimming. The boatman said it was quite safe. Pat dared me to jump in, which I did, though I stayed only briefly and just to be able to say that I swam with crocodiles. They were very far off though…

School holidays in Kenya were generous and a few weeks on the coast looked tempting. We discovered Mweni Cottages, thatched huts for rent twenty miles south of Mombasa, not far from the Tanzanian border. Situated on the shore, each had a bedroom, sitting-room and kitchen with fridge and cooker. A cook cum house-keeper was part of the deal. Each evening a fisherman would visit us carrying the day's catch in a basket on his head and, with the help of the cook, I selected the night's supper. During the day, young girls brought locally grown vegetables and again the cook helped me haggle for the best price. Our days were spent reading, swimming or walking the reef when the tide was out. Pat, being much more adventurous, loved scuba diving. Not I. I lack the courage and I have no desire to consort with sharks, thank you very much. Swimming is different; I can't get enough of it.

Security is always an issue in Kenya, even on the beach. The hut was well protected with shuttered windows and bars everywhere, which seemed odd as any enterprising thief could just put his hand through the thatched roof. On the first night we had an intruder. In the small hours we were awakened by a terrific racket coming from the kitchen, the sound of pots, pans and plates thrown about. Pat, having extricated himself from the mosquito net, grabbed the cutlass that he always carried with him. We listened while the sound continued unabated. An amateur thief perhaps? It took a while for Pat to muster up enough courage to push open the creaking kitchen door. Inside, staring at him with huge innocent eyes, was a little bush baby, beautiful to behold. He had crawled in through the half open window and was investigating the food situation. We had never seen a bush baby before and had to look up the book to identify it. It was with some reluctance that we set him free. It was worth the few broken plates.

Old Kenya hands never tired of warning us about the danger of robbers and it wasn't too long before we found out for ourselves. It was some months after our arrival in Nairobi that we had our first brush with them – well Pat did. He had an appointment with a computer company in town and we parked as usual, paying the watchman the customary fee to keep an eye on the car while we were inside the building. In the past I had sat in the car but for some reason I decided this time to accompany Pat inside. We had our VW Golf Gti with us and as it is very low to the ground, Pat feared that we had done some damage when we hit a fresh pothole as we turned into the street. On our return to the car, the watchman greeted us with a smile but when Pat reversed out he found that the brakes didn't work and he attributed this to the pot-hole, which was confirmed when the watchman pointed to the oil on the ground where we had been parked. The watchman suggested 'mechanic' and we were very surprised at the alacrity with which four of them appeared. Without a word one of them dived under the car and reappeared almost immediately with a contraption of tubing dripping with oil. I had no idea what was happening. They wanted money to go to the garage and purchase new fittings but Pat said that the Gti was not a car used much in Kenya because of the potholes and that even VW garages would not have the parts. Giving money like that was saying goodbye to it. So, Pat suggested he go with them to find a welder and as three of them disappeared with Pat, I stayed behind sitting on the kerb, entertaining the fourth man and the watchman with my beginners' Kiswahili – to their great amusement. After quite a long time, Pat and his escort of three arrived back and in a jiffy they had the strange contraption fitted under the car again. I noticed Pat, though calm, looked a bit dishevelled and his clothes surprisingly grubby. Beckoning me to transfer something into the boot, he whispered that we must go quickly. Just before that, his 'escorts'/mechanics had told me that they'd saved his life from some attackers.

Believing them, I was so grateful that, not only did we willingly give them every penny we had on us but I assured them that, yes, I'd do as they asked and come into town on Monday with more cash to meet the balance they were still demanding. We bade them farewell. Pat reversed out on to the road. It was then, through the rear-view mirror, we saw that a dispute of some kind had broken out between the watchman and the erstwhile 'mechanics' and that the latter were passing money over to the watchman. Driving to the nearest hotel, where he treated himself to a stiff whiskey, Pat told me all. It was a very rough area of the city where he got the brake pipes welded and as he was heading back to the car, he was suddenly jumped from behind and choked unconscious. 'Coming-to' in the gutter he was 'rescued' by his escorts who had, according to them, prevented him from being completely stripped – otherwise there would be nothing left for them, I suppose? The whole thing was a 'set up' he explained, starting with the watchman who allowed the thieves to cut the brake fluid pipe while we were inside the building. I found it all unsettling and disillusioning.

We were reluctant to spend much time anywhere than on the seashore after our experience there. We did spend a few nights camping in the Maasai Mara and elsewhere but, whenever we had any lengthy period of vacation, we headed for the coast, which became a sort of nirvana for us. The journey from Nairoibi to Mombasa and back was hazardous and one always encountered evidence of fatal accidents – once we counted ten. On the roads in Kenya, life is cheap. Because of this and of the ever-changing condition of the road, a journey that normally should take six hours can take up to twelve and more. A few times we had to seek overnight accommodation en route because it was never safe to travel by night. By August 1997 we had spent a year in Kenya and felt seasoned travellers. We had got stuck in the bush, broken down, been robbed, our food had been stolen by monkeys, we had camped in lonely places – we assumed we could handle anything. A weekend at Watamu Bay looked inviting; on the coast, fifty miles north of Mombasa, on the way to the famed island of Lamu.

By now we were well accustomed to early morning departures from Nairobi and driving through the city at dawn helped one see it in a new light. Lazarus carried all we needed for the journey – including jerry cans of petrol, bottles of drinking water, emergency equipment and the inevitable sandwiches. On long journeys we took it in turn to drive, each spending two hours at the wheel. On this occasion we passed evidence of recent very bad road accidents and, as we neared our destination without mishap, we were beginning to count our blessings. I was driving. Pat was sitting cross-legged on the passenger seat, studying a map but fortunately with his safety belt on. It was a long straight road – a narrow ribbon of tarmac flanked by two strips of

loose shingle on each side. Beyond, it was tropical vegetation.
One always tried to keep the two inside wheels on the tarmac and
oncoming drivers made room. It meant survival. We were some fifty
miles out of Mombasa; it was just after midday on a straight stretch
of road when in the near distance we saw a huge lorry approaching,
heavily laden and taking up the whole width of the road. I remarked
to Pat: 'He's going to have to make room for me,' but he didn't. To
avoid a head-on collision I drove off the road but, to my horror, found
myself facing a precipice. I struggled with the steering and managed
to get Lazarus back on to the road only to find, without any warning,
it had suddenly become a narrow one-lane bridge. Luckily there was
nobody else on the bridge. But by now I had lost control of Lazarus.
The barriers along the sides of the bridge had long ago disappeared
and, as Lazarus lurched from side to side, it kept missing the abyss by
inches until, in one final lurch, it toppled over. Luckily a lone iron bar
from the bridge pierced the front of Lazarus and helped flip it over on
to its roof where it got stuck in the undergrowth.

It had fallen about ten metres. Lazarus lay flattened concertina-like
and upside-down in the shrubbery, its metal twisted and torn.
Miraculously we were unhurt. Pat claims he passed out during the fall
but all I remember is each of us asking the other: 'Are you OK?'
I don't remember being afraid – there was no time for it – but, still
strapped upside down, I remember being aware of something dripping on to me and thinking 'the car is going to burst into flames'.
When I voiced this fear, Pat assured me the fuel was diesel and that
there'd be no explosion. In those days I always drove barefoot. Pat
reminded me to put my sandals on because the undergrowth was
rough and spiky. Neither doors nor windows would open and after
Pat kicked out the shattered windscreen, there was just enough space
to squeeze me through. He followed but had to return to the vehicle
to retrieve his safari jacket containing our passports and cash.

Looking up, I noticed several people lining the bridge. At the time
I took it that they were waiting to rescue us but Pat, reminding me
of stories in the newspapers about injured people trapped in road
accidents being stripped of their belongings, murmured: 'They are
waiting to see if we are dead enough to rob.'

For all we know, some in the crowd may have been sympathetic to
our plight. By the time we reached the road there was a sizeable crowd

of onlookers. Luckily, a school bus from Nairobi was passing and the
driver advised Pat that his next step should be to summon the Maasai
herdsman standing nearby and arrange for him to guard the crashed
vehicle and me. The bus driver gave Pat a lift to the nearest police
station to report the accident and organise a rescue vehicle.
Meanwhile, I felt very secure being guarded by the young Maasai,
named Julius. At this stage, I was unaware of any danger. I expected
Pat to return fairly soon but it was some hours before he got back.
Seated under the shade of an acacia tree, I shared my sandwiches
with Julius and with a young woman who had stopped to talk to us.
At one point two men stopped and spoke to Julius. They didn't look
at all friendly, made no eye contact with me and as they talked,
I noticed they kept eyeing the crashed car and the rings on my
fingers. It seemed to me that they were trying to make a bargain of
some sort. The occasional quiet shake of his head made it clear the
Julius wasn't going to play ball. They eventually went away. After that
I quietly removed my watch and my rings slipping them into my
pocket. Pat finally turned up with two policemen in tow.

Their arrival was a relief, but like many things in Africa, the end of
one saga heralds the beginning of another. The police, of course
wanted money, first before they'd even agree to visit the scene and
then in order to reimburse the State of Kenya because we had knocked
down the parapet of the bridge! After much haggling, it was accepted
that the parapets of this bridge had already been knocked down years
ago and that we were not responsible. The police tried several other
tacks to see if Pat would part with some money but eventually they
gave up and it was agreed that we'd return on the following day to
continue negotiations about the report they were going to write for
our insurers. Police in Kenya consider accident insurance money is
something that should be shared – preferably with them. In the meantime it was arranged to have Lazarus towed to the police station for
'safe-keeping'. Luckily, our hand was strengthened when another
European stopped. He was a British Army person en route to Nairobi
and he offered us a lift. Looking at the smashed-up vehicle he
remarked: 'It is impossible to believe that anyone emerged uninjured,
let alone survived that crash.'

He took part in directing the tow truck driver on how best to
retrieve poor Lazarus. He pointed out, something neither of us had

noticed, that our clothes were starting to disintegrate. The seat of Pat's shorts had virtually disappeared. We now found our canvas travel bag had also been affected, so we discarded it in the ditch. What I had thought was petrol dripping on me inside the vehicle after the crash was, in fact, acid from the car battery, stored under the driver's seat. It was now dark and after changing into something more decent, we started the long journey back to Nairobi where we still had Marco.

Deeply grateful to be in one piece, it was after midnight when we reached home. However, early next morning, after a fitful sleep, we set out again for Mombassa, driving Marco. We passed several fatal accidents on the way and we realised any one of them could have been ours. Arriving at the police station earlier than expected, we found that they had removed the radio from the car and were in the process of removing other 'saleable' parts of the engine. 'To keep them safe for you,' they explained cheerfully. The police knew that the insurers required a report from them before they'd pay out any claim. It was a long drawn-out day. Every phase of the crash report had to be carefully negotiated. Lazarus was comprehensively insured. It took a while for the implications of this to sink in. However, once the police understood that, no matter how they phrased the report, there was no money in it for them, things speeded up. In the end and to celebrate, Pat went out and bought a crate of beer to be shared among them. At last we were free to go, but as it was approaching nightfall, the police warned us of robbers. They advised us to spend the night in a local guest house, the only one within fifty miles. It was the most uncomfortable, mosquito-ridden place we had ever slept in. Dawn, when it eventually came, was very welcome. Pat had already arranged with a tow truck in Nairobi to come and pick up the vehicle the next day – otherwise all of it might have disappeared into 'safe-keeping'.

What with being away camping most weekends and Pat teaching all week, we did not consort all that much with the expatriate community in Nairobi. However, there were a few people with whom we got together from time to time. One congenial couple whose company we much enjoyed was Joe and Elsie Emmett. We often met up with them somewhere for coffee, or had lunch with them on the veranda of their attractive home, not far from where we lived in Lavington. While tucking into avocado pears and other produce fresh from their garden, we were able to enjoy the sight of the beautifully plumaged little humming-birds feasting on nectar from the plants Joe had so conveniently planted adjacent to the veranda. The Emmetts were very much part of the social scene in Nairobi. A self-made man, originally from South Africa, Joe had amassed his wealth through his business as a builder. They attended auctions regularly and surrounded themselves with antique furniture. They both had an eye for fine paintings. In fact they had such an excess of these, that they generously lent us some beautiful pictures of Venice to adorn our walls in Lavington for the duration of our stay. They were also acknowledged orchid experts and in the huge greenhouse in their garden cultivated rare specimens for show. Joe had strong views about everything, especially religion, for which he claimed he had no time. We had heard that he liked to push his atheism but in our company he was always courteous and pleasant. His big idea was evolution until he discovered that our ideas about evolution were far more radical than his, which took him aback because he had thought evolution had swept away the foundation of the whole Christian tradition. Pat and Joe got on particularly well and I think Joe was merely tickled when, in the company of others, Pat teasingly addressed him as 'The Vicar'. Joe's attitudes were well known among the expatriate community, so it must have puzzled some why the four of us got on so well together. Once we all spent the weekend in a rented cottage on the shores of Lake Naivasha and for the few days before we finally left Nairobi we stayed with them. Joe was a fund of knowledge about Africa, particularly Kenya, its history and its wild-life. When we first arrived we learnt much about East Africa from the books he lent us. Kind and welcoming people with a sense of humour, the Emmetts were never boring.

There were others whose company we enjoyed from time to time. Like the O'Maras mentioned elsewhere, who lived near Nakuru, and Diarmud Davin and his wife Pity, a quiet dignified Kikuyu who was employed as a social worker in the Nairobi slums. Diarmud was a brilliant teacher and a colleague of Pat's at Peponi. The couple lived in the shade of Mount Kenya on a plot of land inherited from Pity's family.

Then there was Nicola McCutchen, a young teacher colleague of Pat's and her husband Jos. He is a Dutchman, a horticulturalist who in due course took charge of President Moi's successful flower-exporting farms. Between these half a dozen or so, well-informed people we got a good insight into what was happening around us in Kenya.

After its summersault on the Mombasa road, it was to be a full six months before Lazarus was fit to travel again. Having experienced the excitement of the bush in the Landrover and Marco being unfit for that sort of dodgy travel, we decided to invest in a new Suzuki 4 x 4. For some reason we never got round to christening it but it shared many wonderful adventures with us during our final year in Kenya. We had an opening made in the roof so that, as in Lazarus, I could stand up and view the wild life while Pat drove.

One of our earliest adventures with our Suzuki was a camping trip to the Maasai Mara with Nicola and Jos. The once tarred road into this area had crumbled, making the trip a bone-shaking six hours' journey, which didn't really bother us. Our plan was to set up our tents just outside the park and spend a couple of hours exploring the area before the light faded. Dusk was a good time for spotting wildlife. Camping outside the park saved us some expense and had less red tape attached. It was more adventurous but less secure.

We set up our two tents – separated by a huge mound of elephant dung – on high ground overlooking a bend in the river. Jos and Nicola were in their own 4 x 4, somewhat bigger than ours and, for safety, we travelled in convoy. We decided it would be wise to hire an armed Maasai guard, since robbers had attacked campers at this very site only a week previously and we did not want to arrive back and find our tents gone. We were an hour's journey from our camp when we were hit by one of those sudden tropical downpours that makes you literally stop in your tracks; all we could do was sit it out in our vehicles and watch the dense rain cascade. The muddy red laterite roads turned into rivers of treacle but eventually, as the downpour eased, we braved the elements and headed for camp, following closely in one another's tracks. Floating off the road into the undergrowth was a risk we had to take but, eventually, we got back safely. It was late but, fortunately, the Maasai had had the foresight to collect some dry wood for a fire, so we were able to cook a meal. The rain eventually stopped altogether and we chatted round the fire a while before getting into to our sleeping bags.

In the small hours, a fierce hullabaloo from our watchman woke us up. An almighty din – flashing lights, animal noises and flying arrows filled the night. At first we thought it must be another robbery until the Maasai explained that it was only a group of baboons that had been trying to get at the contents of our cold box that Pat had unwisely thought it safe to leave outside our tent. The baboons had just enough time to damage the box but didn't get to the contents. The morning light showed up bits of several broken cold boxes, evidence that the thieving baboons had had plenty of practice on other campers before us.

After the baboon raid we did not sleep again, so rose very early at sunrise to a truly pristine-like golden morning, freshly cleansed by the heavy downpour of the previous night and everywhere now beautifully still. We stirred up our fire and after a leisurely breakfast set out for a full day of exploration in the park. Soon, with Jos in the lead, we were driving along the laterite road, now hardened and dry again. After following up a sighting of elephants, we returned to the road. Rounding a bend, we came upon a large compact troupe of baboons sitting by the verge. Having been in Kenya longer than the newly-arrived couple, the ubiquitous baboons no longer held any interest for us – they had sometimes become a bit of a nuisance on our camping trips – but the front car had stopped to take photographs and we were stuck behind them. Still standing on the back seat with head and shoulders out through the roof and on the alert for wild-life, I became aware of this huge Alpha baboon, twice the size of any of the others, detaching himself from the group and heading for our vehicle. Uneasy, I sat down on the back seat and asked Pat to drive on, but of course he couldn't with Jos at a standstill only a few yards ahead of us. Pat reassured me that all would be well. But suddenly the baboon leapt on to the roof of our Suzuki and sat looking down into the car at me, now huddled in the opposite corner and shooing him away. Perhaps he misinterpreted my gesture as an invitation, for the next thing I knew, this very large, wild animal was sitting very close beside me. It all happened so quickly. I found myself grappling with the baboon and he with me. When a baboon is in a sitting position, his long back makes him much taller so I was now looking *up* at him. He was making loud grunting noises 'humph-hu-hu' into my face. Not only was I grappling with this gigantic wild creature but I was also in the grip of naked fear. Never before had I experienced fear like this and may I never, ever do so again. It is interesting how in moments of terror like this, one's basic instincts come to the fore. As the Psalmist said: 'Out of the depths I cry to you O Lord' (*De Profundis*, Psalm 101). As little children we were taught to call upon God whenever we were in trouble and we all had an armoury of little pleas, prayers or, as they were generally called, 'aspirations'. Quite honestly I was convinced I was about to be savaged. So too was everyone else. Still grappling with the baboon, with every fibre of my being I cried out: 'Sacred Heart of Jesus, I place ALL my trust in you.' People can hardly believe me, and that's understandable, when I recount what happened next. In a split second, the baboon let go of me and, as though on a spring, shot up *backwards*, through the open roof and was gone like a rocket. While all this was happening Pat was not idle. Leaving the keys in the ignition, he jumped out intending to open the back door, only to find it locked. Rushing back into the driver's seat he put the vehicle into reverse. Pat maintains that the gearshift, causing a slight movement in the vehicle must be what alarmed the baboon resulting in his bionic leap. This coincided with my prayer for help. I hold that sometimes God brings about extraordinary results through ordinary happenings. You decide.

Meanwhile Jos and Nicola were rushing towards us, horrified at what they'd observed. They later recounted how they had envisioned carnage with blood everywhere and desperate attempts to somehow get me to hospital in Nairobi, etc, etc. All of us were very shaken and we sped off. With lions and leopards now the last thing on our minds we headed for the nearest Tourist Lodge where the men had stiff whiskeys and the women double coffees.

During this period also we often spent weekends with Robert and Fleur O'Mara near Nakuru, in the shadow of Mount Kenya, a few hours' drive from Nairobi. Robert, a well-known painter with clients from around the world, has built his own unique eco-friendly house that only an artist could have designed. Over breakfast on the veranda we enjoyed our own 'stage-show', put on free by colobus monkeys swinging in the trees in front of us. The name is derived from the Greek word for 'mutilated', because unlike other monkeys, they do not have thumbs. Even their heads looked theatrical, a triangle of white fur topped with a black fez-like 'hat'. It was another opportunity

for me to play table tennis which I enjoyed doing from time to time
with the pupils at Peponi. Fleur, a New Zealander, was as beautiful
as her cooking was scrumptious. They have three remarkably good-
looking sons, all products of Glenstall Abbey, the only Benedictine
school in Ireland. We still keep in touch.

Pat's two-year contract at Peponi finally ran out. Though the school
wanted him to commit himself for another two years, we felt that now
was the time to see other parts of Africa. When school closed in June
we headed straight for the coast where we spent a glorious two months
living in our thatched cottage, eating fresh fish, making the odd foray
into the countryside and even out to sea, where Pat swam with
dolphins and encountered the occasional shark while scuba diving.
After our crash earlier in the year, we had decided to go to Zanzibar
for two weeks – 'cheaper than a double funeral,' Pat quipped. Pat was
also partial to Tanzania because, as a student in the 1960s, he had followed the political career of Julius Neyrere and studied his particular
brand of socialism called *Ujamma* – or self-reliance. All this was very
new to me but not without some interest. Leaving our car in Mombasa
with members of Pat's family visiting us at the time, we flew to
Dar-es-Salaam for a day to get a flavour of the place. A friend, Padraig
Devine, showed us around Dar and next morning dropped us back at
the airport in time for the 9 am return flight. The check-in girl eyed
us glumly and told us the flight had just left.

'But it couldn't have,' exclaimed Pat in disbelief, 'we are an hour
early. My brother is waiting for us at the airport in Mombasa. We confirmed the booking when we flew in last night.'

At that moment, several other irate passengers came running along,
shouting at the hapless girl manning the Air Tanzania desk. One man
claimed his luggage was on the plane, even if he wasn't. He had
checked in and was left sitting in the waiting room when the plane
took off.

'I'm booked to fly on to London this afternoon. And the next flight
from here to Mombasa is in two days.' The poor man was fuming.

We made a note not to fly Air Tanzania ever again. But there was
nothing anyone could do. This was a fairly frequent occurrence in
Africa. A government minister had come along and commandeered

the plane, ordering the pilot to fly him to Kilimanjaro. It was several hours before we found a small plane going to Zanzibar and from there we booked, yes, you guessed it, an Air Tanzania flight to Mombasa. Showing our tickets to the girl at the desk, she said we could try for a refund but she had never yet heard of anybody who had succeeded.

Pat's eventual replacement at Peponi had undertaken to continue renting the place in Lavington. This was something of a relief since it ensured the continued employment of our staff, people of whom we had grown fond over the two years we were with them.

Muthoni warned us not to tell anyone we were leaving because it would be an invitation to all the local robbers, so we did not have any celebrations. The staff, of course, knew we were going. Instead of the usual going away celebrations, we offered to train each of them in a new skill of their choice. Muthoni could not think of any new skill but wanted us to buy her a plot for a house in her Kikuyu homeland, something beyond our budget. She had assumed we were very rich, that is, until one day I showed her a photo of our thatched home in England. That confused her somewhat. A thatched house in Kenya wasn't much of a status symbol. She was a formidable but likeable woman, early middle-aged and authoritative, not to be trifled with. Her father had been a local government policeman in the days before independence and she had seen him cut to pieces in front of the family by the Mau Mau. She had one daughter but no husband as far as we could make out. She had little time for politicians or, for that matter, for men in general whom she considered surplus to requirement.

Everyone had a soft spot for Reuben, our Luo gardener and day watchman. Muthoni told us his young wife had died of typhoid, that she had been quite a harridan, and had not made the gentle Reuben happy. But he was devoted to their little five-year-old son, Ephraim. He was totally reliable and I clearly recall one disquieting episode when he kept me safe. Pat had wisely instructed me to take Reuben with me into the city centre and, having parked the car, we walked together through Uhuru Public Park to a building on the hill where I had to sign some papers. It was mid-morning, with people passing quietly in both directions along the wide central pathway. Task done, we were heading back through the park when Reuben, close by my

Reuben

side all the time, said very quietly: 'Mama, a man has been following us ever since we parked the car.' Boy! Was I glad when we reached our vehicle.

Reuben told me that he had been robbed several times. Shortly before we arrived in Africa he had spent three years languishing in gaol because there was nobody to pay the bribe that would free him. He had been picked up in the street after a house nearby was robbed; he was just a passer-by. When I asked him how on earth he had coped with this injustice and the awful prison conditions he said simply: 'Prayer'. He had hoped to be a teacher but his people were too poor. Reuben liked to read and spoke English quite well, though he was far from talkative, going quietly about his duties. Once when he did not turn up for work for several days we got worried and sent Muthoni off to investigate. She found him extremely ill, so we promptly got him into hospital, where he was diagnosed with typhoid. A day or two more and he would have died. When I visited him in hospital with Muthoni, he was well on the road to recovery and seeing this, kind-hearted Muthoni shed a few tears of relief. He told us that a child of his had also died of typhoid. For his going away gift, Reuben wanted to learn carpentry.

Wycliffe, our night watchman, was one of Reuben's brothers and chose to learn to drive so that he could get a driving licence and become a lorry driver. Wycliffe was an altogether darker person than Reuben, less educated, more taciturn. We assumed that he'd take driving lessons, pass a driving test and get his lorry drivers' licence so we did our calculations accordingly. To our surprise he arrived with his driving licence a couple of days after we had given him the money. He'd bought his licence on the black market. He would now learn to drive and had arranged with a *matatu* driver to teach him. He would hop on to a *matatu* at a street corner as arranged, drive a couple of blocks and hop off again. Next day it would be a different corner. After so many weeks of this he'd be an expert driver and with his fake driving licence he would soon join the others clogging the streets of Nairobi. In fact, while still our night watchman and before we left Nairobi, he had already started to drive a lorry. We also set up his physically handicapped brother Job as a shoemaker. I did drawings of each of them and the one of Muthoni sits in our kitchen to-day, a reminder of our two unforgettable years in Kenya.

At one stage we had considered driving home to the UK from Nairobi – hence the purchase of the new Suzuki. However, after several visits to the appropriate authorities, Pat concluded that the red tape was too much. It left us at the mercy and whim of too many petty officials, all requiring *kidogo*, the Swahili for 'something small' or bribe. So we sold our Suzuki, and Marco also, but we still kept Lazarus in Nairobi hoping, Macawber-style, that something would turn up and bring us back to Africa.

Shortly before we flew off, Pat was offered the Headship of a Moslem secondary school in Mombasa. This was very exciting and completely unexpected. Much was discussed over the phone but the

Muthoni asleep

official interview took place in a hotel near the airport on the day we were leaving for London. Pat and Mr Bin Yamu, the chairman of the Mombasa Aga Khan Education Board, thrashed out the final details and Pat agreed to accept the offer. Two air-tickets would be sent to our home in England by mid-October and Pat would assume his duties by mid-December. It was agreed that if the tickets did not arrive, the deal was off.

The prospect of two full years on the coast greatly appealed to us and our departure from Nairobi in mid-September 1998 was a quiet but happy occasion.

CHAPTER 17

Africa Still Beckons

OR THE NEXT couple of months we forgot all about Africa as
we sorted out our problems with Rivendell and its garden and
the myriad small things that have to be 'seen to' in a house built
in 1667. We assumed Mombasa would come back to us with two air-
tickets but if they didn't – we'd accept that. We were game to try
something different. For that reason Pat did not contact Bin Yamu or
Mombasa or make any further enquiries about the proposed posting.
Mr Bin Yamu wrote to tell us that they had acquired a house for us
on the beach but no air-tickets were enclosed. In Africa, time is elastic, even more so than in Ireland, but when we had not heard from
Mombasa by the end of November, Pat concluded that the appointment had fallen through and decided to forget it.

Dublin, early December 1998. The weather was miserable, cold and
wet and we found ourselves wishing we were back in the sun and heat
of Africa. The Irish government's Ministry of Foreign Affairs recruits
many people to work in underdeveloped countries and before we left
Kenya a branch of that ministry, called APSO, tried to recruit Pat to
work in a school in Burkino Faso, West Africa. Pat knew the country
and declined the offer. But as we were passing the APSO office in
Dublin, we decided to call in and enquire. They already had Pat's CV
and were aware of his background and his work in Kenya, and in
Nigeria before that. They had just advertised about twenty overseas
positions for what they described as 'Development Workers'. After our
period in Kenya, Pat knew exactly what he wanted and he told them:
(1) any new post had to be in the tropics, i.e. between 20° north and
20° south of the equator; (2) it must have some element of IT in it
and (3) it must be by the sea. With such criteria we soon narrowed

down the posts available at APSO to three – one in the Cameroons
in West Africa; one in Asia; and another in Dar-es-Salaam, Tanzania,
at The Tanzania School of Journalism (TSJ), now part of the University
of Dar-es-Salaam. With regard to the TSJ job, along with suitable
academic qualifications he was required to have a professional quali-
fication in teaching, which Pat had. The successful applicant was to
teach Journalism, Public Relations and Advertising to post-graduate
students. APSO had been trying for several years to fill this post but
without success. They offered Pat the post, subject to his passing the
medical and the interview. They also advanced the return airfare from
England for the interview. We told one another what a good thing it
was that the Mombasa offer had fallen through. We were delighted
the way things were working out and never gave the miserable
weather another thought.

Elated, we drove on to Galway where we were spending some days
with Pat's brother Michael. At 6 am next morning there was a telephone call from Mombasa; Mr Bin Yamu was ready to mail our tickets. But he was almost two months late and he knew it. He would
hold the post open, he said, and would not re-advertise it until after
the interview with APSO. We now knew in our hearts that Mombasa
was not on. Dar was by the sea and even more attractive than
Mombasa, with the island of Zanzibar only a two hour ferry ride away.
And that's how we ended up in Africa for another two years, which
we later extended to four.

The understanding with APSO was that we'd travel out together to
Dar-es-Salaam in time for Pat to start teaching after Easter. APSO
had a strict schedule of initiation and language courses for all newly
recruited Development Workers (DWs) and their spouses. The majority of volunteers were bachelors and single women, mostly young
graduates. As merely the wife of a DW, I could have opted out of
attending these courses but I decided not to. We were both keen that
I fit in and we opted that I go through the full DW process. This
meant a two-week Kiswahili course in Dublin before setting out for
Dar, another two-week 'orientation course' in down-town Dar-es-
Salaam immediately after arrival, followed by a six-week Kiswahili
'immersion course'. This latter was held in Arusha, a small town

nestling among the lush green foothills of Kilimanjaro, near the border with Kenya and about ten hours drive north from Dar.

However things did not work out as planned. The Tanzania School of Journalism, pleading dire shortage of staff, badgered APSO to have Pat out there before Christmas. And so it was that late December 1998, Pat flew out with a group of other newly recruited APSO Development Workers, leaving me to follow once he had found a house for us to live in. Pat had to skip the Dublin course but went straight into the orientation course in Dar and then the Kiswahili immersion course in Arusha. The phone lines to Tanzania were unreliable, so we kept in touch via email, which enabled Pat to paint a very realistic picture of day to day life in Tanzania. It seemed as unpredictable as it was exciting and I was looking forward to the new challenge with enthusiasm. The picture that came across was that Tanzania was less developed than Kenya but, sadly, equally corrupt; the people, even more friendly, if poorer. Unlike Kenya, Kiswahili was spoken everywhere, along with local languages and the use of English was less widespread. This gave me even more of an incentive to concentrate on my Kiswahili, a language I had already started to learn in Nairobi.

Pat's main task in preparation for my coming was to find suitable accommodation. He himself was prepared to live in a mud hut, and had done so in Nigeria; no running water, no plumbing – just the 'long drop' in the yard, minimal utensils, oil lamp, wood fire or cooking outside. We had agreed without any debate that this time he'd insist on a proper house, well secured, with running water and electricity and plumbing that worked. Though the School of Journalism (TSJ) was contractually obliged to provide accommodation and transport, we were by now sufficiently experienced about Africa not to bank on contracts. We intended to have our own transport (Lazarus was still waiting in the wings in Nairobi) and pay for our own accommodation but we thought that the least TSJ could do was to find us somewhere to live. Government institutions such as TSJ had several properties all over Dar-es-Salaam. Julius Nyerere, as part of his *Ujamma* socialism programme, had confiscated most privately owned properties in Dar and handed them over to government departments like TSJ, who immediately and automatically set about looting and vandalising them – easy come, easy go – stripping them of everything of value, including plumbing, doors and windows. TSJ lined up seven of those for Pat to inspect. Of course they'd repair whichever one Pat selected! Knowing Africa, one would be foolish to count on that. After a week of showing him around these uninhabitable properties, Mr Moshiru, the Principal of TSJ, was getting very frustrated at Pat's lack of enthusiasm and murmured that he expected a dedicated volunteer worker like Pat to 'put up with some suffering' – for the sake of Africa, I suppose. Pat, well aware of this mentality, looking him straight in the eye, said: 'Listen Mr Moshiru. I came to Africa to share my skills with you not for you to share your suffering with me.' Mr Moshiru, who had a very good sense of humour, laughed heartily at this and later on quoted it at staff meetings. After that he and Pat developed a good working relationship and **we** soon had our own house.

Unlike Nairobi, and thanks to Julius Nyerere's brand of socialism, Dar had no ghetto, or 'no-go' areas; most of the city was a mixture of modest private homes and shanty, all connected with sometimes impassable mud roads and ditches full of dirty water and rubbish. Our house was situated near the main road, in an area known as Kinondoni B, a noisy sprawling mixture of dwellings, some fortified, some not. It had barred windows and was surrounded by high walls and iron gates. It had, of course, to be guarded day and night. Unfortunately it lacked a garden, which would have been very welcome in the stifling heat of Dar, but it was within easy drive of TSJ and thus saved Pat the fumes and stresses of the snarling traffic jams that seem to plague every African city. It was rented from a local Tanzanian woman, Mary Lois Rugambage, an attractive well-educated woman in her thirties who could not do enough for us. We soon became friends. She had grown up by the shores of Lake Tanganyika on the western border of Tanzania, where her much loved father was a wealthy farmer.

We arrived during the dry season but when the rainy season came, we found that two of the bedrooms flooded. It happened suddenly, day or night and it emptied just as quickly. It was a design problem that could not be easily rectified, certainly not by us, so we moved our bed to the front room that did not flood and decided to live with our problem. In Africa flooding quickly dries up and one makes do. Waking up in a big bed with a mosquito net and surrounded by a quiet lake with the faint sound of trickling water is certainly a novelty. One of our visitors christened the place 'The Lake District'.

In any case, we had by then become accustomed to the house; it was conveniently situated near the market and the sea and only twenty minutes from the centre of town. The prospect of searching for another property was too much.

Pat had been in Tanzania for almost two months before I joined him. He had done his two weeks in the slums, his six weeks' language training and had collected our various bits and pieces in Nairobi, including Lazarus, our Landrover. He had also moved into our house in Dar, bought all the necessary pots and pans, made some changes to the plumbing such as putting up a water storage tank and installing showers, and hired two watchmen, one for day-time and one for night-time. He had checked into his office at TSJ and tried to sort out their computer system, which he hoped to use for his teaching. He now discovered he would not be required to begin teaching until after Easter, the time initially planned.

Just before I joined Pat I was contacted by my old monastery, Stanbrook Abbey, who forwarded an email to me from John Misto, a talented award-winning young Australian playwright. In it he said how, in vain, he had been trying to track me down for several years and had almost given up the search until one day he idly 'Googled' Stanbrook Abbey. Thrilled to get a positive response from there, he now wrote to say that about seven years earlier he'd read *The Scent of the Roses*, 'fallen in love with the story' and wanted my permission to dramatise it. Very wary at first, my instinct – surprise, surprise – was to say my usual NO. I contacted Pat immediately and he reminded me of our four-point arrangement of old. So now I was more circumspect in my response to John Misto. As Pat further pointed out, any play would be the playwright's responsibility, not mine. My nephew Sebastian Barry has written several plays based on family members, one particularly close to home, the award winning *Our Lady of Sligo*, based on my mother. And I am not unfamiliar with poetic/dramatic licence – creative freedom – which is precisely why I refrained from ever reading or seeing *Our Lady of Sligo*, much as I love my nephew Sebastian. Besides, I know that in all probability I would be incandescent with irritation at the liberties that were bound to be taken with my own story. Soon, through our emails, a very good rapport was established between Misto and myself. Finally I gave John Misto the go-ahead – on condition that he would not ask or expect me to read the script or see the play. One cannot give more of a *carte blanche*. And, as Pat reassured me: 'It will probably never happen anyway.'

My first experience of Tanzania was a brush with the law on the day of my arrival. After he picked me up at the airport, Pat, accompanied by George our Nairobi Maasai, decided to drive into town. Passing along the beautiful sea front, I could not resist the urge to bathe my hot feet in the cooling waters. I asked Pat to stop the car. With George in tow, I sauntered down to the water's edge and paddled around in my bare feet. It was such a lovely feeling to be back in Africa. Suddenly we were summoned back to the car: Two well-dressed men claiming to be 'presidential security officers' wanted to arrest us for parking in a prohibited place. They wanted to know what I was doing down by the water and who was the person with me.

'This is the Presidential Palace. You cannot stop here. There is a notice at the end of the road.'

'But we came from the other direction and there is no notice there,' exclaimed Pat amicably, as usual.

'Even so, you should know that this is the Presidential Palace. You have broken the law of Tanzania.'

Pat explained to me in Gaelic that this was a regular occurrence and not to worry. The men wanted money. Pat was very good with the police and after much laughter and banter and for the price of a few beers, we were forgiven for 'breaking the law of Tanzania' and allowed to go.

In Nairobi all slum dwellers were squatters. There were no services in the slums, only what the squatters provided – sporadic electricity perhaps, no running water, no sewerage, no roads. By Nairobi standards there were no slums in Tanzania, only rundown areas where maintenance had ceased and properties, though still lived in, had become derelict; roads were broken up, culverts collapsed, and services like running water and sewerage discontinued. It was a country in decline, even decay. Many of the people living in these areas had jobs to go to but their meagre salaries were so eaten up by corruption and bribery that they were permanently poor, living from hand to mouth. Unlike in Kenya where all the rich people lived in one area hogging all the available services and the poor in another, living in relative squalor, in Tanzania the houses of the better-off were evenly sprinkled throughout, thus perhaps benefiting the poor through some sort of 'trickle down' effect. Our house in Kinondoni B would be considered one of those better-off houses where the security lights that burnt all night also afforded a measure of reassurance to those who lived nearby.

I had taken a few lessons in Swahili in Nairobi and a further two weeks' training in Dublin had given me more confidence so, I looked forward to my initial two weeks 'inculturisation' in down-town Dar when I hoped to practise my new found language skills for the first time, however haltingly. There were eight of us on the course, all, apart from me, newly recruited APSO Development Workers (DWs). I was billeted on a family with whom Pat had spent two weeks, so, in a way, I wasn't a total stranger to them. Mohamedu was a civil servant and his wife Fatima a nurse in the nearby hospital, so by local standards they were fairly high up the social scale. They had three grown up children, all unemployed. The modest fee paid by the likes of me was a welcome addition to their stretched budget. By the looks of them they did not seem short of food but the house badly needed some repairs. They cooked on a fire in the yard. Much of their leisure time was spent in the yard where it was cooler than inside. The house was properly plumbed with wash basins and a bath but there was never any water. Every week a large tanker of water arrived in the locality, further breaking up the roads but obviously bringing a handy income to the driver or owner of the vehicle. The bath and every available container was filled, enough to suffice the household for the week. When Pat suggested it might be possible to get some money and repair the water mains, they shook their heads. This had been tried but each time the system was vandalised again almost immediately. The water tanker, they explained, was owned by an important politician, a member of the ruling party. Though there were several wells in the locality, all had their tops sealed, making the populace completely dependent on the corrupt politician for their water.

When Pat arrived to drop me off, he was very warmly welcomed by my hosts. Fatima showed me what was to be my bed (the only one in the house) for the next two weeks. It had no mosquito net but one was promised. Pat warned me that on no account was I to sleep in a bed without a mosquito net. That evening I shared the family's tasty meal, which consisted of *ugali* (maize), *sukumuwiki* (a leafy green vegetable) and beans – good wholesome East African food that I enjoyed. In the afternoon the neighbours started arriving, no doubt for a friendly inspection of the visitor, and they joined the family and myself sitting on mats on the veranda. The neighbours kept piling in and when someone went to roll out an extra mat, out jumped a huge terrified rat who ran for his life. The company never turned a hair, just laughed all the more and continued with their jollity. With night fast approaching and still no sign of the promised mosquito net, I followed Pat's instructions and went out to the telephone kiosk in the street (to my surprise and relief, it worked), to let Pat know the situation. I was to say to the man of the house that unless a net was provided immediately, Pat would be back at once to collect me. Suddenly, a net magically materialised. After that initial settling in, the rest of the week went well.

There were about six of us on the APSO 'inculturisation' course and we learnt about the cultural differences to expect in Tanzania and how to avoid upsetting the locals; we practised the correct greetings in Swahili, how to deal with different social situations, how to behave in public or at the market and which areas in town to avoid. It was a very useful introduction, which I could have done with in Nairobi but had managed to survive without. Living with a local family and attending these courses gave me an opportunity to observe another side of African life that I would not otherwise ever have had the chance of doing. And I was grateful. The young teacher at the school was excellent – always cheerful and courteous. Some months later it was a shock to hear that he had suddenly died of malaria. During our short stay in Tanzania, it was sad how many of our young acquaintances died either from malaria or AIDS.

My slum 'inculturisation fortnight' over, I returned to Kinondoni B for two nights before going two hundred miles north to Arusha for my six-week 'immersion' Kiswahili language course. I can't pretend that I enjoyed my time in Arusha. Even in my youth, I disliked organised lessons; I learn best on my own, in my own way, at my own pace. In Arusha, the fault was principally my own. I have an aptitude for imitating foreign accents and I had already done a bit of Swahili and so, I had some basic conversational Swahili at the ready when we were interviewed to see which group we joined. So, I was placed in a group too advanced for my actual knowledge. I was relieved when the course was over. I returned to Dar to join Pat and start our new life together in Tanzania.

Compared to Nairobi, Dar was permanently very hot and humid. We chose not to have air-conditioning installed, preferring instead the large ceiling fans already there. The windows did not have glass but all had the essential mosquito netting. Much of the time, there was no electricity. It took us a couple of weeks to find a suitable house girl, mainly because our landlady objected to anyone from the nearby slum – like building a hornet's nest in your kitchen, she used to say. But I needed someone to help clean the house. I could train her to cook and perhaps, when we finally left, find her a steady job with some other European family as we had done in Nairobi for Muthoni. A young woman named Regina had approached me several times after Sunday Mass and told me her story – two children to feed, deserted by her husband, and now forced to live in the nearby slum with her parents. Plump and pretty, although not very agile-looking, she was very friendly. Eventually we persuaded the landlady to give her a chance.

When Pat first arrived in Tanzania and acquired a lease on the house, he inherited a night watchman called Musa who lived at the other side of town, a two hour walk each way. Most watchmen were armed either with a gun or a cutlass (panga) but we decided that ours would not be armed. Pat instructed them not to resist a robbery but run away.

'I don't want to be visiting you in hospital or bailing you out of jail,' he told them.

Besides, after a robbery, the staff are the first to be blamed by the police and invariably end up in police custody, which means the house-holder has to bail them out. Soft targets for the police and a nice source of income too. Apart from that, everybody in a locality knew who the robbers in that area were and could point them out to you. The locals believed that the police were in league with them and also received a cut of the takings. We saw clear evidence of this when some friends of ours were robbed.

Musa, our inherited night watchman, came across as a disgruntled character, a born malcontent. One got the impression that he felt hard-done-by. With his first month's salary he bought the usual pair of sunglasses, a peaked cap, a new suit and a camera. One morning we found him decked out in all his finery, draped across the bonnet of our car as if all set for a photo shoot. After a few months with us he asked for a fortnight off to visit his home town, far away on the border with Mozambique. A month's advance on salary would also be very nice, thank you. He promised to be back at his post in two weeks but it was three months before he turned up.

That's how we came to hire John, Regina's father, as our stop-gap askari. The landlady was now thoroughly up in arms. What! Both father and daughter from the nearby slum in charge of her house. She predicted that we'd soon rue the day and be robbed. But we weren't. As far as we could make out, neither father nor daughter ever had any job before we took them on, though John brought a very elegant-looking freshly-typed certificate of reference, which anyone would know was a fake. He could have saved himself the money. We got to like our two workers, though neither would win a prize for competence. Regina, nicknamed 'Sputnik' by one of our visitors, went about her work in slow motion but steadily and we trusted her. She was averse to learning any new skills or making any plans for the future. Pat had some of his students come and talk to her and try to motivate her to avail herself of her opportunities but she had no concept of planning for the future. She lived for now. Since she had very little English, I was further stimulated into getting a move-on with my Kiswahili. As time went by we grew very fond of Regina but never really understood her philosophy of life. When we first hired her, she lived in one room with her parents but, eventually, we found her and her two children another room in town. Sometimes I drove her there after work and she was always concerned about my safety. She warned me about the danger from thieves (one of whom we noticed had an iron bar under his jacket) and she told me to keep the car windows shut and the doors locked. One day she pointed to a heap of ashes in a narrow street and gave me to understand it was the remains of a young neighbour of theirs caught stealing a bicycle. He'd had his hands tied, she said, a tyre put around his neck and set on fire.

An *askari* (watchman) is essential in Africa. In Nairobi we had two, one for night-time and another for day-time, the day-watchman also serving as gardener. At first we did not have a garden in Dar-es-

Leonard

Salaam, so, Leonard, our day-time *askari*'s main job was to watch by the big iron gate, opening and closing it quickly to let our car in and out. Robbers, we were warned, favoured such moments to strike, so one automatically took note of who was in the vicinity. Leonard spent much of his time sitting under the big coconut tree by the wall. He chatted with passers-by but mostly snoozed, jumping to attention at the sound of our approaching car. The house was surrounded with walls three metres high and apart from a few patches of soil for flowers, the ground was cemented all round. We got some flowerbeds going which Leonard enjoyed tending. For his own amusement, but mainly to give him an excuse to be outside the gate, which was where he preferred to be, he created another flowerbed outside. There being no dormant season in Africa, flowers bloom all year round, provided they are well watered. Water is always scarce, yet, when available, it never seems to occur to anyone to use it sparingly. Perhaps it is the influence of the Moslem culture that requires water to flow during their ritual ablutions. Leonard got a great kick out of washing the car and missed no opportunity to do so.

Drunk or sober, but mostly drunk, John was always cheerful but as a watchman he was a disaster. He was well-meaning and very likeable just like his daughter Regina. But in the end his partiality to palm wine was his undoing. Like his predecessor, his first purchase was a radio and the trademark dark sunglasses. Thieves soon relieved him of both as he staggered to work drunk. We were happy enough to employ him and when Musa failed to return, John's position was made permanent. This caused some problems, first with the landlady but also some months later when, out of the blue, Musa arrived back and automatically took up his duty as if he had never been away. It took some while to sort this one out. John remained at his post — for much of the time anyway. When he became too much of a liability as a watchman, Regina understood we had to let him go. We gave him some money but he soon came back for help because his wife had spilt a pot of boiling water over his leg. I spent the next few weeks ferrying him to and from hospital. A couple of times during the rainy season I had to turn back because the water in the street was too deep for my Suzuki to drive through. Eventually we had a meeting between John, his daughter and some of Pat's students to hammer out a plan, which resulted in my no longer needing to run the gauntlet of travelling through the slum every week. We discovered at the hospital that John also had AIDs and probably did not live long after that.

It took some time to get used to living with the heat in Kinondoni B after the relatively cool climate of Nairobi, but we had the glorious sea within half an hour's drive. It was a hotter version of Mombasa. Probably the feature of Tanzania we enjoyed most was its beaches, one or other of which we visited almost daily for lengthy immersions in the Indian Ocean. Our favourite was White Sands, a few miles beyond where Pat taught at the Tanzania School of Journalism.

Pat's teaching load was light compared to Peponi and, as his students were post-graduates, all of them adults of varying ages, we had, for the first time, the opportunity to consort with a very different type of African from those we'd known in Kenya. Pat supervised their theses and from time to time some of them would come to our house in Kinondoni B for advice. They were all very polite and hard-working and appreciated very much what Pat was trying to do. In fact one student from out of town stayed with us over Christmas when her young man was abroad.

During all of our two years in Nairobi, we never laid eyes on our neighbours either side of us. They might have been empty houses. Not so in Dar-es-Salaam. Peter and his family on our left were what might be labelled comfortably off and very much involved with their local Catholic Church. The fact that one of their children was mentally handicapped may have explained why they were very quiet and more or less kept to themselves.

On the other side, the neighbours to our right were much more extrovert and vocal. Salima, a 'traditionally built' matriarchal figure, was a Muslim and the centre of everything happening around her. Which was usually a lot. Except when it rained, the entire day was spent outside where she held court under a huge mango tree. There she and the several related young people around her prepared, cooked and ate their meals – I never could work out their exact relationships. Some lived with her permanently in her little bare house further up the steep slope – people such as Mwajuma, an exceptionally good-looking, high-spirited very young woman, who during our stay in Dar gave birth to a beautiful boy. Her handsome young husband called to see them only now and then, doing the rounds, I suppose, of visiting his several wives. And finally, little eight-year old Taabu whose widowed mother lived in town and could not cope with both Taabu and a new baby. It spoke volumes when we learned that Taabu, the name she was given when she was born, meant 'sorrow'. Taabu was very keen to learn English and I did my best, teaching her in the shade of our yard. Very occasionally a row erupted next door invariably caused by the hot-tempered Mwajuma. In fact on one occasion, the police arrived and hauled her off to jail for a night or two until her step-

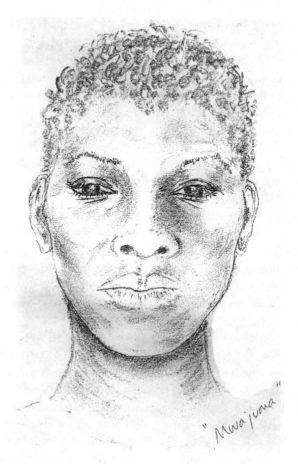

"Mwajuma"

father paid a bribe for her release. She was unusually docile for a good
while after that. Mwajuma's parents had died of AIDs and Salima had
taken her in. But the general mood was light-hearted. I once attended
a wedding celebration with them all, the very young bride so quiet
and docile that I suspect she was drugged, sitting there speechless on
the only sofa in the entire dwelling. Everybody else sat on the floor.

I can still hear the chorus of the irrepressibly cheerful little children
from houses around, who whenever they espied the white Suzuki
turning into our rutted road would come running alongside the
car shouting excitedly: 'Auntie Mailee! Auntie Mailee!' and 'helped'
me unload my purchases. They might well have preferred sweets to
the pieces of fruit I brought them. I didn't enquire. Despite all the

obvious poverty, the little ones were always dancing, laughing and playing without a care in the world – I never saw an African child sulking.

One of our first visitors in Dar-es-Salaam was George, our Maasai godson and friend from Nairobi. The Maasai move at will across country borders, generally without travel documentation, and the police do not usually bother them. Soon after arriving, George appeared in our sitting room dressed in his full Maasai regalia and, uninvited, launched into the traditional Maasai dance. After an earlier visit to us, George was returning to Nairobi with a sizeable sum of money he planned to use to set up a small business. Pat, ready to drop him off at the bus station, was surprised to find him emerging from our spare room decked out in a suit, shirt and tie (all somewhat shabby) and carrying a briefcase; and to crown it all designer sunglasses – all completely unnecessary and surely uncomfortable on the hot twenty-four-hour bus trip to Nairobi. Obviously we thought George might have put his new-found riches to better use but refrained from saying so in case his feelings might be hurt. It came as no surprise therefore to learn some months later that the police had stopped him at the checkpoint half a mile from the border and fined him for not having travel documents. When paying the fine he foolishly took out the wad of notes Pat had given him. The police put him back on the bus only to take him off again before the bus crossed into Kenya, relieving him of everything, leaving him no choice but to hike the one hundred miles to Nairobi. Undaunted, he visited us again the following year with new plans that required more money. This time we made sure to give him advice regarding the police and how to dress when travelling. At that time he was eagerly preparing himself and indeed, it seemed to us, looking forward to killing his first lion, the Maasai man's badge of courage. Needless to say, that was the one endeavour of his we were not prepared to support. Sadly, he later fell in with some dodgy company in Nairobi and we lost touch with him.

Gradually my days in Dar-es-Salam took on a fairly regular pattern. If Pat was teaching and I needed the car for anything during the day, say to go shopping or to Silver Sands beach for a swim, I'd drop him off at TSJ in the morning and pick him up at the end of his day. Otherwise I occupied myself in the house – reading, writing and answering letters, studying my Swahili, doing a bit of drawing, a bit

of writing, teaching Taabu some English and occasionally sitting with
Salima *et al* outside beneath the shade of her big tree. People constantly passed up and down the narrow mud road and sometimes one
of them might stop to talk to Leonard our Malawian day-watchman.
Or one of the neighbouring children might knock on our gate with
any and every excuse, hoping to be admitted. Our yard was very small.
It was impossible to see in or out over the high walls. In the rainy
season we were fascinated to discover the tall lilies, in the small area
we had developed for flowers, harbouring miniature frogs, no bigger
than the nail on the little finger.

In vain I also tried to introduce Regina to the art of cooking – an
uphill battle – but, being Dar-es-Salaam, there was always plenty of
other work for her to do, not least sweeping and dusting. Occasionally
there was some exceptional commotion like the time we were visited
by a large (about three metres) monitor lizard, first sighted by a frightened Regina earlier in the day as he lay lounging in the sun on the wall
overlooking her kitchen window. Later in the evening on our return
from a swim, when we opened the garage door, this large terrified
creature ran up the wall. Monitor lizards are not aggressive or dangerous – they just look that way – Peter next door told us that, if excited
or cornered, a swish of its long tail could break human bones. They
are called 'monitor' because they warn of the presence of a crocodile.

I was always hoping to see a mongoose. No such luck. Then one
day, shortly before we were to leave Africa forever, I went off to pick
up Pat at TSJ. I was driving carefully to avoid the potholes in the dirt
road, when suddenly there, right in front of me, crossing the road at
a leisurely pace and in single file were four beautiful mongooses. I
stopped the car to savour the unusual sight. Perhaps, as Pat maintains,
word had got round among the mongeese and it was a display put on
especially for me?

As in Nairobi, there were several modern supermarkets and a
remarkably wide choice of fresh fruit and vegetables at the various
local markets close to where we lived. Once I got to know those
manning the stalls I got quite adept at shopping there. Occasionally
I visited the fish market on the sea front on the way into town. My
first visit there, within days of my arrival, was such a memorable one
that I decided to write down my impressions as soon as I got back to
the house.

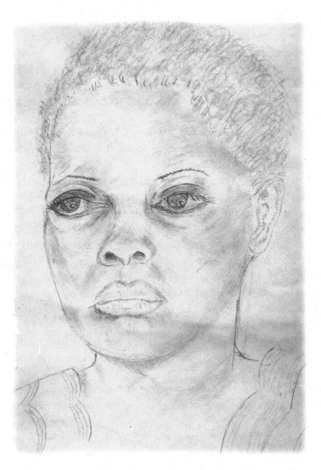

Regina

It might have been a film set we'd stumbled onto. Perhaps Palestine by the Sea of Galilee two thousand years ago? ... the huge numbers of men and women gathered there to see and hear for themselves the Fabulous Preacher who taught and healed, about whom everyone was talking? But no, far from it. For one thing, this fresh, sunny morning we were in fact by the shores of the Indian Ocean. The motley crowd, with doubtless, plenty of Semitic blood coursing through the veins of many of them, was all black-skinned Tanzanians. Who can say, but maybe their forebears had been meeting like this, thousands of years ago anyway. And, if nothing else the brightly multi-coloured kangas worn by most of the women would have told us that we were in late 20th century Africa.

In the high blue sky not a cloud. Barely a ripple on the water. On land bustle, noise and shouting of wares everywhere – and there was no escaping the all-pervading smell of fish.

Michelle, an English girl of Caribbean origin familiar with this scene, had invited us along to experience the Saturday morning fish market in Dar-es-Salaam, and should we decide to buy some fish as well she'd be there to help us do so.

Bargaining over the price – something Africans *expect* you to engage in, is something that neither of us would relish. We'd leave that to our friend, well versed as she is in this.

Other markets I'd visited before had been held in relatively enclosed spaces. But this one was all taking place out in the open. Everyone there seemed intent on either buying or selling. Groups of women sat in circles here and there on the shore bidding for the morning's catch which was being auctioned. Fruit vendors plied these customers with sweet, fresh oranges, already peeled and halved for easier consumption. An air of good-cheer prevailed everywhere.

Eventually, we were lured back into the shade of the huge shed at the entrance. There we watched our friend banter and bargain energetically on our behalf with several eager young men vying good-humouredly for her custom. In the end we purchased some kilos of prawns from an arrestingly handsome, Nilotic-featured youth, who spoke excellent English.

While this transaction was coming to a close, my husband nipped off to investigate the hand-woven baskets on sale nearer the shore. He arrived back with three.

Quite an experience. I think we'll be going there again.

After a year in Dar-es-Salaam I felt confident enough to accept the invitation to help a doctor friend who ran an AIDs Clinic at the other end of town. Driving there through the morning traffic was just as hazardous as Nairobi. Some time after our return home to Rivendell, Coral Barry, my nephew's daughter, asked me to write a few lines about my stay in Africa for her school magazine which was promoting charitable causes in Africa. This is it:

There was something almost heart-breaking about it. All these children had been born with AIDS. As I approached the clinic for the first time that sunny morning, I could hear a child's toy loudly playing, over and over: 'Happy Birthday to You'...

For an adult knowing the probable fate of these children, the whole situation was quite disheartening but the children mercifully could not know any of this. We played ball together, the little girls showed off their pretty dresses and everyone listened attentively as I read stories to them. For me the most poignant sight was of the elderly grandmother and her three orphaned grandchildren. All they had was their grandmother and all she had left in the world were her eight-year old grandson and his twin brother and sister, barely one year old.

Once a week this four-some trudged the dusty road to this Medical Missionary clinic of hope. They came from afar, I was told, several bus journeys away with a long walk at the end. I watched them arrive and leave, one twin strapped to the back of the eight year old and the other strapped to the aged granny's back. After a day at the Clinic they left for home again, provided with several plastic bags full of the coming week's food and medicines. They were a sorry sight but to me they were ever smiling, very gracious and so full of hope. From time to time, I still wonder what happened to them.

Apart from a few such sad-making recollections, I remember Tanzania as a stunningly beautiful part of the world: azure waters, rich in fish, an abundance of delicious fresh fruit and vegetables, postcard perfect white sandy beaches, the slow relaxed pace of existence.

Though life for the average Tanzanian is hand-to-mouth, people seem to be very happy and contented. Piles of cheap second-hand clothing donated by richer countries, which somehow end up on sale in Dar-es-Salaam, puts the local cloth industry out of business and likewise the shoemakers, thus denuding the populace of so many transferable skills that help make communities independent and proud. As a result people are made dependent on handouts as nobody can compete with donated products sold at rock bottom prices. One can buy designer brand names for a relative pittance, virtually new or unworn. A Luis Vuitton bag for a dollar, sweaters made in Italy and France, brand names I would think twice before buying at home because of the exorbitant price. It is disquieting to see the misguided charitable intentions of the rich in Europe and America making the poor African even poorer, stripping him of his native skills and making him dependent on Western Charity. I suspect all Foreign Aid, whether governmental or private, has a similar result.

Jacqueline Kirwan, one of my favourite cousins, who lives in Persia came to visit us in Dar-es-Salaam. Her husband Ali lectured at Teheran University and could not come, which was a pity for he too was such good company. One day we passed a hotel called The Viagra Inn and Jacqueline insisted that we stop and take a picture of her standing in front of the sign to send to Ali as an email attachment. Top of her list of 'must see' was Zanzibar. The island was of special interest because a relative of hers (and mine) had worked as a nurse there during the early 1930s and 1940s. We took her to Stone Town and other favourite haunts.

On our return we all spent a day at Mikumi National Game Park. Everything went swimmingly until the incident of the elephant. Sighting a large lone elephant close by the track, Pat slowed down. Maybe my mistake was that I made eye-contact with the elephant – something we learnt later one must avoid doing – but, for whatever reason, the animal started to flap his ears and trot towards the car. Pat, curious to see what the animal would do next, ignored my increasingly urgent pleas that we drive off. Cool as a cucumber, he kept on driving very slowly, and taking his eyes off the road ahead, watched through the rear view window for the animal's next move. The elephant started to trumpet at us – a bad sign. Suddenly Pat struck the steep bank, the vehicle wobbled and almost overturned. By then I was crouched down on the back seat, my face in my hands ready for the worst. Echoes of baboons... By now even Jacqueline had joined in my pleas for Pat to make a getaway. Always until then, elephants ignored us and we often just stopped in our tracks to let them cross our paths. After that there was no dallying with elephants.

It was at the same Mikumi National Park that I had an unforgettable near-encounter with a crocodile and here is the story as I related it in an email to a friend a few days later.

> Training for the Olympics wasn't in it. That mad dash of mine for the safety of the vehicle may well have broken some kind of a speed limit. The alacrity with which I ran back and straight into the car would qualify me for the Olympics.
>
> Yesterday, as we were coming to the end of an interesting eight hour drive through Mikumi National Park, and heading for the exit, we turned a corner and, unexpectedly, saw before us the first clear, deep water we'd seen all day – the Hippo Pool. Not a wild animal in sight,

so, contrary to warnings posted prominently at the entrance, we decided it was safe to get out of our two vehicles and explore.

The little hill overlooking the pool afforded a good view of whatever inhabitants might favour us with a sighting, however minimal and brief. We were in luck, for there in the distance, at the far side of the pool, we made out a dark spot in the water indicating that there were some now-you-see-them-now-you-don't hippos below the surface. We waited quietly in the gentle, late afternoon sun. Eventually we were rewarded with a partial view of two small groups of adults and their young; all typically crowded on top of each other with the top of the heads, snouts and bulging eyes briefly visible, when they surfaced every now and then for air.

In between times we scanned the pool's edges and caught sight of, was it? Yes, it was: a crocodile, half submerged. With the aid of the binoculars we saw his vigilant eye and vicious teeth quite clearly, before, at the sound of our excited whispers or possibly at seeing us, however far away, he slithered into the water and out of sight. I remember thinking that looking at him through the binoculars was quite near enough. Not to be listed among endearing wild beasts. While the others turned their attention back to see what the hippos were up to, if anything, I wandered idly away to see what might be visible from the far side of the small bush right beside us at the crown of the hillock. Rounding the corner, on the opposite side and out of sight of the rest of our little party of four I suddenly came upon him. I swear that had I been concentrating hard on looking for the hippos, I might easily have stepped on the huge crocodile which was lying alarmingly near, about 3 or 4 metres from my feet, so unexpectedly far from the water's edge, a good 7 metres up the bank. He was in profile, with his head tilted to one side away from me, so that even if, at that moment, I'd been foolhardy enough to stay to investigate, I wouldn't have been able to tell whether or not he had his eyes open, like his relative on the far side and was on the alert for enemies. Had he heard my approach? Was he playing possum? Was he asleep? Was he dead? At that point I did not linger to find out. Swift as an arrow I turned and shot back to the car, jumped in and slammed the door shut whilst warning the others in a loud stage whisper, about the proximity of, as the Chambers dictionary has it, the large long-tailed tropical reptile, with powerful tapering jaws and a thick skin covered with bony plates, a few metres away on the far side of the bush. Unfazed, Pat quietly made his way round to see for himself, our two female companions staying put, just in case...

Then all of us had another wary look, moving back round the bush to view him from the other angle, from where they took snaps. I was careful to stay at the back of the group and had no wish to be included in any photographs. 'He's dead,' someone whispered. Eventually Pat threw a stick in the crocodile's direction and he was off like a flash down the slope and into the water. Later when I questioned Pat, he said: 'Yes, the eyes were wide open.' So, indeed, my croc had been on the alert all along.

Me: 'Do you think he heard us before I found him?'

Pat: 'Oh yes.'

Me: 'Well why didn't he come and eat us?'

Pat: 'Maybe he was full.'

I recalled the Swahili proverb: never call a crocodile 'Big Mouth' till you've passed him by.

Later, I read that crocodiles can travel overland quite far from water and that from a stationary position they can take off at a speed of 40 mph, without the need to rev up, in other words, out-run a 4x4 on rough terrain. A disturbing thought. A European acquaintance of ours told us that her grand-daughter (only weeks before we arrived in Tanzania) was eaten by a crocodile.

The road past our house in Dar was rutted and potholed and it took all one's attention to negotiate it in the Suzuki. One morning, rushing to pick up Pat at the School of Journalism, I saw a soldier coming towards me picking his way between the potholes. Normally people pull to the side and let you pass but this fellow kept to his course in the middle of the road and as I was slowly driving past, he gave the bonnet a hefty thump with his fist. I thought no more about it until about a week later we were alerted by loud banging at the outside gate. Pat went out to see what was up. He soon returned: 'I did not know you had a car accident involving a soldier?'

'No, I didn't.' And I told him the story.

The soldier was claiming the equivalent of several hundred pounds to have his wrist treated. Only his sister, a nurse, could do it and she lived a couple of hundred miles away in Arusha. There was also the question of his army badge that came unstuck from his cap when he thumped the bonnet. We examined his wrist and could see nothing wrong with it. He had no English and in order to make sure we were hearing him correctly we called our neighbour Peter, who spoke per- fect English and often helped us sort out problems such as this. Peter

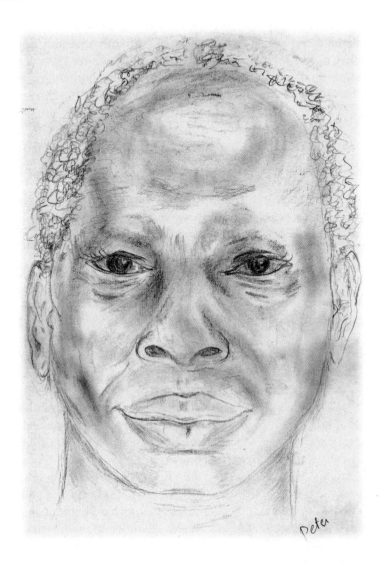

could see nothing wrong with the wrist or indeed with the badge, which could easily be sewn back on the cap, but he pointed out to us that any 'palaver' with a soldier was bad news. This soldier wanted money. Soldiers had guns and often manned road-blocks and they could make life miserable for a person. It was best to pay him something but not the huge sum he was demanding. It was a lengthy negotiation, with Peter as intermediary. Eventually we paid him the equivalent of ten pounds. All this ended in smiles. And I distinctly remember parting with a spontaneous mutually fraternal hug.

Another time we were approaching traffic lights in town just as they were changing. We stopped. A car went speeding through the lights and we heard this almighty bang like a shot and saw newspapers fly up into the air. The speeding car had hit the paper-boy who, taking advantage of the red light, had rushed across the street hoping to make a sale or two. He was now an inert bundle in the middle of the road with his newspapers floating about him. The culprit sped on. We stopped but nobody else paid any attention.

During our six years in East Africa, family and friends from Europe came and went. Pat's mother, Bid Villa, a dear person who enjoyed life, flew out with the youngest of her seven children, Michael, and his family. When she came to Nairobi she was in her early eighties – with a heart condition but game for any adventure. That trip was a great success and she enjoyed herself with ne'er a murmur when unforeseen hardships cropped up, like the time she was subjected to an extra eight-hour long diversion to Amboseli National Park. A little older now and once again, against the counsel of her GP back home on Aran, and of Pat who had also gently tried to dissuade her, pointing out that Dar was even hotter than Nairobi and very humid, she was nonetheless determined to visit her firstborn. The night she arrived, I was recovering from a bout of bronchitis and I did not accompany Pat to the airport to pick up his family. The flight was delayed by several hours, their baggage lost with Bid Villa's heart tablets among the missing luggage and it was after midnight when they finally arrived at our house in Kinondoni B. Later that morning, Bid Villa died quietly in her sleep. It was three days before Christmas. A doctor friend, the wife of Nestor Ilahuka, one of Pat's postgraduate students, most generously insisted on taking charge of everything, even organising the requiem Mass in our local church, from where the body was brought to the nearby Hindu crematorium to be cremated. Later the ashes were brought back to Aran for burial.

Towards the end of 1999, TG4, an Irish television channel sent a team to Dar-es-Salaam to record a programme about Pat's work in Tanzania. It proved an interesting diversion. Though I tried hard not to be involved it was difficult for me, as Pat's wife, to avoid appearing in the programme. I did not relish the prospect, especially as the programme was done on a shoe-string and they could not afford make-up or special lighting. Producer Micheál Lally, reporter Róisín Ní Eaghra and their cameraman were very pleasant company and, all told, it was an enjoyable week of filming. Never before had I appeared on a TV programme without being professionally made-up. Vanity dies hard. The unforgiving harsh sunlight of Africa flatters no one, least of all a woman in her sixties. Luckily for me, TG4 had a lot of pre-recorded footage from past recordings with Irish TV available to them, which they were able to use along with the Tanzanian footage. The TG4 team filmed us in and around Dar-es-Salaam, at the Tanzania School of Journalism, haggling at the local market, playing 'smash-ball' on the beach and sailing in a dhow in the harbour. During those same days we happened to have a very dear friend of ours staying with us, Professor Adrian Hastings, a specialist on Africa and a controversial polemicist who, like so many others, was keen that Pat write about his African experiences.

The day came when we both 'knew' it was time to leave East Africa for good and we started preparing for that departure. All told, it had been six rewarding and enriching years. No, we didn't get to Turkana in Northern Kenya, or to Lalabela in Ethiopia, because of the highly dangerous situations obtaining in these places each time we tried to visit. But there were plenty of other places on our list, so to speak, which we managed to see. It took all Pat's skills in our doughty little VW Gti to get us to the wonder that is Crater Lake. At times the road, deep in sand, looked impassable but the 'red dragon' battled on. Once at the rim of the crater we left the car, climbed down the slope and, enveloped in the peaceful stillness, dared to swim in the weirdly beautiful pea-soup green waters said to have medicinal properties beneficial to the cattle regularly brought down the steep slopes by their Maasai owners. Then there was the prehistoric site of Olduvai Gorge in the Rift Valley, made famous by the findings of the renowned Leakey family. Archaeologists believe this area to be the cradle of mankind, the place from where our ancestors first emerged, something awesome on which to reflect as one looked out over the ancient quiet land. Memories of gazing out for the first time over the spectacular Rift Valley, or of early mornings in the bush sitting on some low hill with miles of savannah stretching as far as the eye could see, the world and nature enwrapped in a golden silence, the peacefulness of which is not interrupted but rather enhanced by the distant cry of a wild bird or animal.

Memories of our week-ends with the O'Maras at Naro Moru. The times we drove to the Serengeti to watch the annual migration of the wildlife. On one occasion, we sat in our Landrover with our visitors from Ireland, Dermod McCarthy and Marguerite McCurtin. We watched the tide of wildebeest and zebra, oblivious of our presence, flowing past us in the single-minded pursuit of their call. The adventures of roughing it with our backpacks to places like Zanzibar and getting visiting friends to do the same — like our sedate seventy-five-year old Dutch woman Jean Heitz. Never before had Jean travelled with fewer than three suitcases. The unbelievably beautiful black men and women sometimes glimpsed on the streets of the towns and cities of Kenya and Tanzania; the matchless elegance and grace of the most beautiful of all the African women I've ever seen, one still sunny afternoon when we had arrived to spend a few days in a small Massai village in northern Tanzania. I had been walking alone not far from where we had pitched our tent outside the settlement and had stopped to gaze around. Very faintly at first there came a tinkling sound that grew steadily louder. Suddenly, through the long grass and at first unaware of my presence, there passed before me this stunningly beautiful young Maasai woman in all the splendour of her Maasai attire, the tinkling sound being made by the multitude of bangles and other adornments she wore. Catching sight of me, the woman shyly approached and was joined by another, older woman, whom I found to be her mother, also splendidly attired but considerably smaller in stature. Both were of a delicate build and held themselves beautifully. Addressing me in a gentle and courteous manner, they managed to convey to me, first that I was welcome and that the younger woman had just had twins and that her mother had suckled one of them for her. One of the most impressive things about this encounter was that this exquisitely lovely woman was unaware of how remarkably beautiful she was. No trace of hubris. As dusk approached, the chief (father of the young woman) persuaded us, for safety's sake he said, to be their guests in the community compound. As dawn broke, still snug in our tent, it was fascinating to observe the village come to life, each person carrying out his or her particular domestic chore.

Then there was the liturgy. People in Africa 'love to celebrate life and God in their midst', as someone has written. Amen to that. Nowhere else in the world have I taken part in celebrations of the Eucharist so exuberant and joyous as in the local Kiswahili-speaking African Catholic churches we attended down at the coast in Kenya or in Tanzania. Whether in the cathedral in Dar-es-Salaam or in our own very capacious parish church, which was always packed to the rafters, overflowing into the compound, we had to arrive early if we wanted a seat. It was impossible for a believer not to get swept up in the general rejoicing. Nor can I forget the wonderfully disciplined choir of a few dozen young men and women, always in (instinctive?) harmony, and with several indigenous musical instruments to accompany them. 'Rejoice in the Lord! Again I say rejoice!' – that injunction from St Paul was always followed with gusto by the entire congregation. One particularly memorable occasion was the Easter Vigil, celebrated down at the coast in Kenya. Halfway through the ceremony a power-cut left everywhere in darkness and from there on, the rest of the liturgy, including the baptism of dozens of adults, was conducted by candle-light.

It is the memory of positive happenings such as these that linger on after leaving Africa. They far outweigh the memories of the occasional unpleasant happening that befell us. Two nights before we left East Africa for good, our house was broken into and we were robbed. It was the monsoon season. The heavy pounding of the incessant rain on the tin roof, allied with the familiar whirring of the ceiling fan, ensured the drowning out of all extraneous sound. Just after dawn, when the rain had abated, we were awakened from our sleep by Leonard, our night watchman, tapping on our window frame (there was no glass in our windows, only mosquito netting) and urgently whispering: 'Mama! Mama!'

I shot out of bed, parted the heavy mosquito netting around our bed and went to the window.

'Mama, all is not well!'

Behind me, Pat said in a quiet, very controlled voice: 'They came for the computer.'

And so it was. We had been warned that once it became known that we were leaving, there was a danger of being robbed but the date of Pat's departure would have been known at the School of Journalism. We worked out that the watchman must have let them in the front

gate and, once inside, they used their acetylene equipment to cut
through the one-inch thick iron bars on the kitchen window at the
back of the house. We never heard a thing. They cleared us of com-
puters, suitcases and boxes ready for shipping home to the UK, mobile
phones, cameras, money – everything they could lay their hands on.
Doubtless they would have been armed and would have placed armed
guards outside our *unlocked* bedroom door. Pat thinks they must have
had instructions not to harm us. We could have been killed or maimed
and for that I heartily thanked God. The watchman claimed that the
robbers had climbed over the wall but the neighbours on examining
the walls very carefully, found no footprints on the whitewashed bricks
and came to the same conclusion as Pat. We didn't blame Leonard
because Pat, as pointed out earlier, had told him not to risk his life
resisting thieves. The owner of the house, who came to replace the cut
iron bars, advised us to move out of the house immediately since we
were now marked targets. We'd rather not have moved but Nestor,
one of Pat's post-graduate students, warned: 'They'll come for your
car tonight. Don't be seen driving around town with it either.'

We switched cars with Nestor and spent the final two nights with
friends. We were advised against reporting the robbery to the police.
It would only result in our staff and neighbours being incarcerated –
the last thing we would have wanted. Involving the police would only
drag out the incident in the hope of extracting money. We were in
fact thankful that during our four years in Dar we were robbed only
that once. The diary that Pat encouraged me to keep since we came
to Africa was among the things taken. But I had spent many a pleasant hour sketching those who peopled our lives and, fortunately, the
sketchbooks survived. Sometimes it was an excuse to give them a
kidogo, a 'little something' for letting me draw them though they
seemed delighted to sit for me.

On our last day in Dar we were dropped off at the airport by one
of the Sisters who had kindly taken us in after we were robbed. We
had a few big suitcases and some extra baggage that Pat had arranged
for with the airline. We joined a lengthy check-in queue and soon
noticed that those in front of us with heavy bags were being offered
some sort of a deal by airline staff and their heavy bags seemed to
bypass the weigh-in system. As we had paid for extra baggage
anyway we refused to participate but Pat was afraid that because of

this refusal, bags might be 'mislaid' as once happened to me in Durban when all my luggage simply disappeared for ever. Also, if baggage went on board un-weighed, what might that do to the registered weight of the plane? After going through 'check-in' we reported the incident to a British Airways official, who seemed quite shocked. He said it was illegal and dangerous. Another even more worrying matter came to light as we approached Emigration: my passport was one day out of date. This was very serious because if the man at the desk spotted the error we would not be able to board – unless we paid a hefty *kidogo*. Pat decided that I should have a go at exercising my best Kiswahili to distract the desk. And it worked. We were out of Africa within the hour.

Back home in England we were kept busy with plenty of work in and around Rivendell after our six years abroad. I was content with the prospect of catching up on my reading, continuing where I had left off with an anthology on the subject of 'Colour' and carrying on with my drawing. I even took up playing the piano again, something I hadn't done since I was fourteen. I never gave a thought to the harp. Then the World Harp Congress (WHC) intervened and put paid to these leisurely plans of mine.

Sheila Larchet, the doyenne of Irish orchestral harpists, approached me about taking part in the WHC in Dublin in 2005. I declined the invitation because by now I had retired. In Dublin a few days later, I went to see Sheila. Undaunted, the organisers asked if I would give a talk instead. I said I'd think about it. Sheila also suggested that I get a book of song and harp accompaniments ready and make it available for the Congress – I had never written down my accompaniments. I memorised them. Another challenge.

We were staying with Dermod McCarthy and over supper the subject of the WHC came up. Dermod was enthusiastically in favour of both a talk and a book. I was still in my 'no' mode. Then Pat sighed and said to Dermod: 'It's always been like this. You get excited about a project and she says *no*. It's all very disheartening.' That did it. Feeling considerably chastened, I went away and slept on it. At breakfast next morning I announced that I'd prepare a talk *and* get a song-book ready. Eventually five song-books resulted from that decisive 'about-turn' as well as talks on three continents. So, thank you Dermod. And thanks to Pat also, without whose expert help there would not have been any talks *or* song-books.

These decisions had a considerable impact on my life for the next few years. Friendship is something I've always cherished and, over the years, I have been blessed with many good friends. Dermod McCarthy and Marguerite McCurtain are two of our long-standing friends who live very busy, separate lives. Every now and then, we four managed to meet up in different parts of the world and holiday together. After Pat and I returned from Africa (where they had come to visit us), Dermod was very keen that our next get-together would be in Australia to coincide with the opening in Sydney of John Misto's play *Harp on the Willow*. Dermod, unaware of my pact with the playwright, was assuming that we would all attend the opening night at the end of our holiday. We started off in Alice Springs and, having visited Uluru (Ayer's Rock) and drunk in all its wonders, we spent the next couple of weeks touring parts of Australia that that I hadn't visited before, finally ending up in Sydney for the opening of the play. The night before the opening of *Harp on the Willow*, Michael Bach, a friend of Dermod's, hosted a party in his home so we could meet John Misto. Our friendship, established through email, gained a new dimension and the friendship continues. Sticking to my decision never to see the play, I had the pleasure a few days later of meeting Marina Prior, who played the leading role, and the rest of the cast at a tea-party I gave for them at our hotel. Incidentally, the play ran for thirteen sold-out weeks. Of course, I did not see it. We got to know Marina better when she played the role again in Melbourne in 2007.

In 1957 in New York, I recorded a Gaelic song called 'Seóladh na nGabhna' on *Songs of Ireland*. Then in the early 1980, just as I had finished reading Marian Zimmer-Bradley's novel *The Mists of Avalon*, what did I get but a letter from her asking for the words and music of 'Seóladh na nGabhna'. She loved the song, as did her little daughter Moira who, because of it, had now started to learn the harp. Little did I know that about two decades later Moira Stern, by now a well known singer and harpist in America and mother of three little boys, was to play a key role in persuading me to put together my song books *Travels with My Harp Vols. 1-5*. As with John Misto, Moira, Pat and I have become and remain good friends via the internet.

Since returning from Africa in 2002 Pat and I spend some of the colder winter months in La Carihuela, a little fishing village in Spain. I like to walk along the beach while Pat goes off to check his emails in the local cyber café. One day he returned saying: 'There was an email for you from a student named Michael Angelakos in Chicago. He wanted permission to 'layer' one of your Irish songs, '*Óró Mo Bháidín*', a favourite of his.'

'What did you tell him?'

'I told him to go ahead. He'll let you have the finished product for your verdict.'

'What is 'layering'?'

'I don't know. We'll find out shortly.'

Pat is always pleased when some foreign person expresses an interest in his mother tongue: Gaelic. I'd forgotten all about the episode until several months later Pat mentioned that the 'layering man from Chicago' had been in touch and had sent a sample of what he had done. When I asked if I could listen to the result, Pat sheepishly admitted that he did listen to it but had deleted the attachment by mistake. He blamed the unfamiliar cyber café equipment.

'What was it like?' I enquired.

'To me it sounded like a bag of cats and I didn't think you'd want to hear it.'

Recently I've learnt that six million people have downloaded it from the web. It has been used for advertising and TV programmes in America and' Top Gear' used it as their theme tune in Australia.

Had I listened to the demo then, undoubtedly, the composition which is entitled *Sleepyhead* would have elicited a very emphatic NO from me. Pat is delighted and I am glad to say that his *felix culpa* has so far resulted in a steady source of healthy income. A nice change from being ripped off because of unpaid royalties over the years. Such are the vagaries of the music world. That particular recording of '*Óró*' was for the Clancy/Tradition label on *Songs of Ireland* in New York in 1957.

For some time we have been doing up a place on Inis Mór, the Aran Islands, Pat's place of birth, so our trips to Ireland have become more frequent. It might be said that I've had an ambiguous relationship with Ireland. Though I love the country, its history, its culture, its language and people. Though Richard and I had talked of the possibility of living on Aran. I never even considered the idea of moving back there for good – until now. To my own surprise, I'm doing that very thing: moving back to Ireland after about half a century of living abroad.

This updating of the original autobiography, *The Scent of the Roses*, which was first published in 1980, has been written as a final addition to the collection of my papers housed at the Burns Library, Boston College. Towards the end of 2009, I sent off several crates of my papers to the Burns Library where they were put on exhibition for six months. Boston College also has my first Briggs harp, my steadfast companion over many years of unexpected twists and turns. Included with the papers is the Gold Medal presented to me some years ago by the Éire Society of Boston. As part of the Burns Library Exhibition, I gave a talk. In the late 1980s I had given at least one concert at Boston College, but this particular presentation which I entitled *Travels With My Harp* was to be, my husband and I both felt, a closure of sorts.

Now that I have entered my mid-seventies, fit as a fiddle, hail as a harp and with plenty of energy, thank God, Pat and I have decided that it is time to move from Rivendell, the 17th-century thatched cottage which we have made our own and where we have lived so happily together, with friends coming and going for the past thirty years.

But life goes on. And we have just received news from Australia that John Misto's play, *Harp on the Willow*, has had another very successful run. As I sit here at my desk, I can see the young rabbits disporting themselves on the lawn in the summer sun; some of them may well be visitors from nearby Watership Down. They are not at all bothered by the arrival of the deer, or the pheasants or indeed by the woodpeckers – all daily visitors. These will continue to visit bird and animal-friendly Rivendell, as they have done down the centuries, playing and nibbling away, long after we have passed through. Perhaps we'll miss lovely peaceful and peace-filling Rivendell. But I for one try never to forget that we are all pilgrims, *in via*, birds of passage. To quote St Paul, 'our homeland is in heaven'.

Appendices

APPENDIX I

THE PHILLIPS GALLERY
Sunday Afternoon, February 10, 1957
At 5 o'clock

A Recital of Irish and Scottish
Traditional Songs

Sung and accompanied on the Irish Harp by
MARY O'HARA

REBELLION, EXILE AND FAMINE
The Minstrel Boy
The Quiet Land of Érin
Sliabh an mBan
Famine Song

OCCUPATIONAL SONGS
Weaving Song
Waulking Song
Hebridean Cattle Croon
Milking Song
Óró mo Bháidín

LOVE SONGS AND BALLADS
The Bonny Boy
Ballynure Ballad
Eibhlín a Rún
I have a Bonnet Trimm'd with Blue
Cucúin a Chuaichín

FAIRY SONGS AND LULLABIES
Dia Luain, Dia Máirt
Shohín Seó
The Song of the Water Sprite
The Gartan Mother's Lullaby

Note: Miss O'Hara will explain and translate as much as necessary.

APPENDIX 2

STANBROOK ABBEY
Sr Miriam accompanying herself on the Irish Harp
(Recital c.1973, end of)

1. *Bó Luaithreach Thú*
   (Scots Gallic Traditional)
2. The Quiet Land of Érin
   (Irish exile song – translation)
3. Come Lord!
   (God song – M O'H)
4. Bubbles
   (Poem – Richard Selig/M O'H)
5. Eros
   (Poem – R Selig/M O'H)
6. Cucúín
   (Irish Gaelic Trad)
7. The Lord of the Dance
   (Sydney Carter)
8. The Uist Cattle Croon
   (Scots Gallic Trad)
9. I Have a Bonnet Trimmed with Blue
   (Irish Traditional)
10. Judas and Mary
    (God Song)

11. *Tant Con de Vivre*
    (French Trad – 11th Century)
12. *Sliabh na mBan*
    (Gaelic Trad)
13. The Frog and the Mouse
    (Irish Trad)
14. Litany
    (God Song – M O'H)
15. *Óró Mo Bháidín*
    (Gaelic Trad)
16. Poll and Nancy Hogan
    (Irish Trad)
17. Sweet Child of Glory
    (Irish Trad – translation)

APPENDIX 3

Mary O'Hara
at
ROYAL FESTIVAL HALL
Saturday 5th November 1977

1. *Lúibín Ó Lú*
2. The Bonny Boy
3. Kitty of Coleraine
4. *Plaisir d'Amour*
5. *Is Ar Éirinn Ní Neosfhainn Cé Hí*
6. A Shetland Spinning Song
7. Morning Has Broken
8. When I Need You
9. The Clown
10. Prayer of the Badger
11. Forty-Five Years
12. *Ruban Roughes* (Scarlet Ribbons)

13. The Lord of the Dance
14. *Cucúín A Chuaichín*
15. The Wee Cooper of Fife
16. *Úna Bhán*
17. Trotting to the Fair
18. Among Silence
19. The Quiet Land of Érin
20. A Hebridean Milking Song
21. A Hebridean Milking Song
22. The Snail
23. Tapestry
24. Rocky Raccoon
25. Bring Me a Shawl from Galway
26. Bridge Over Troubled Water

Mary O'Hara – Celtic harp, vocals
Paul Bennett – Woodwinds
Mike Barker – Acoustic guitar
Bunny Thompson – Piano, celeste, harpsichord
Martyn David – Percussion
Brian Jones – Double bass
Musical Director: David Gould
Production supervisor: Dee Lustig
Sound co-ordinator: Bernard Doherty
Stage manager: Paul Brown

APPENDIX 4

Mary O'Hara's UK Tour programme 1979

The programme will be chosen from the following:

A Ballynure Ballad
A Friend of Mine
Drink To Me Only With Thine Eyes
Eros
It's A Me O Lord
Killing Me Softly With His Song
Lord of the Dance
Mon Pays
My Lagan Love
Plaisir d'Amour
Pussy Willows, Cat Tails
Rainy Day People
Seán A Bhríste Leathair
Sliabh Na mBan
Song For a Winter's Night
Spinning Wheel
Streets of London
Sweet Child of Glory
Tant Con Je Vivrai
The Clown
The Frog and The Mouse
The Minstrel Boy
The Snail
The Sun is Burning
The Twa Corbies
The Weaving Song
Too Much Magic

APPENDIX 5

SASKATCHEWAN CANADA September 1985

Guide for Lights Person
One-person show: *c*.2 hours excl. Intermission

Mary O'Hara
Harp & Voice

Titles	Mood
Greensleeves – Elizabethan English Trad	Moderate
I Know My Love – Irish Trad	Quick
Óró Mo Bháidín – Gaelic Irish Trad	Lilting
Song for a Winter's Night – Canadian G Lightfoot (MOR)	Nostalgic
Kitty of Coleraine – Irish Trad	Quic/amusing
Eibhlín a Rún – Irish Trad	Slow/romantic
A Reading – from *Celebration of Love*	
The Garden Song – Mallett (MOR)	Quick/light
It's-A-Me-O-Lord – Negro Spiritual	Unaccompanied
Wiegenlied – Schubert	Lullaby
The Fairy Tree – Irish art song/spiritual	Quick/dramatic
The Riddle Song – American Trad	Slow/Romantic

20 minutes Intermission

My Lagan Love – Irish Trad	Slow
'S Ar Éirinn Ní nEósfhainn Cé hÍ – Gaelic Trad	Moderate/lively
The Laird o' Cockpen – Scot Trad	Quick/amusing
A Reading from *Celebration of Love*	
Caleno Custure Me – Elizabethan English Trad	Moderate
The Snail – Levi/O'Hara contemporary	V Slow
Ceól a' Phíobaire – Irish Trad	Quick
Pussy Willow Cat Tails – Gordon Lightfoot MOR	Moderate
Róisín Dubh – Irish Trad Gaelic	Unac/Dramatic

Prayer of the Badger – O'Hara/Moncrief   Moderate
Plaisir d'Amour   Slow/sad
Lord of the Dance – Sydney Carter   Quick

Other songs that may be substituted from time to time

An Peata Circe – Gaelic (The Pet Hen)
Na hAori – U-Scots Gallic (Child of the Woodland)
I Know Where I'm Goin' – Irish Trad
An Fhideag Airgid – Scots Gallic (The Silver Whistle)

APPENDIX 6

UK TOUR December 1982

Mary O'Hara accompanying herself on the Irish Harp
Also: Piano & Flute accompaniment

The Spinning Wheel – Trad. (Irish)
Song for a Winter's Night – Lightfoot
Plaisir d'Amour – Martini
A Hebridean Milking Song – Trad. (Scot Gallic)
Were E'er You Walk – Handel
The Sun is Burning – Campbell
A La Claire Fontaine – Trad. (Fr. Canada)
The Fairy Tree – Laine/O'Brien
Never Weatherbeaten Saile – Campion
She Moved Through the Fair – Trad/Colum
Gens du Pays – Vineault
Forty Five Years from Now – Rogers
In an English Country Garden – Jordan
The Song of Glendun – O'Neill/Hardeback
The Wee Cooper of Fife – Trad. (Scot)

314

TRAVELS WITH MY HARP

Sliabh na mBan – Trad. (Ir. Gaelic)
Among Silence – Selig/O'Hara
An Peata Circe – Trad. (Ir. Gaelic)
Say That I'll be Sure to Find You – Brahms/Sherrin
A Song for Ireland
Too Much Magic – Knight/Johnson
Bailero – Trad/
Bring Me a Shawl From Galway – Neil/Croft
The Lord of the Dance – Carter

Interval: 20 Minutes

Occasionally a song from the following list may be substituted:

Perhaps Love – Denver
Mon Pays – Vigneault
Róisín Dubh – Trad Gaelic
Tant Con Je Vivrai – Trad Fr.
Chansons Por Les PetitsEnfants – Buffet
Rubans Rouges – Trad. Trans. Twinberrow
The Quiet Land of Érin – Trad Ir.O'Hara
The Snail – Levi/O'Hara
Willie's Gane to Melville Castle – Trad. Scot
Rainy Day People – Lightfoot
Danny Boy – Trad Ir.
The Clown – Levi/O'Hara

Index

Magdalen College, Oxford 51, 64, 77, 125, 186
Magdalen College, Cambridge 186
Mahon, Caroline 191
Manchester 155
Manchester Guardian 32
Manns, Johnny 243, 244
Marlin, Brigid 30, 252
Marshag 130, 131, 132
'Mary O'Hara and Friends' 222, 225, 234, 236
Mary O'Hara Live at the Royal Festival Hall 180
Mary O'Hara: Recital 182, 190
Mary O'Hara's Ireland 152, 177
Mary O'Hara's Monday, Tuesday – Songs for Children 152, 178
Mary O'Hara's Scotland 152, 177-8, 217
Massey Hall, Toronto 214
Matthews, Jackson 63
Melbourne x, 143-4, 231, 304
Melbourne University 66, 143
Mercier, Peadar 199
Merton, Thomas 170
Mike Douglas Show, The 214
Miles, Ann 231, 232
Mitchell, Adrian and Maureen 74, 92, 125
Misto, John x, 279, 304, 306
'Mo Cheól Thú' 189
Mombassa 252, 254, 265
Monkstown 154
Monroe, Marilyn 163
Montague, John 194
Montreal 200
Moore, Dudley 87, 219
Moore, Gerald 208
Moore, Thomas ix, 21-2
Moose Factory 200
Moray, Anne 98
'More Contrary' 27, 79, 80, 86, 87
Morley, John 110
'Mount Street Master Tapes' 152-3, 176
Moyne, Lord – *see* Bryan Guinness and family

Moynihan, Father Anselm 109, 143, 145-6, 148-9
Mulcahy, Father Columban 147-8
Murison, David 137, 219
Murphy, Richard 45, 200
Museum of Modern Art, New York City 62
Music Association of Ireland (MAI) 200
'Music for the Millions' 86
'Music Speaks Louder Than Words' 190, 209
Muthoni (house girl) 250, 251, 255-6, 271, 273, 283
'My Friends: A Fable' 106
'My Lagan Love' 153, 174, 311, 312

Nairobi 247-74 *passim*, 277-92 *passim*, 298
Nantucket 111, 113-14
Newcastle-on-Tyne Arts Festival 198
Newman House 43
'News of the Day' 139
New York 62, 83, 96, 99, 100, 101, 106, 110, 112, 114, 115, 118, 123, 128, 151, 199, 200, 204, 214, 215, 237, 304, 305
New York Times, The 214
New Zealand 111, 142-3, 225, 231, 234, 270
Nice, John 176-7, 181, 216
Nigeria 3, 219, 246, 247, 275, 277
Norham Road, Oxford 58, 83, 92
Northern Ireland 9, 234
    See also Belfast
Nunraw Monastery 147

Oban 40
Observer 203
Occidental College, Los Angeles 62
O'Connor, Ulick 48
Ó'Dálaigh, Cearbhall 191
Odetta 111, 151, 176
O'Donnell, Mary 191, 215
O'Dowd, Brendan 151